*Secrets for Success
and Happiness*

SECRETS FOR

SUCCESS

AND HAPPINESS

OG MANDINO

Fawcett Columbine • New York

Grateful acknowledgment is made to the following for permission to reprint
previously published material:

The J. Peterman Company: Excerpts from the OWNER'S MANUAL copyright ©
1991 by The J. Peterman Company. Reprinted by permission of Mr. J. Peterman.

Success Unlimited, Inc.: "A Letter to Two Sons" by Og Mandino, appeared in
SUCCESS UNLIMITED Magazine in December 1968, Vol. 15, No. 12. Copyright © 1968 by Success Unlimited, Inc. "Father's Day" by Og Mandino appeared in SUCCESS UNLIMITED Magazine in June 1971, Vol. 18, No. 6.
Copyright © 1971 by Success Unlimited, Inc.

Library of Congress Cataloging-in-Publication Data
Mandino, Og.
Secrets for success and happiness / by Og Mandino.
    p.   cm.
ISBN 0-449-90691-4
1. Success.   2. Happiness.   3. Conduct of life.   I. Title.
BF637.S8M265 1995
158'.1—dc20   95-12226
CIP

Manufactured in the United States of America
First Edition: November 1995
—— 10 9 8 7 6 5 4 3 2 1

Dedicated to that special guardian angel who has loved and cared for me through all these years . . . my wife, Bette.

Pursue, keep up with, circle round and round your life, as a dog does his master's chaise. Do what you love. Know your own bone, gnaw at it, bury it, unearth it, and gnaw it still.

However mean your life is, meet it and live it; do not shun it and call it hard names. It is not so bad, as you are. It looks poorest when you are richest. The fault-finder will find faults even in paradise. Love your life, poor as it is. Humility, like darkness, reveals the heavenly lights. Superfluous wealth can only buy superfluities. Money is not required to buy any necessary of the soul.

—*Henry David Thoreau*

Secrets for Success
and Happiness

1991

A life that is worth writing at all, is worth writing minutely and truthfully.

HENRY WADSWORTH LONGFELLOW

Welcome . . .

Take my hand. Become my companion and friend in these pages. Fly with me to strange cities and follow me onto theater and convention hall stages, before large crowds, when I give my speech on success and happiness. Then relax with me here in my studio, in the glow from the fireplace, and take long walks by my side through the pines and birches behind my old farmhouse while the snow is falling and the squirrels are waiting to be fed.

Most important, please listen to me as I touch upon a large variety of subjects, some trivial, some vital, while we pass through weeks and months together. If you do, listen closely . . . our time together just might give you an idea or two that will help to improve the conditions of your life.

What are you planning for the years ahead? Are you looking forward to them with joy and excitement and anticipation, or have you already raised the white flag of surrender and decided that your life has been a waste? Did you intend to write one life story and now sadly realize that you have written another? Are you filled with remorse and self-pity when you compare the volume as it is with what you had hoped to make it?

Hold my hand. Tightly. It is not too late. Pay attention to my words and you will soon discover that mixed in with my rambling are ideas and suggestions, many not mine, that can change your life. All of us are beset by fears and pain and doubts. We let ourselves get turned away from our goals by obstructions. But it is possible, as Marie Curie once reminded us, to change our world so that nothing in life is to be feared, only understood.

January 4

Although this is truly a personal journal, it is being kept with eventual publication in mind. Henry David Thoreau once wrote, "He is not the great writer who is afraid to let the world know that he ever committed an impropriety. Does it not know that all men are mortal?"

From the age of twenty Thoreau spent his entire adult life keeping a journal. At first, perhaps, his entries were for his eyes alone, but as years passed, his journal commentaries were often rewritten and polished with the intention of having others read his words.

Thoreau's *Walden*, as well as all his other writings, including the thirty-nine volumes of his journal, have brought great joy and contentment and understanding to my life ever since high school, and yet although I have written seventeen books, I have never considered keeping a journal of my own until the seed was planted by an old friend, Robert Conklin. It had been my honor to speak at a convention of the Conklin Company years ago, and we have kept in touch, through the years, via mail.

Three closing paragraphs in a letter from Bob were the prime motivation for my daring to undertake this journal:

Og, I don't believe you have any idea how much of a legend you have become. Your works will live far beyond our present generation. Although all of your books are, in a way, self-disclosures, I hope you find a channel of some kind to allow those of the future to have an even more intimate knowledge of the "spirit behind the pen."

Personal essays? Biographical sketches? Diary? A journal, perhaps? Five hundred years from now people will be writing about you. What they don't know they will invent. Why not give them authentic material?

I hold your success in awe, my friend. You accomplish in a month what most authors and speakers would relish for a lifetime.

High-powered flattery that would turn anyone's head.

Not long after reading Bob's letter I happened to be engrossed in Thoreau's Journal Ten. His entry for October 21, 1857, stated, "Is not the poet bound to write his own biography? Is there any other work for him but a good journal? We do not wish to know about his imaginary hero but how he, the actual hero, lived from day to day."

I am neither a poet nor a hero but I have traveled a long and bumpy road—from the horror of being a drunken bum to the delight of being a best-selling author. Experience has been a stern but excellent teacher. So . . . come on along. You just might enjoy the trip, and I *know* I'll enjoy being with *you*.

January 5

The first few days of each new year have always seemed to be filled with a special magical quality of anticipation. What will the new calendar produce in our lives? In an old edition of *Elbert Hubbard's Scrap Book*, published in

1923, the year I was born, I discovered a special collection of New Year's requirements, by W. R. Hunt, that would make any of our lives a heaven on earth:

> The sun is just rising on the morning of another day, one of the first of a new year. What can I wish that this day, this year, may bring to me? Nothing that shall make the world of others poorer, nothing at the expense of others; but just those things which in their coming do not stop with me, but touch me rather, as they pass and gather strength:
>
> A few friends who understand me, and yet remain my friends.
>
> A work to do which has real value without which the world would feel the poorer.
>
> A return for such work small enough not to tax unduly any one who pays.
>
> A mind unafraid to travel, even though the trail be not blazed.
>
> An understanding heart.
>
> A sight of the eternal hills and unresting sea, and of something beautiful the hand of man has made.
>
> A sense of humor and the power to laugh.
>
> A few moments of quiet, silent meditation. The sense of the presence of God.
>
> . . . and the patience to wait for the coming of these things, with the wisdom to know them when they come.

January 7

I am making these journal entries in my studio on an old IBM Selectric typewriter, my only writing instrument for many years and at least a dozen books. Since the outside temperature is well below freezing, the gas fireplace, close to my desk, is glowing brightly.

What are we doing in an old farmhouse on a narrow dirt road in a small southern New Hampshire town after spending more than a dozen years in a lovely Scottsdale home complete with swimming pool, my own putting green, and a bright sun that made its appearance at least three hundred days a year? There have been many moments when Bette and I looked at each other and wondered. We are still not certain what forces caused us to move across the country to the tiny hamlet where Bette spent her childhood and where we were married thirty-four years ago, when we had about ten dollars between us.

As the story goes, this chapter in our life began in June 1988 when I was scheduled to give a speech at the Hynes Convention Center in Boston. Although Bette rarely travels with me, she decided to come along, also taking her aging mother and father with us. Instead of flying to the Boston airport, we would fly to Manchester, New Hampshire, and from there we could drive the old folks, in our rented car, to Grampa's brother's house and leave them for a week or two to enjoy, perhaps for the last time, the tiny hamlet where they had spent most of their lives.

The trip went well, and after we had deposited the old folks with Uncle Bill, we still had a day to ourselves before I was expected in Boston, so we decided to videotape the area to show our two grown sons where their mother spent her youth and where we were eventually married. And so, with Bette driving and doing the narration, I managed to capture most of the important landmarks on videotape, including Main Street with its few stores, the old church where we were married, the homes where Bette spent her youth, her schools, the tiny library, and even the Grange Hall, where she had been a member.

The small hamlet of less than three thousand is spread

over several square miles, and eventually, with me still working the camera, we found ourselves on the outskirts where there were only a few scattered houses but plenty of pine, birch, and maple trees of all sizes. As we were driving along, Bette suddenly pointed out the window to her left at a small dirt road and said that in all the years she had lived in the town, she had never been down that road. Near several huge boulders was a metallic sign displaying the words FOR SALE in bright orange. I remember Bette wondering what could possibly be for sale on such a lonely road. While I kept my finger on the camera trigger, videotaping out the front windshield of the car, Bette stopped, circled around, and then turned down that small dirt road, so narrow in many places that tree branches touched one another as they leaned from one side of the road to the other.

After driving through perhaps a half mile of trees without seeing a house, we climbed a small rise, and ahead of us, on our right, was an old gray farmhouse. Out front, on the uneven lawn, was another bright orange FOR SALE sign. Bette turned toward me and then, saying nothing, pulled into the driveway. Since it was obvious that the house was not being lived in, we began peeking into the windows, through which we could see massive ceiling beams and old-style wide floorboards. I remember Bette saying that while it was an old place, it had certainly had a lot of love. While we were still looking in windows, a car pulled up in front of the house, and a smiling man came walking across the lawn, extending his hand toward me. He lived up the road about a half mile, he said, and was on the way into his office when he saw our car. Bob was a realtor and a builder and shook his head in amazement when he said that he had just listed the house on the previous day and because of its out-of-the-way location he didn't expect to have any interested visitors for months. He asked us if we would like to go in and look around, since it was a very special place.

I thanked him and told him that we weren't house hunting, since we already had a lovely home in Scottsdale and if he had come by five minutes later, we would have been gone. "Well," he replied, not knowing that he was talking to someone who made his living telling stories about how fate works, "maybe this was all meant to be." I looked at Bette, who shrugged her shoulders. "Okay," I said, "show us the place."

It was love at first sight. We went through all nine rooms, many needing work, and saw it all . . . the bright, oak-paneled living room . . . the wide-planked floors with old countersunk nail holes . . . the old floor-to-ceiling fireplace loaded with character . . . the aged oak beams extending across the kitchen ceiling . . . even an old room with no insulation and rough, unfinished walls that had obviously been used for storage, although Bob said it was called the summer room. In better times it had probably entertained families as they sipped their lemonade on hot summer days.

Five hours later Bette wrote out a check covering the deposit on the farm. We returned to New Hampshire in late August for the closing. Our oldest son, Dana, who should have been an architect, came along, did a lot of measuring, and then drew up some plans for us. The "summer room" would be my insulated and carpeted studio with built-in floor-to-ceiling bookcases to hold all my books. A thirty-by-twenty-foot new addition, off the hallway, would be our giant family room and the perfect spot for our six-foot Sony projection television set, with a huge master bedroom directly above on the second floor. On the house's western side we would add a three-car garage and build a four-room apartment over it for Bette's mom and dad, since we couldn't possibly leave them in Arizona. We then turned the plans that Dana had drawn over to Bob, and his construction people went to work.

We put our Scottsdale home on the market in March 1989, and luckily sold it in September. In late October, with all our belongings, we moved across the country, and on November 1 we moved in, with Bette's folks moving into their new place, thrilled at once again being back in the town of their youth.

Carpenters, plumbers, electricians, and painters became part of our household during the following year or so, even laying down their tools and taking a coffee break every morning at ten in our kitchen. They have finally completed all the building and refinishing that Bette and I wanted done, just a month ago!

I do believe we have finally found our own "Enchanted Haven."

January 15

A heavy snowfall, now many hours old, made this a perfect day for me to tackle and respond to what I can only call fan mail. Most of it is sent to me with love and gratitude for the help that one or another of my books has provided and very often the letters will share words of wisdom written by some wise individual of the past.

One of the letters I answered today contained a marvelous treasure written by Bolton Hall who, my *Dictionary of Thoughts* tells me, was a nineteenth-century minister.

Take not anxious thought as to the results of your work nor of our work. If you are doing all that you can, the results, immediate or eventual, are not your affair at all. Such seed of truth as we plant can but grow. If we do not see the fruits here, we know nevertheless that there or somewhere they do spring up.

It would be great if we could succeed now; it will be greater if we patiently wait for success, even though we never see it ourselves. For it will come. Do not be fretted by abuse. Those who abuse you do not know what they are doing. We also were at one time deluded and cruel, therefore forgive.

Do not be worried by bigotry. We cannot help it, we are not responsible for it—we are responsible to ourselves and for ourselves and for no one else. Do not be angry at opposition either; no one can really oppose the order of Nature or the decrees of God, which are one and the same. Our plans may be upset—there are greater plans than ours. They may not be completed in the time we would wish, but our works and the work of those who follow us, they will be carried out.

Do not grieve over your own troubles; you would not have them if you did not need them. Do not grieve over the troubles of "others"; there are no others.

Therefore, let us keep God in our hearts and quiet in our minds, for though in the flesh we may never stand upon our edifice, we are building that which shall never be pulled down.

January 22

Our local historical society met in the library last evening to hear a lecture on the history of our small town. Bette and I learned plenty.

The price of real estate in these parts was around nine cents an acre in 1766. In 1767 the population of our town was twelve, but by 1774 there were fifteen families living here. The entire eligible male population fought in the

Revolutionary War, and the first town meeting was held in 1771. An old history of the town states, "Of course, it could not be expected that a history of this quiet town would be very romantic or great. We have had no Indian tragedies, no national battles, no men of extensive fame, no mines of wealth, and no very remarkable record in any way. Our town has little that is brilliant; much that is solid, honorable and good."

I suspect that any current town historian would probably come up with the same evaluation as he or she looked back over our most recent hundred years or so.

We truly hit the jackpot last night at the historical meeting, finally discovering how old this special place is that we now live in. With a little help in digging among old records we discovered that our dwelling was first built by a Nathan Cole in 1792. 1792! He lived here with his wife, Nabby, and later with a second wife, Molly, until 1800, when the place was sold to David and Mehitable Hills. Apparently a bad fire almost destroyed the old farm somewhere along the way.

Now I know why the wind, blowing through the pines at night, sounds almost like a chorus of voices . . . voices from two hundred years of laughter and tears, tragedy and joy, victory and disaster from people like Nabby and Mehitable and Nathan and Jeremiah and Ella and Franklin.

1792!

February 12

In that great musical *A Chorus Line* I can still remember a young dancer in one scene being asked what she wanted to be when she grew up. "Young" was her reply.

I have been playing a game of sorts with myself ever

since I reached my sixty-fifth birthday on December 12, 1988. That date, according to my new calendar of life, is the date of my second birth, and my goal now is to live at least twenty-one "new" years, attaining a second coming of age on December 12, 2009!

I like what Shakespeare once wrote about growing old: "Some men never seem to grow old. Always active in thought, always ready to adopt new ideas, they are never chargeable with fogyism. Satisfied, yet ever dissatisfied, settled, yet ever unsettled, they always enjoy the best of what is, and are the first to find the best of what will be."

Today therefore I am only two years and two months old in my new life. The best, I am certain, is all ahead of me.

February 19

Arrived early last evening in Vancouver, British Columbia, one of my favorite cities in the entire world. I arrived early so that I could do a radio show or two today to promote my speech tonight. What a wonderful feeling to have the program's sponsor, Peter Legge, publisher of many Canadian magazines, inform me before my scheduled appearance on Julie Brown's noontime radio show that the Orpheum Theatre was already sold out. When I asked Peter what that meant in terms of live bodies, he said, "Two thousand seven hundred and fifty, plus a wheelchair or two!"

February 22

Flew from Canada down to Monterrey, Mexico, to speak at the First International Leadership Congress. More than two thousand young people packed the Luis Elizondo Auditorium, at the Monterrey Institute of Technology. What impressed me most was the intensity of the group. Both the young men and the young women leaned forward, unsmiling, concentrating on every word I said, which was immediately translated into Spanish, and their questions following the speech were more on target than those from any audience I have faced in years.

Sitting in my hotel room after my appearance, I couldn't forget the faces of the young, eager Mexicans, nor could I help thinking that if our American young don't wake up, these Mexican kids are going to outproduce, outmarket, and outperform our bunch in the next twenty years.

The world is gaining on us . . . fast!

February 23

Bette was knitting in the family room when she spotted him, a giant owl, perched on the limb of an oak tree in the backyard just at the beginning of our woods. His feathers were grayish brown, and he was at least two feet tall. He had no visible ear tufts but had large, staring eyes, which silently surveyed the ground, perhaps thirty feet below, probably looking for food. We hastily checked our bird guidebook while he sat patiently and calmly, but found no owl that looked exactly like him or fit his description. The drawing of an eastern screech owl looked most like our visitor, but the book said that they rarely reached larger than eight inches at maturity. Finally our visitor lifted his huge wings, soared up through the tree branches, and was gone.

We were honored by his visit and so grateful that we are far enough away from the congestion of man to be able to see and enjoy some of God's other creations who, under civilization's crushing advance, are gradually disappearing from the earth. It is a loss that cannot even be measured. How sad.

March 4

A few memorable moments at the airport in Baton Rouge. I had been booked several months ago as guest speaker for the Baton Rouge Eighth Annual Business Awards Banquet, and received a letter from the program chairman informing me that Louisiana's governor, Buddy Roemer, would be introducing me. Then, about a week ago, I received another letter informing me that the governor's plans had been changed so that he would be unable to attend the banquet.

When I arrived at the airport, I walked down a long corridor, pausing as I reached the main lobby, puzzled as to why no representative from the awards banquet was meeting me as arranged. Getting a little hot under the collar at this foul-up, I trudged across the lobby toward the down escalator in order to pick up my luggage, scarcely noticing the dapper but tieless gentleman standing by himself and staring intently at each passenger who had disembarked the plane.

At the bottom of the escalator a young man approached me, smiling. He had been sent to pick me up, but rather than explaining why he was waiting down at the luggage area instead of in the lobby, he greeted me with, "Mr. Mandino, did you see the governor?"

"The governor? No."

"Well, he's upstairs in the lobby somewhere, waiting to greet you as you came off the plane, but I guess you missed each other. He said he felt so badly about not being able to introduce you tonight that he wanted to apologize to you himself. Hey, here he comes now!"

I turned and saw Governor Buddy Roemer coming down the escalator. So did a couple of hundred other citizens, pointing in dismay and wondering what their governor was doing, all by himself, waving on an escalator.

We embraced as he stepped off the escalator, and chatted for a few minutes. He said he missed me because he wasn't expecting to see Mandino in a white sport shirt and blue jeans. I didn't recognize him because I wasn't expecting to see the state's governor not surrounded by a convoy of state troopers.

Still the evening went well, and the mayor of Baton Rouge, Tom Ed McHugh, presented me with a plaque making me an honorary mayor and president of the city of Baton Rouge, parish of East Baton Rouge.

April 12

I was reading somewhere today that a cubic foot of granite weighs 150 pounds or more and that a single yard of stone wall, three feet high, calls for about a ton of granite.

We have old granite stone walls around just about all our property. As closely as I can figure, there are at least 1,200 feet of stone wall, which means that we have 1,200 tons of granite guarding our place—2.4 million pounds of stone!

Took a short walk through the woods this morning. Found a lovely and iridescent spiderweb strung across two large blueberry branches. Dew still covered it, and I stopped and watched its creator as he moved slowly across the shimmering strings. When I was a kid, I remember that I would always knock down and remove, with a stick, any spiderweb I would find, and now I just watch . . . and eventually walk away.

April 19

The town of Marshall, population 11,736, is in southwest Minnesota, and it is the perfect example of small-town America at its best. The town has eighteen churches, a municipal hospital, a newspaper, three radio stations, five motels, a railroad station, and even a small airport with twice-daily commuter flights to Minneapolis–Saint Paul.

Last night I spoke to well over a thousand people in the Marshall High School Auditorium, sponsored by the Rural Business Support Team. The audience was warm and friendly. They applauded so long when I finished that I began to feel tears running down my cheeks. America, the beautiful!

April 22

Went on a little exploration trip that I've been promising myself for a couple of months. In midmorning, with the sun shining brightly and spring in the air, I crossed our old road and walked down the steep bank into the woods beyond. We own approximately two acres on this side of the road, land where the trees are not much more than ten feet tall, probably because the area was cleared at one time in the past. Beyond our small chunk of earth the pines and oaks and birches still grow tall and dense where I entered the woods through an opening that probably was the beginning of a long-ago pathway.

The woods erupted in noise as I walked along. It seemed as if every bluejay, crow, woodpecker, and squirrel resented my presence in their virginal forest and were letting me know exactly how they felt. Nevertheless I forged ahead, often having to alter my forward course in order to continue, but eventually I came upon the object of my search, a very special place called Heron Lake. From what I had been able to learn, this unique and almost unknown body of dark water was probably created by some long-ago glacier and apparently had increased in size through the centuries until it now enveloped several acres of trees that still stood, rising out of the water with their leafless branches reaching toward the sky.

I wanted to visit this enchanted place now because several local citizens had warned me not to go near the pond in late May or early June. On top of most of the dead trees, rising out of the water, I could see huge nests. This pond has been for many years a rookery where great blue herons come each year in May and June to hatch and then nurture their young. If I had waited to visit this special place in early June, chances are that I would disturb the big birds during their parental duties and they would immediately depart, leaving their eggs or young offspring to the elements.

Splashing sounds in the brackish water just below my feet alerted me to a family of beavers, who were swimming by with large sticks of wood in their mouths. I watched fascinated, listening to the strange sounds around me and inhaling smells that were completely unfamiliar to me. Had this pond really been here for millions of years? Standing there, I felt very insignificant and small. Another family of beavers swam by, each one carrying wood for its home. Even here, in a place that time has forgotten, among the cranberry bogs, sphagnum moss, sedges, and tall grass, life goes on.

April 28

Yesterday was a hectic day in Dallas. Spoke to the Baron's Club, representing the top salespeople of New York Life, in the morning and then went to the studios of the Automotive Satellite Television Network, where I was interviewed on tape for a program on cable to the nation's automobile dealers who subscribe to the service. Afterward Kathy Davis, ASTN vice president, rode with me to the airport saying that she had loved every minute of our time in the studio and that there wasn't a dry eye in the house when I told the "Disco Duck" story. "I am amazed," she exclaimed, "at your gentleness and serenity. You had our production crew and programming staff mesmerized." What nice words. Almost better than getting paid.

April 29

Bette and I have finally decided to put our wild-growing two acres across the road to good use. This morning a local construction company arrived with lots of heavy equipment and commenced clearing the area of trees. Then with all sorts of bulldozers and steam shovels they will excavate a hole approximately ten feet deep, a hundred feet long by seventy feet wide.

Water from our artesian well, which currently drain its surplus overflow into a pipe under our front lawn and under the dirt road until it empties into the woods beyond, will now drain instead into the new pond and, along with the rain, gradually fill the huge cavity. Hopefully by the end of the summer our new addition to the landscape, which we plan to christen Little Walden, will look like all the other old-fashioned New England ponds.

We also plan to plant grass seed around its newly cultivated, wide bank as well as a row of tall birches all the way around the east and south side plus purchase at least a couple of comfortable Adirondack wooden chairs for some heavy-duty reading and relaxing, with the pond at our feet.

I think that Mr. Thoreau would approve.

May 1

I see that the great pianist Van Cliburn, after twenty years of retirement in Fort Worth, will be performing the Tchaikovsky Concerto with Zubin Mehta and the New York Philharmonic tonight at Carnegie Hall.

Reading about Van and how, as a young man, he stood the world on its ear with his upset victory in the Tchaikovsky International Piano Competition in Moscow reminded me of a special evening, almost two years ago, when it was my honor to drape the Napoleon Hill Gold Medal for Achievement in the Arts around the great man's neck.

Ever since the award dinners were initiated years ago, W. Clement Stone had always been the individual who hung the gold medals around each recipient's neck. He even hung one around my tense neck a few years ago. However, Mr. Stone was not feeling well, so I was contacted by the awards committee, with not too many days to spare, and asked if I would join actress Florence Henderson at the head table. When each winner was announced, I was to stand, congratulate the individual, and gently drape the huge gold medal with its wide ribbon around the person's neck.

It was a fun evening, presenting the gold medals to Wally "Famous" Amos; *Parade* magazine's editor, Walter

Anderson; NBC's Nancy Foreman; and also to representatives for Amway's Rich DeVoss and old friend Paul Harvey.

What I remember most vividly about the evening, however, is Van Cliburn's acceptance speech. He said that one of the things he found most inspiring about the evening was that while he sat next to Og Mandino at the head table, it gave him a personal thrill to observe people come up to Og with the "kind of warmth and sincerity of deep gratitude for the words that he has written in his very successful life."

I hope Van knocks them dead tonight.

May 12

Mother's Day ... and although my beloved mother has been gone for half a century, I still miss her as much as if her funeral had been yesterday. She was the greatest influence in my life.

Even before I commenced school, my mother, a tough little redheaded Irish lady, had mapped out my future for me. She was constantly reminding me that someday I would be a great writer, not just a writer—a *great* writer. I didn't fight her; I bought the idea. She even had me reading grown-up books and writing short compositions long before I ever sat behind a classroom desk. Yes, someday I would be a *great* writer!

We held on to our dream through the growing-up years, and in my senior year of high school I was editor of our school paper, writing many articles for the various editions. Also, we pored through scores of college catalogs for many months and finally selected the University of Missouri because we believed that it had the very best journalism school in the country. I was all set—in the fall of 1940 I would be in college, and my career would truly be under way.

Then, only six weeks after I graduated from high school, my mother dropped dead in our kitchen while she was preparing lunch for me, and that tragic event put an end to my dream of college and a writing career. Bitter and brokenhearted, I joined the Army Air Corps as swiftly as I could, and a year later I received my silver wings as a bombardier. Eventually I flew thirty missions over Germany, earned several decorations, and came home in one piece.

I had managed to save about a thousand dollars while in the service, so I rented a small walk-up apartment just off Times Square, planning to test the waters as a writer. Somewhere deep inside, my mother's dream was still alive in me. I remember buying a secondhand Underwood typewriter and began to write. Since so many of the nation's book and magazine publishers were in Manhattan, I would bring my finished work, articles, short stories, even poems, directly to their doors. I failed miserably. Sold nothing, not even a single filler piece. Finally ran out of money and returned to New England, land of my birth, got a job selling life insurance, and married a lovely lady.

The next ten years or so were a living hell, for me, for my wife, and even for our new and precious daughter. It seemed that no matter how hard or how many hours I worked, we were always in debt up to our eyeballs, and as time went on, we kept sinking deeper and deeper into the pit. Somewhere along the way I began doing what so many still do to hide from reality. No matter how late I worked to try to make a sale, I would stop on the way home for a drink. Soon that one drink became two, then four, then six, and I eventually, and deservedly, lost the two people who meant the most in my life. My wife took my daughter and left the miserable drunk who was her husband. Of course then I really went to hell, drinking more and more until I lost my job and our mortgaged home. With my few clothes tossed into the back of my old Ford, I traveled the country, taking any kind of work I could find in order to earn a few more bucks for that next bottle of cheap wine.

Then, on a cold and dark morning in early winter in Cleveland, I almost ended my life. I was in one of the dingiest parts of the city, freezing, no topcoat, when I passed a pawnshop and saw, inside the window on a shelf, a small handgun. Attached to the gun was a yellow tag that read twenty-nine dollars. I reached into my pocket and removed three wrinkled ten-dollar bills, all I had in the world, and I thought, *That gun is the answer to all my problems. I'll buy that damn thing, get a couple of bullets, take them back to that dingy room where I'm staying, load the gun, put the gun to my head, and pull the trigger. Then I'll never have to face that miserable failure in the mirror again!*

I don't remember what happened next. Through the years, in countless interviews, I've been asked why I didn't buy that gun, and I've now learned to joke about it, saying that even taking one's life requires some form of courage, and I had fallen so low that I couldn't even do that. I don't know what happened. I heard no voices, no angels singing, but I slowly turned away from that pawnshop and trudged up the street in the driving rain and sleet until I found myself on the steps of a public library. I entered. It was warm—and it was free. I wandered slowly through the aisles of books until I found myself standing in front of that special section that is in every library, that gold mine containing books on how to succeed and how to hold on to one's success after it has been achieved. I began that morning to read book after book by the great masters of success—people like Norman Vincent Peale, Napoleon Hill, Elbert Hubbard, Maxwell Maltz, Dorothea Brande, Percy Whiting, and Russell Conwell. Gradually, starting that morning, my life began to change.

I continued to wander, gypsylike, from city to city in the months that followed, but now I was spending a good deal more time in libraries and less in barrooms, searching for some answers. Where had I gone wrong? Could a thirty-five-year-old bum with only a high school education still make something of himself? Or was it too late for me?

I continued my search and discovered W. Clement Stone's great book, *Success Through a Positive Attitude*, in a library in Concord, New Hampshire, and his words inspired me so much that I wanted to work for that special man. The book stated that he was president and founder of the Combined Insurance Company of America, and I began searching for the company. I found one of their branches in Boston, applied for a job, and they actually decided to take a chance on this thirty-five-year-old loser. They hired me! Also, at the same time that I was searching for W. Clement Stone, I met a woman who had a good deal more faith in me than anyone ever had before. I married Bette.

Within a year my excellent record earned me a position of sales manager, and my first territory was northern Maine. I hired several young guys right off the potato farms, taught them how to earn five times what they had been making, and soon our sales totals were attracting national attention within the company. I was flying high now that I had learned and applied Stone's positive-mental-attitude philosophy every day.

Then I took a long step into the future, although I didn't realize it at the time. I rented a typewriter, took a week off from work, and wrote a sales manual on how one sells insurance to rural people. The writing dream was still alive! I typed the manual as neatly as I could and mailed it to the company's home office in Chicago, just praying that someone back there would recognize the great talent they had working for them in northern Maine. Well, someone did, and soon Bette and I and our new young son, Dana, were moving to Chicago, where I went to work in Combined's sales promotion department, writing sales bulletins. At last, despite all the tough years, I was finally earning my living writing!

After a year or so of creating motivational material for salespeople, another break came my way. The editor of W. Clement Stone's monthly magazine *Success Unlimited* retired, and I boldly applied for the job, although I truly didn't know a galley sheet from a roll of toilet paper. Well, by then Mr. Stone and I were friends, so he gave the job to me.

I didn't know what I was doing, but I sure learned in a hurry, and since we had a tiny staff, I was not only editing but also writing a good deal of the material that went into each monthly issue. One month I wrote and ran an article on Ben Hogan and his brave comeback from a terrible automobile accident, and after the magazine was published, I received a letter from a New York publisher telling me that he had read my story and was very impressed. If I ever decided to write a book, he would be very interested in seeing it, and a year and a half later we published a tiny volume titled *The Greatest Salesman in the World*.

The book's first printing was only five thousand copies with no advertising promotion, yet it began to sell in great volume as soon as it hit the bookshelves. The publisher had to go back for printing after printing, thanks to word-of-mouth "advertising," until sales had exceeded 300,000 copies—and that was way back in the late 1960s! Somewhere along the way my little book had also attracted Bantam Books' attention, and the publishing giant was interested in obtaining the paperback rights. The sum of money being discussed for the rights was $350,000, which I was certain was more money than there was in the entire world. However, before Bantam would purchase the rights, they wanted to meet with the author to determine if he, too, was promotable along with the book. And so, on a day I shall never forget, I found myself nervously sitting in a large oval-shaped boardroom at Bantam's New York headquarters being grilled by at least thirty executives. Apparently they decided that they could do something with me because the chairman of the board finally rose, walked down to where I was nervously sitting, smiled, and extended his hand as he congratulated me. They had bought my book—for all that money!

I couldn't wait to be done with the hand shaking and get out of that huge office so that I could hurry back to the New York Hilton, where I was staying, to call Bette with the great news! I hadn't gone very far along Fifth Avenue when the sky opened and the rain fell, in buckets. I had no topcoat to protect me, so I dashed into the first open doorway I could find—a tiny church. There was no one in the church when I entered, and the sound of heavy rain pounding on the roof echoed loudly throughout the silent building. Then I heard music coming from the basement or cellar beneath me—an organ, or a recording of an organ playing "Amazing Grace."

I walked slowly up to the front of the church, fell to my knees, and began to sob—and all I could think of was my mother. Half aloud I heard myself saying, "Mom, it took us a long time, but we finally made it!"

I was forty-five years old. It is never too late.

May 17

Fiddleheads. Our woods are filled with them, these baby fern, their emerging heads shaped in a spiral that does indeed look like the head of a fiddle before they uncoil upward, reaching toward heaven until they become giant sprays of lush, green fern. What a lovely accent to the dark pine needles from which they emerge.

All known families of ferns have existed on our fragile earth for more than 150 million years, enduring a range of climates extending from the Arctic Circle to the hot, wet lowlands of equatorial jungles. Ferns were nibbled on by dinosaurs long before these magnificent creatures ever saw a fruit tree or a flower in bloom.

I've never eaten one, but I understand that fiddleheads are considered a delicacy by many, especially here in New Hampshire. Maybe instead of cholesterol-filled cheese chunks I'll try some in an omelet one of these days.

May 19

It's been some time since I've had to endure Mexico City's terrible pollution problem for more than a few hours, and I see that several entrepreneurs have now opened special booths in local parks and malls, charging $1.60 per minute to breathe clean air through a mask!

May 23

The Inn At Spanish Bay, on the Monterrey Peninsula, is probably one of the loveliest spots on our globe. Spoke there yesterday morning to more than a hundred members of the President's Club of National Education Centers, a group of schools that offers vocational training in electronics, business, and allied health.

My objective was to inspire the members not only to achieve bigger things themselves but to go back to their schools and lead others to a greater level of experience. Did I succeed? From the reception after the speech it would appear that I did, but only time will tell.

The golf course just outside my hotel window looked so tempting, but I never bring my golf clubs when I'm "working" because of a sorry experience I had several years ago. I had been booked to keynote a convention of the top producers of an American insurance company who were being rewarded for their achievements with a luxurious week, along with their spouses, in the faraway Algarve region of Portugal. The company president phoned me, several days before departure, inviting me to play a round of golf with him. I told him that I never mixed business with pleasure, but he insisted that he wanted a chance to win back some of the outrageous fee I was charging them, so I brought my golf clubs across the Atlantic to the lovely resort overlooking the Mediterranean.

It was raining when I arrived, and it was still raining when I departed three days later. I did get to use my putter, hitting golf balls from one of the rooms in my suite to the next, trying to get them to go into the drinking glasses I had placed on the lush carpet.

I learned a lesson. . . .

May 31

I doubt that I will ever forget the events of yesterday evening. I shared the speaker's platform with an old friend whom I hadn't seen in ten years or so, Norman Vincent Peale.

Presented by LIFE Seminars, Dr. Peale and I spoke at the Cobb Great Hall at the Wharton Center for Performing Arts on the campus of Michigan State University in East Lansing, Michigan, and all 2,500 seats were occupied when my old friend walked out on stage at seven P.M.

I was sitting backstage, close to Ruth Peale, when her husband was introduced. Dr. Peale opened by saying, "Ladies and gentlemen, I hope you all realize that I am not the feature speaker here tonight. On this program with me is not only a great speaker but a great writer, Og Mandino." As Dr. Peale continued with his testimonial, I turned to his wife and said, shaking my head, "Ruth, will you listen to him." She smiled and nodded and patted my shoulder.

Dr. Peale didn't know that we had a surprise planned for him. Nancy Vogl, the bright lady who heads LIFE Seminars, had arranged for a huge birthday cake to be baked, containing ninety-three candles. When Dr. Peale finished his speech, I pushed this huge cake, with every candle lit, out on stage, to the old boy's great surprise. Then a local group of children from the People's Church came up on stage and sang "Happy Birthday" as well as "I Never Touched a Rainbow" to the great man.

Dr. Peale broke down and cried and kissed my cheek as we walked off the stage together, arm in arm. Backstage he actually apologized to me for the time that was being taken away from my speech for his birthday festivities!

June 5

I am at the Doubletree Hotel in Santa Clara, speaking tonight in the ballroom downstairs for a firm called Motivation Marketing. Flew into San Francisco yesterday in time to appear on Jim Eason's KGO talk show to promote ticket sales for this evening. It was a phone-in show, and the callers were very kind to me—as was Jim.

Planned to spend this day doing some writing but haven't even opened my attaché case. I try, again and again, but I just can't seem to work away from my studio. Lolled around most of the day in my pajamas, with room service bringing me food while I tried to develop interest in the daytime television talk shows until my disgust overrode my boredom.

It is now slightly past five on a bright, sunny California afternoon, and I step barefooted from my twelfth-floor room out onto the concrete balcony. I lean against the pitted metal railing and gaze out in awe at part of the Silicon Valley. Every road and side road, it seems, from those passing close to the hotel to the multilane freeways almost as far away as the horizon, are choked with late-afternoon traffic. Nothing seems to be moving, even at the proverbial snail's pace, while a thick grayish-black cloud floats menacingly not far above the thousands trapped in their vehicles as they struggle to get home for supper plus a little playtime with the kids.

Gradually, day by day and year by year, we are strangling ourselves to death as we cluster closer and closer together, not because we want to but because we have to in order to be within a couple of driving hours of our jobs, God help us. I thought of my buddy, Thoreau, who almost a century and a half ago wrote that "we live thick and are in each other's way, and stumble over one another, and I think that we thus lose some respect for one another. It would be better if there were but one inhabitant to a square mile, as where I live. The value of a man is not in his skin, that we should touch him."

The *San Jose Mercury News* was delivered with my breakfast this morning, and I read about the horrible problem facing the nearby city of Campbell, population 35,000, sitting right in the middle of a horrendous transportation crossroads in the valley. One traffic intersection in Campbell, the corner of Hamilton and Bascom avenues, is now handling—trying to handle—125,000 automobiles, trucks, and vans every day—every twenty-four hours!

Counting Paula, our mail person, I figure that four cars per day, on the average, go past our old farm on our sandy road. That means that as many cars go through the Hamilton and Bascom avenues intersection in Campbell every day as will pass our house in eighty-six years! As Thoreau added, "I have, as it were, my own sun and moon and stars, and a little world all to myself." How lucky we are!

June 15

Our vegetable garden, just across the road, is now completely filled, awaiting the proper blend of sunshine and rain to produce baskets of food for us, I hope.

I planted three kinds of corn this year, all sugary enhanced hybrids—Kandy Korn, Double Delicious, and Quickie. Also, four rows of bush and wax beans for Bette to can, tendersweet carrots, Cherry Belle radishes, and Ruby Queen beets.

From a local garden supply house I had also purchased several boxes of small plants, including Serrano, which is supposed to have more "fire per inch" than any other pepper, King of the North bell peppers, Straight Eight cucumbers, and six Super Beefsteak tomatoes.

I found a small cluster of wild violets growing in the midst of my cultivated garden. Put a stake into the ground to keep me aware of their special presence and planted my vegetables around them.

A special calmness comes over me when I am planting, a calmness I cannot even explain.

June 21

An important part of setting goals is developing the ability in one's mind to picture that goal vividly and clearly as already attained. A nineteenth-century wise man, Joseph Appel, once wrote,

> You want a better position than you now have in business, a better and fuller place in life? All right, think of that better place and you in it as already existing. Form the mental image. Keep on thinking of that higher position, keep the image constantly before you and . . . no, you will not suddenly be transported into the higher job, but you will find that you are preparing yourself to occupy the better position in life. . . . your body, your energy, your understanding, your heart will all grow up to the job . . . and when you are ready, after hard work, perhaps after years of preparation, you will get the job and the higher place in life.

I've always found that this "mental imaging" works well for material things as well . . . a new car, a new house, new golf clubs. Picturing that those things are already in one's possession is a powerful step toward actually acquiring them.

Many years ago, when we were struggling just to make our mortgage payments each month, my dream was to own a Jeep Grand Wagoneer, which for many years was the ultimate in a four-wheel-drive automobile with its luxurious leather interior and electric controls, weighing more than two and a half tons and carrying its riders high above those in normal automobiles.

In the room where I was trying to write my first book, back in Arlington Heights, Illinois, I had several color photos of the Grand Wagoneer on the walls. There were several more nailed to a wall of the garage. Every day I would see those photos and dream.

Well, we didn't buy our Grand Wagoneer until we moved back here to New Hampshire, where four-wheel drive is a necessity in the winter. The car now looks big and boxy compared with some of its competitors, and the gas mileage is lousy, but Bette and I still love the old wagon, which Rock Hudson introduced to the world in a 1963 movie and which has a devoted group of owners. Ours has only twenty thousand or so miles on it. The motor needs to be coddled, and we are now burning high-test gasoline to keep things from knocking, but the big box on wheels has become one of the family, and neither one of us wants to part with her.

After almost thirty years, yesterday must have been a very sad day when the last model, a dark green one, came down the line, discontinued because of declining sales.

June 23

The Kellogg School of Business at Northwestern University in Evanston, Illinois, has been one of the nation's leading business schools for many years.

Yesterday morning Bette and I sat proudly in McGraw Memorial Hall at the university and watched our youngest son, Matthew, receive his master of management degree.

Where did all the years go? It was only yesterday, wasn't it, when I peered through a window in the maternity ward in Highland Park and saw his little face for the first time?

June 25

The first tiger lilies exploded into bloom today. We must have several hundred plants, east of our house, lining both sides of the dirt road, and within a week or so orange will be the prevailing color. Also, Bette made a major discovery this morning. Across the road, to one side of the circular path that swings around the mailboxes, is a family of wild honeysuckle. Reds and yellows and soft whites, with provocative-looking petals, look down on us from vines that have tenaciously wrapped themselves around young maples. Somehow I always thought honeysuckle only grew around old southern plantations and New Orleans mansions.

July 8

Bette and I are still exhausted even though we almost slept through all of yesterday. We have just returned from exploring one of the last untamed wilderness routes in the world, Alaska's Inside Passage, on Holland-America's luxurious cruise ship, *Ms. Westerdam*.

So many great memories . . . the famous Butchart Gardens, blazing with color in Victoria, capital of British Columbia; Vancouver's bustling Chinatown; Ketchikan, acclaimed as the totem-pole capital of the world; Juneau, Alaska's capital city, where we shopped for gold nuggets and, in a motorcoach, were driven to the giant Mendenhall Glacier, a constantly moving jagged sheet of blue ice. In a gift shop at the visitors' center I purchased a small vial of glacial flour with the label stating that it was "a sample of finely pulverized sediment resulting from glacial action, collected from the beach area in front of the Mendenhall Glacier."

Icebergs, whales, eagles, and a vast panorama of trees and glaciers spread before us as we traveled through the waters of Glacier Bay National Park. In Sitka, a center of rich Russian heritage, we visited Saint Michael's Orthodox Cathedral with its immense onion dome and priceless holy paintings. The trip was a change of pace that we both needed, seemingly a journey back in time. I even bought Bette a mug of beer in Juneau's Red Dog Saloon and a couple of gold nuggets in one of their many jewelry stores.

We truly enjoyed our "northern exposure."

July 23

Took a long walk, alone, deep into the woods behind our farm. Woodpeckers seemed to be doing their thing in almost every pine tree, and yet there was a stillness and peace among the trees that I could almost feel as I moved through the deep underbrush. It seems that whether nature smiles and preens herself on her loveliest days or becomes pale, gray, cold, and rainy in autumn or winter, there is something in her that not only touches our soul but awakens thousands of memories of the past for those who were fortunate enough to spend some of their youth exploring the woods.

In my constant search for words with power and grace, I found this piece by an early-nineteenth-century American author, Donald G. Mitchell:

> Thank heaven every summer's day of my life, that my lot was humbly cast within the hearing of romping brooks and beneath the shadow of oaks. And from all

the tramp and bustle of the world, into which fortune has led me in these latter years of my life, I delight to steal away for days and for weeks together, and bathe my spirit in the freedom of the old woods and to grow young again, lying upon the brookside and counting the white clouds that sail along the sky, softly and tranquilly, even as holy memories go stealing over the vault of life. I like to steep my soul in a sea of quiet, with nothing floating past me, as I lie moored to my thoughts, but the perfume of flowers and soaring birds and shadows of clouds.

Two days ago I was sweltering in the heat of the city, jostled by the thousand eager workers and panting under the shadow of the walls. But I have stolen away and for two hours of healthful regrowth into the darkling past I have been, this blessed summer's morning, lying upon the grassy bank of a stream that babbled me to sleep in boyhood. Dear old stream, unchanging, unfaltering, never growing old . . . smiling in your silver rustle and calming yourself in the broad placid pools, I love you, as I love a friend.

Memories. . . .

August 1

Bette and I walked around our pond, now almost filled, soon after the sun had set. She counted 101 frogs along the water's edge, each sitting a foot or so from its neighbor with only its head out of water, sounding off with the others in a loud chorus. Little Walden is looking better every day. I'll have to build a beach with white sand along the western edge so that the grandchildren can have fun when they visit.

Construction commenced today on the stone wall we

are having Bobby and his landscape crew erect between our flower garden and the newly planted orchard beyond. The boulders he is using look new and a little strange contrasted with the stones on our north and south wall, which have probably been in place for at least a century and are covered with that grayish-blue magical organism called lichen. Bobby says that he has developed a liquid that, when sprayed on bare stone, will speed up the lichen-growing process. He's talking about marketing it someday.

The perennials in our flower garden continue to thrill us with their colors. Tall white spires of Icicle Veronica, dark red Starfire phlox, purple Stonecrop sedum, pink astilbe, each seemingly served by their own crew of butterflies in matching colors. Amazing!

I know that autumn is waiting in the wings, although the thermometer reached ninety degrees today. We have some Baby Tears chrysanthemums, and they are already beginning to show flat yellow buds. Hated to see the mums getting ready to bloom when I was a kid. They were the early warning that school bells would soon be ringing.

August 2

The war between the "haves" and "have-nots" just increased a notch in intensity. I see where the rental-car companies in Florida are in the process of removing any bumper stickers or other emblems indicating that their automobiles are rentals. Apparently rental cars, loaded with tourists' belongings, have become prime targets for thieves, especially in vacation meccas.

August 7

Bette and I spent the day at the fifty-eighth Annual Craftsmen's Fair at Mount Sunapee State Park in Newbury. Hundreds of artists and craftspeople, in their booths under eight huge tents, were not only displaying their creations but also demonstrating how they were made. There was an amazing array of talent and ingenuity, and we tried to take it all in, from rug weaving to birdcarving to blacksmithing to chain-saw sculpting to quilting to hand-coloring photographs, pressed-flower bookmarks, and stained glass. And the entertainment! Better than a month of television's best efforts. There was a marvelous group playing contemporary international jazz, a fashion show, Cajun- and Shaker-style music, storytellers, folk music, even a children's tent where the young could spend hours cutting and pasting under careful supervision.

American independence, ingenuity, and self-reliance are not dead. These special people, artisans and merchants both, despite the terrible recession that has engulfed New England, continue to smile and talk about a better tomorrow. Tomorrow. Tomorrows will be better . . . if we, all of us, just hang on.

August 8

Took another journey back in time this morning. Not since I was a young schoolboy have I picked wild blackberries. Dressed for protection from the sharp thorns, Bette and I moved slowly through the brambles across from our place, and when we had finished, we had two quarts of the succulent jewels. I don't know why, but as I was picking, accompanied by a loud chorus of birds singing in the woods behind us, an image came to mind from the morning paper of Albanians being fired upon in the water as they tried to escape their impoverished nation. I closed my eyes for a moment and thanked God for all my blessings.

August 9

The long, dry spell has ended. Beginning at around noon today a heavy rain has soaked the gardens, and the dirt road was getting a little soft as darkness fell.

My writing has been nearly stalled for the past hour or so by a catalog from Miller Nurseries. Already the fall garden catalogs are arriving, not to mention toy and gift catalogs for Christmas shopping. I love looking through Miller's catalog with all their exotic nursery items such as Hosui Dwarf Asian pear trees; kiwi vines; Saturn, a new red seedless grape; Cardinal strawberry plants; and even a single apple tree, multiple-grafted so that five different varieties—Red Delicious, McIntosh, Yellowgold Delicious, Northern Spy, and Cortland—all grow on the same main stem! I always get the urge to order at least one of everything, but, fortunately I guess, the other thirteen acres of our land is heavily wooded and it's going to stay that way. Dinner tonight included corn and squash from our garden followed by a huge chunk of delicious blackberry pie baked by Bette from the berries we picked yesterday.

August 16

Four murders, in the poorest neighborhoods of Boston, violating our sensibilities on the eleven-o'clock television news. The morning papers had carried a piece about nine swastikas being painted on the Newton Free Library scheduled to be opened in September.

And then, in the same paper, like words from one's

mother assuring us that "everything is all right," is the story of Daniel Perez, who didn't like the mess of beer bottles, newspapers, garbage, and weeds that grew in the center strip of Broadway in upper Manhattan. Daniel cleared the area, worked the soil, fertilized it, and planted corn. Rustling in the breeze, as traffic passes, are more than a hundred stalks, now at least six feet tall. Swastikas . . . or corn. The choice is ours. This country's future can go either way, and where it leads will be up to us. We cannot hide behind locked doors and drawn curtains and wait for others to remake our world. This life of ours needs constant cultivating, like Mr. Perez's corn, or it will bear no fruit.

Samuel Taylor Coleridge was entertaining a visitor one day when the conversation got around to children. "I believe," said the visitor, "that the children should be given a free rein to think and act, thus learn at an early age to make their own decisions. That is the only way they can grow to their full potential."

Coleridge interrupted the man and said, "I would like you to see my flower garden," and the poet led the man outside. The visitor took one look and exclaimed, "Why that is nothing but a yard full of weeds!"

"Well," smiled Coleridge, "it was filled with roses, but this year I thought I would let the garden grow as it willed without my tending to it. And you can see the results."

September 3

Bought a life-size white rubber duck this morning. McNeil's Backward Look Antiques, on Route 9, always has its lawn cluttered with old horse-drawn vehicles, wooden Indians, carousel horses, and an ever-changing collection of folk art, and for several weeks I had noticed a white duck that had been placed close to the side of the road. Every time I drove by, I thought of our real live duck that we had back in Scottsdale for so many years, a duck who is still an important part of my speech on success.

One day, when my youngest son, Matt, was in the eighth grade, he came home from school carrying a shoe box, with holes punched in its cover. In the box was an adorable yellow duckling. The kids had hatched him in their biology class, nurtured him for five weeks, and then they held a raffle, and my son won the duck! Just what we needed!

In any event Matt and I built this little guy a great-looking home in a corner of our backyard. Matt painted it white and over the doorway, in bright red, he painted the word DISCO . . . Disco Duck! Then we went to the hardware store, bought a roll of eighteen-inch chicken wire, and erected a fence around Disco's hut so that he wouldn't go wandering off and get lost.

We had Disco for thirteen years, and of course Matt finally went off to college, leaving me to attend to Disco's every need. One morning, after many years of tender, loving care, Disco commenced quacking loudly before dawn and the quacking continued for days. After all our years together I knew Disco pretty well, and this quacking sounded different from his usual sounds. It almost had a whining, complaining pitch. Something was wrong. Disco obviously was not happy. Either the water in his pool was not being changed often enough, or the food was lousy, or the straw in his hut was wet, but there was no getting around it—Disco was miserable and he was letting us all know about it.

Yes, Disco had a problem. Disco just didn't know how capable he was. He had no idea that if he was unhappy with the conditions in his life, he had all the power and ability necessary to change them. If he truly wanted to change his life and his environment, perhaps for the better as far as he was concerned, all he had to do was flap his wings and *leave*. However, I remind my audiences, poor Disco didn't know how good he was. Disco had no idea that he could fly—just as most of those listening to my words have no idea what they can accomplish.

A couple of years before we moved from Scottsdale, I went out one morning to feed my old friend and found him floating facedown in the pool. At the far corner of our yard I dug a deep hole and buried my old buddy.

The duck I bought at our local antique store looks exactly like Disco, and as soon as I returned home, I carried my new friend, who was quite heavily weighted so that he wouldn't blow away, around to the far side of our little pond and set him close to the water's edge. He'll stay there until the snow flies, and then we'll bring him in until the following spring.

How great it is to look out our kitchen window in the morning and see the little guy with his image reflected in the pond. Disco lives!

September 13

It is almost too much for the mind to comprehend. For almost fifty years our nation has had to live with the possibility that sooner or later that big bad Russian bear might force us into a war that would probably end life, as we know it, on this planet. Who knows how many hundreds of billions of dollars have been spent for defense, through the years, that could have gone, instead, to making our land, and our world, a better place for all to live?

And now we are watching, in awe and disbelief, as our

archrival falls apart before our eyes. The enormity of what is transpiring as the Soviet Union disintegrates was made easier to grasp for those of us who have lived with the "red menace" for all or most of our lives by an Associated Press photograph in today's newspaper. Three young female students, taking a break from their studies, are smiling and conversing as they sit on a huge, toppled statue of Joseph Stalin in Gorky Park. The age of miracles is not over.

September 23

Fall officially arrived this morning, at 7:48 A.M., although at least half the maple trees near our farm have already altered the color of their coats to bright scarlet and every possible shade of orange and yellow.

Two strangers helped us greet the new season, early today. We were awakened by a horrible cacophony of moans and bellows and ran to the front of the house. In our pond were two large Canadian geese, loudly announcing to the world that they were in town. As we watched, one of the geese suddenly noticed my lifelike rubber statue of Disco Duck standing quietly, close to the water. He turned and swam hurriedly toward Disco, followed closely by his companion. When they had reached land, one of the geese approached Disco from the rear and the other from the front until they were so close they could have pecked at each other. After sniffing around the duck for several minutes, they raised their long necks, looked at each other, apparently decided he was no threat, and returned to the pond, where they swam slowly and quietly for perhaps another ten minutes before lifting their long brown wings and heading south accompanied by several shrieks of farewell. Hopefully we will be visited by many more winged travelers as they pause to rest on their journey to warmer climes.

I cannot understand why William Cullen Bryant once called these days of autumn the "melancholy days . . . the saddest of the year." The sky is bluer than ever, the air is crisp and sweet, and the fireplace, still unlit, is beginning to look very inviting. We are already Christmas shopping. No melancholy thoughts allowed.

September 26

In my speeches I am forever asking my audiences to take inventory of their skills, asking if there was anything they learned during all their years of school that could help them to change their lives for the better if they were to begin to apply that special ability immediately, regardless of their present condition, occupation, or age.

Then, as dramatically and forcefully as I can, I remind my listeners that they all learned *how to read*, and with that talent alone they can work miracles with their lives if they wish.

Thomas Carlyle, many years ago, wrote, "What we become depends on what we read after all manners of professors have done their best for us. The true university of today is a collection of books."

Unfortunately this nation of ours has a difficult task ahead before my assurance that everyone can transform their lives through the magic of reading becomes a reality, because the latest figures indicate that at least ten percent of our population is functionally illiterate, unable to read much more than the sign on the street where they live. No accomplishment in our entire history would give off a stronger and brighter glow than our eradication of this terrible handicap, because if one cannot read the map, he or she will never find that gold mine.

Back in 1981 my selection of the ten greatest how-to-succeed books was featured in *The People's Almanac #3*. If I had to recommend just three books to anyone looking for some answers to a better life today, I would suggest that they read *How to Stop Worrying and Start Living* by Dale Carnegie, *Psycho-Cybernetics* by Maxwell Maltz, and *The Power of Positive Thinking* by Norman Vincent Peale. However, I always have a personal struggle with that advice because I am frequently tempted to suggest a couple of my own books along with the others.

October 1

Lack of willpower has ruined more lives, destroyed more careers, and brought anguish and tears to more families than the lack of any other asset or quality, even including the lack of wealth and ambition.

A generation has now grown to adulthood since the United States surgeon general warned us that if we continue to smoke, those harmless little white sticks called cigarettes would kill many of us. More than fifty thousand Americans are now dying from lung cancer each year, yet a quarter of the adult population is still smoking!

Now a new government report tells us that there are almost eleven million alcoholics in the country and that more than seventy million—*seventy million*—individuals are affected by alcohol abuse because of a problem drinker in the home. Seventy million??!!

So many of us realize, too late, that life was a special gift but we never even removed the wrapping paper. For thirty years or more I have been trying to tell the world, in books and talks, that by following a few simple rules, such as counting one's blessings and going the extra mile, it is possible to live a life filled with pride and peace. My major problem is that I'm afraid I'm going to run out of years long before I run out of people who need help in conquering life.

October 4

First frost last night, and today the giant ash, whose limbs extend protectively over most of our house, has commenced shedding its hundreds of thousands of tiny gold leaves. In an effort to stay ahead of the deluge, I swept off our deck around noon, but by dark the wood was covered again by another foot or so of leaves. Also pruned and sawed away a good deal of old wood on several of our wild blueberry bushes today before giving them their annual feeding of aluminum sulfate.

We have just about hit our peak season of fall colors in all the trees, and the roads are filled with tour buses containing people that the natives call leaf-peepers.

October 5

Completed chapter 5 of *The Twelfth Angel* today. More than any of my books, at least as far as I can remember, this one seems to be writing itself. I have completely fallen in love with my little fictitious hero, Timothy Noble, as he attempts to play Little League ball despite a handicap that the other players and coach know nothing about. It seems that I just sit at this typewriter, put in a sheet of paper, and watch what takes place as if I were in front of a television set. Hope this magic is sustained for at least seven more chapters.

October 7

Our pond, Little Walden, is now filled to capacity, and the overflow drain that Homestead Landscaping installed is working around the clock. The drain is just a wide piece of plastic pipe that was erected with its open top at the height we had decided was as tall as we wanted the pond to rise. When it reaches that point, the rising water then flows into the pipe, which extends down to the bottom of the pond, takes a right angle under twelve or fifteen feet of soil, and then drains into the sloping woods beyond the pond. The wind was so strong this morning and the waves so pronounced that we were looking for whitecaps. Can't wait to see ice on it. Our own personal skating rink.

October 8

Leo Durocher, the fiery baseball player and manager, is dead at age eighty-six. Back in the mid-1960s, after working late in my office one evening, I remember stopping at the old Plantation Restaurant and Bar that was directly across the street on North Broadway in Chicago. Leo was at the bar, drinking, and I joined him.

We chatted for a couple of hours, but for the life of me I cannot remember a single subject that we touched upon or a solitary wise thought put forth by either of us.

October 15

For the past several days, like most of the nation, Bette and I have been staring at our television set watching the Senate Judiciary Committee fumble and bumble their way through countless hours of questioning in order to attempt to resolve the sexual-harassment charges brought against Supreme Court Justice nominee Clarence Thomas, by Anita Hill, a University of Oklahoma law professor—charges that concern events alleged to have occurred ten years prior.

Since there were never any witnesses to the alleged sexual innuendoes that Thomas was accused of speaking over a period of several years, it became a question of whom one believed, and both seemed to be telling the truth. A no-win situation, no matter how the Senate finally voted, which was 52–48 to confirm Thomas.

October 18

Spoke in the lovely auditorium at the Georgia World Congress Center in Atlanta last night. Of course, when New Century Productions booked me several months ago, they had no way of knowing that the Atlanta Braves would be playing Pittsburgh in the National League Championship Series and that the series would come down to the seventh and final game, tied at three games each, and that the last game would be played in Pittsburgh *on the evening of October 18th*!

By seven last evening the streets of Atlanta were practically deserted, as almost everyone began settling down at house parties or their favorite bar to watch the deciding game on television, scheduled to begin at eight, the same time I was due to walk out onstage and commence my presentation.

Backstage, at least fifteen minutes before "showtime," I was told by New Century's boss, Vern Morgan, that he doubted the crowd would be much more than four hundred, and he apologized to me for the sparseness of the turnout. I told him that if he were presenting Elvis reincarnated, he probably would not have done much better on an evening when the Braves were fighting to get into the World Series after finishing absolutely last in their league the prior year.

Waiting to go on, a crazy idea hit me, and I managed to get one of the young men backstage to cooperate. First I asked if any of them planned to listen to the baseball game while I was speaking. One of them finally admitted that there was a small radio in the office to the right of the lobby and that when he wasn't helping out, he would probably be close to the set.

So . . . we worked out our stunt. After I had been speaking for about forty-five minutes or so, he was to come into the auditorium and walk down the aisle, but not so far down that those sitting in the farthest back row of seats could see him. Then, first, he was to hold up fingers to indicate how many full innings of the game had already been played. After he was certain I had picked that up, he was to hold up the number of fingers representing the number of runs scored so far by Atlanta. Then he would point down with the number of fingers representing runs scored by Pittsburgh.

Worked like a charm. Approaching the end of my speech, I saw the fellow walk slowly down the side aisle, hold up five fingers, then place both his hands behind his back, then hold up three fingers, place his hands behind his back, then point down with only a closed fist.

At that point I stopped my speech, looked around, and asked, casually, if anyone was wondering how the Atlanta Braves were doing. A loud moan erupted, followed by a sea of nodding heads.

I smiled and said, "All is well. The Braves are doing fine! At the end of five innings they're leading the Pirates three to nothing!"

Loud gasp. Then applause. Then puzzled faces looking at each other wondering, "How did he do that?????"

It was a fun night, and even though New Century Productions didn't fare so well financially, they still insisted their efforts were well rewarded and they were proud to have me.

The Atlanta Braves won that seventh game, 4–0!

October 19

I doubt that Bette and I watch much more than ten hours of television a week, including the news programs, but last night we sat enthralled as the 1940 award-winning classic *The Philadelphia Story* was retold before our eyes in living black and white.

Watching the boyish and match-thin Jimmy Stewart trying to hold his own in a cast filled with the likes of Cary Grant and Katharine Hepburn, I recalled, very vividly, another day when Jimmy was neither very shy nor bashful.

Lieutenant Colonel James Stewart had completed flying his tour of missions in a B-24 Liberator before my crew and I ever arrived at the 445th bomb group field in Tibenham, England, early in 1944. We would see the famous colonel when we dropped in at the officers' club for a drink, and of course we looked upon the man with both admiration and awe.

Prior to Jimmy being transferred to wing headquarters, after his missions had been completed, he performed many duties on our base, and I shall never forget the day that our entire wing was dispatched to bomb an important bridge near Magdeburg. When the other two groups had passed over the target, cloud cover had been so heavy that any chance of their scoring a bull's-eye on the bridge, with radar, was almost nil. However, when we began our bomb run, the clouds suddenly parted ahead of us. We were able to see the bridge and we clobbered it.

Upon our return a worried Colonel Stewart met us with his clipboard as we climbed down out of the Liberator. Headquarters already knew that the other two groups had failed to accomplish their mission, and when I informed Jimmy that we had truly hit the target, he made me repeat it three times, along with my assurance that when our strike photos were developed, he would know that I was telling the truth. He finally smiled, congratulated us, patted us all on the shoulder, jumped into his jeep, and headed for the tower, looking and acting not much like the shy scarecrow Bette and I had watched on film last night.

By the time Jimmy Stewart had completed his combat missions, I remember that his hair was either white or light gray. I returned to the United States after completing my tour of duty, months before Stewart did, and I can vividly recall the day he walked down the gangplank in New York Harbor. The photo of him, waving his hat to the crowd, on the front page of the *New York Mirror*, showed Jimmy with a full crop of lush black hair! Miracles, miracles, miracles!

October 26

Had a surprise visitor on our road this morning. There he was, a huge moose, ambling past our house slowly and calmly as if he did it every day. He was truly a giant and he lifted each of his excessively long legs high in the air as he strolled past, giving our house only a casual glance while he waved those massive antlers from side to side.

Perhaps the old boy knew what I had just read in the morning paper, that the ten-day moose-hunting season had ended in New Hampshire, two days ago. This year, according to the report, eighty-nine of these magnificent creatures of God were ambushed and slain by so-called "sportsmen" with their high-powered rifles and telescopic sights. This is sport? I call it murder!

As I watched, the old boy went behind the tiny storage building across the street that we call Matt's Shack, circled around Little Walden, paused and looked back toward Bette and me, who were watching from the house's front steps. Then he tossed his head high in his own strange farewell and disappeared behind the small ash trees beyond the water.

Stay well, big guy—and know that you've at least got another year's reprieve from man and his deadly toys.

October 28

Spent most of this morning trying to catch up with my mail. Probably answered forty or so letters, thanking most of those who wrote for their kind words about one or more of my books. No one but myself has ever read or responded to any of my "fan mail." I figure that if someone cared enough to take the time to write, he or she certainly deserves a response from me, not some secretary.

I was deeply touched by a small note from a woman who enclosed a clipping. The clipping, apparently torn from a greeting card, was a statement of profound wisdom from William James: "The greatest use of life is to spend it for something that will outlast it." Who could ask for a better gift of praise than that?

My books continue to sell very well. Royalty statements are now all in for the first half of the year, and the paperbacks alone, in the six-month period ending June 30th, sold 1,107,100 copies!

October 29

It is not too difficult for anyone convinced that this nation is on a downward course toward eventual third-world status to come up with figures to reinforce his or her viewpoint. Two sets of numbers carried by the news media in only the past few days would be a good place to begin for any doomsayer.

Teenagers are now having more than three thousand illegitimate babies in our country *every twenty-four hours!*

Food stamps are now being dispensed to almost ten percent of our population. Almost twenty-four million people received federal food stamps in August!

Watched a one-hour television program last night whose promotional pieces, all week, had promised that it would show you how to handle things if anyone ever attempted to mug you. It was awful and a waste of time. Final conclusion of program, just before it went to its last commercial: "If someone comes up to you and tells you to give him your purse and your valuables, do it. It might save your life." Do any of us really need that advice?

Maybe what we do need is a new Sermon on the Mount. Or, better still, someone to remind us of the first Sermon on the Mount. If all our lives are truly plans of God, someone had better call a meeting soon to remind us, once more, what great miracles we really are.

November 1

One of the prices one must pay for living in a rural area is acknowledging the fact that there are not very many decent department stores nearby to serve you. Consequently, since our return to the country two years ago, Bette and I are doing more and more of our shopping via catalog and telephone.

By now of course we must be on every possible mailing list in the nation, and I'm sure that between September 1st and December 1st we receive a wide variety of at least two hundred catalogs, from L. L. Bean to Tiffany's, J. Crew to Victoria's Secret, Saks Fifth Avenue to Eddie Bauer, Bloomingdale's to Norm Thompson, Wolferman's to Williams-Sonoma—but my favorite of all of them is mailed out several times a year from the J. Peterman Company of Lexington, Kentucky, each one titled "Owner's Manual" followed by a number.

The "Owner's Manual" is a long and narrow catalog, perhaps 5½ inches by 10½ inches, printed on fairly heavy stock in four colors. Two of its features make this catalog stand high above most others: the unique merchandise being offered and, most important, some of the most colorful and exciting copy I have ever read. Even if their goods were not high in quality, which they are, I would still buy things from them periodically just so they never drop my name from their mailing list.

For example, a Gatsby shirt is offered. According to the catalog copy,

Gatsby was amazing. He even managed to see to it that the book about him was regarded as a novel, as pure fiction, as though he didn't exist. Even Fitzgerald, by the time he was through writing it, believed he'd made the whole thing up. . . . Gatsby walked into rooms wearing a shirt with no collar. Even a little thing like that made people talk. And probably will still make them talk. The Gatsby shirt, of course, has no collar. Only a simple collar band. . . . the cotton we have used in our uncompromising replica of Gatsby's shirt is so luminous, in and of itself, that even a person who notices nothing will notice something. . . . Two-button cuffs. Stud at neck. . . . white overlaid or solid white with narrow dark-blue stripes, widely spaced as Gatsby wished them to be.

On page 14 is Lindbergh's coat:

He was 25. He just made it over the tops of those trees, and now he was far out over the Atlantic somewhere. . . . At Paris they were waiting. . . . He did it. He did it alone. Lindbergh's coat. Tough, supple goatskin. Belted. Luxurious dark mouton fur collar. Flapped handwarmer pockets. 2 communicating side pockets, zippered. Exterior map pocket, zippered. Interior chest pocket. Windproof full-length zippered front, windproof cuffs, quilted lining. . . . Price $980.

On page 19 a James Dean jacket:

Dead in a car crash. Age 24. Killed but unkillable. 36 years later he's everywhere. . . . Classic American windbreaker. No better, no worse. . . . No, it isn't red. The movie's over. This is for life.

On page 54 is the famous J. Peterman coat, the product which I suspect started it all for this special company:

Classic horseman's duster protects you, your rump, your saddle and your legs down to the ankles. Because it's cut very long to do the job, it's unintentionally flattering. With or without a horse. Although I live in horse country, I wear this coat for another reason. Because they don't have Dusenbergs anymore. J. Peterman Price $184.

And then of course there is Hemingway's cap:

> He probably bought *his* in a gas station on the road to Ketchum, next to the cash register, among the beef jerky wrapped in cellophane. Or maybe in a tackle shop in Key West. I had to go to some trouble to have this one made for you and me but it had to be done. The long bill, longer than I, at least, ever saw before, makes sense.... Price $33. (He probably got change from a five when he bought the original.)

I've already circled a few items I'd like Santa to bring me this year, especially that leather 1928 Air Corps briefcase.

November 6

Flew from Manchester to New York's La Guardia Airport yesterday evening on one of those dreaded tiny commuter planes. Would much rather fly another combat mission over Germany. My trip had two purposes. To meet, for the first time, with the editorial people from Fawcett, my new publisher, and to buy Bette a Christmas present at Cartier.

There is a special aura surrounding Fifth Avenue that always makes my pulse beat a little faster. Perhaps it's just remembering back to the hungry days after the war when I lived in a tiny fleabag apartment, just off Times Square, writing, but not selling anything I wrote, and walking to Fifth Avenue whenever I felt most depressed. Although I couldn't afford anything in the stores, just being there and using my imagination lifted my spirits.

And now it was almost fifty years later, but I felt young again as the cab dropped me off at Fifth Avenue and Forty-ninth Street. I stood on the corner, for I don't know how long, just watching people, then I turned and headed north on my own yellow-brick road.

I fought the temptation to go into Brentano's to see how many Mandino books they had on their shelves and lingered outside Saks Fifth Avenue, admiring their elegant window displays. At the sudden smell of hot pretzels I turned as a vendor passed, pushing his cart slowly.

I stopped outside Saint Patrick's Cathedral, walked up its many marble steps, and entered. In all the years since my last visit nothing had changed. How wonderful. I lit two candles, one for my mother, one for my father, knelt to say a brief prayer, and then stepped out into that other world once again.

I paused at Rockefeller Plaza. Sadly this year's huge Christmas tree had not yet been erected. My loss. Then I went into a tiny building with marble-framed windows at the corner of Fifty-second Street. . . . Cartier.

I remember so vividly visiting New York in the late sixties and going into Cartier to price one of their famous Tank Watches, which I wanted to buy Bette. Well, the watch cost around three hundred dollars at the time, and I had nowhere near that amount. That watch has increased in price over the years so that it is now four digits plus, but I bought it for my lady, black alligator strap and all.

I stepped out of Cartier with my glossy vivid-red Cartier shopping bag, a perfect target for muggers, and quickly did some shuffling of items. I folded the shopping bag and stuffed it into one of my overcoat pockets and in the other I placed the gift-wrapped Cartier Tank Watch.

I continued north on Fifth, past Bulgari and Liberty of London. At the corner of Fifty-fifth, facing north, I could see two hotels. To my left the new Peninsula and, just ahead, the Saint Regis, where I was scheduled to have lunch with my agent and new editors. I checked my watch. Then I continued north, window-shopping and sight-seeing. There was Henri Bendel, with its Lalique windows, and Bergdorf Goodman, with its haute couture for women on the right side of the avenue and its store for men directly across the street.

I passed the Plaza Hotel and paused outside FAO Schwartz. Never have been able to pass a toy store. I entered that special fairyland and walked downstairs to be greeted by a giant clock with an animated face singing "Welcome to Our World." Would like to spend the day there.

Outside again, I paused and turned south. Almost time. I stopped in at my literary agent Alice Martell's office, and we hugged and visited. Then, arm in arm, we walked to the legendary Saint Regis, just reopened after a hundred-million-dollar renovation.

Lunch was lovely, and I felt completely at ease with my new editor, Susan Randol, and her editor-in-chief, Leona Nevler, whom I have admired for many years. It appears we have a good marriage. The atmosphere was warm and cordial, and now I feel at home with my new publisher.

Most important, I did buy Bette her watch. Finally.

November 10

I may talk and write about the secrets of success that anyone can learn and apply in order to change his or her life for the better, but like every other public speaker, I do contemplate, now and then, the sheer terror of being introduced only to walk out on some stage to discover that just a tiny group has come to hear me.

Fortunately that scenario has never unfolded (yet), and

today the spacious Ballroom of Bally's Grand Hotel, in Las Vegas, was sold out, when nearly a thousand realtors, attending their national annual convention and trade exposition, came for lunch and to listen to me.

Their warm response and standing ovation when I finished my talk made yesterday's sixteen-hour ordeal, involving canceled flights and long hours of sitting in airports, all seem worthwhile.

Bette is with me, and as I write these words she is downstairs, in the casino, indulging in her only vice, I think, playing the slot machines.

Tomorrow we shall fly down to Phoenix, where we'll spend a week with our youngest son, Matt, and his wife, Lori, while we do some Christmas shopping. I can still recall our early years together when buying even a single gift for each other and our children called for budgeting and sacrifice, and yet there were as many smiles and hugs and kisses then as now. I think it was Anatole France who once wrote that some of us have no idea what to do with this short life, yet we want another that will be eternal.

November 21

No two humans possess the same perspective on life. Approximately forty thousand people from other nations are congratulating themselves today because their name has just been drawn in our nation's largest immigration lottery. A new life, one hopefully filled with promise and joy, awaits them on our shores, and yet . . . and yet the Labor Department has just announced that more than a million United States citizens have now abandoned their fruitless search for employment, the first time we have topped that figure since the 1981–82 recession.

How do the immigrants and the unemployed survive?

Most of us who write and speak about that mysterious Shangri-la called Success have been trying for centuries to isolate those mysterious factors that enable one human to make it big while another scarcely remains alive without the help of others. Samuel Goodrich, an American author of another era, undoubtedly pointed out one of the traits absolutely necessary for survival and growth when he wrote, "Perseverance gives power to weakness, and opens to poverty the world's wealth. Perseverance spreads fertility over the barren landscape, and bids the choicest fruits and flowers spring up and flourish in the desert abode of thorns and briers."

No matter how tough things appear to be, one must never give up. Winston Churchill, addressing a graduating class during his years as Britain's prime minister, stood after he was introduced, walked slowly to the podium, looked over the crowd for several minutes, and said, "Ladies and gentlemen, and all you young graduates . . . never, never, never, never, never, never give up!" He then slowly returned to his seat as the applause built to a crescendo of sound. Powerful story. It has survived for almost sixty years, and I am using it as the underlying theme for *The Twelfth Angel*. Never give up! Never! Never!

November 28

This special day, Thanksgiving, has become a day of memories, like Christmas and perhaps the Fourth of July. Unfortunately I cannot wave a magic wand to produce my two sons, their spouses, and my grandchildren at our Thanksgiving table as in past years when we were living in Arizona, but Bette and I will *see* them and *hear* them in our hearts while we are at the table this day. There is so much to be thankful for, and our kids are at the top of the list.

I walked out into the woods for a few moments, which always makes me feel closer to my own mother and father. Under my feet was a heavy cushion of fallen leaves, and the bright sun, shining through now barren branches, cast strange silhouettes on the woodland floor. I looked up, through the trees, blew a kiss at the heavens, and wished both Mom and Dad a Happy Thanksgiving. Strange behavior for an old geezer, I guess, but no one was looking. Thank you, God, for allowing me to hang around for so many Thanksgivings.

November 29

As a World War II bombardier, I was fascinated by news in today's paper that there is a gentleman in Spanish Fort, Alabama, E. C. "Ned" Humphreys, Jr., also an old bombardier, who has been collecting names and addresses of every Army Air Force World War II bombardier for more than ten years, and his total is already over thirty-five thousand. He is now even publishing a newsletter called, what else, *Crosshairs*. Mr. Humphreys is being assisted by Max Springer, sixty-eight, who was an air force major with twenty-one years of active duty. Both gentlemen agree that they are in a race against time in accumulating their lists since, as Max said, "We're dying off like flies." Most of us, if we're still alive, are in the neighborhood of seventy, so I guess he's right. I understand that they even have reunions, and they must be not only touching and sentimental but also hilarious. Hell, we exaggerated our accomplishments on every mission while we were flying combat, so I can just imagine how the tales of most missions have grown in quantities of courage, heroism, and marksmanship during the past half century.

December 4

It is early afternoon. I am scribbling some notes for my journal as I sit comfortably in a lounge chair resting on the outside balcony of my sixth-floor suite, one of the more than fifteen hundred Crystal Palace and Casino rooms in Nassau, the Bahamas. Below, on the white panorama of beach sand, nearly all the plastic lounge chairs are occupied by human bodies of various sizes, shapes, and colors. Piercing shrieks from children constantly fill the air as they plunge downward and around and around the largest winding water ski slide I have ever seen.

The Crystal Palace boasts fourteen restaurants, six bars and lounges, and more than an acre of slot machines intermixed with gaming tables. The facade of its many buildings and towers, extending far down the beach, is painted in alternating bands of tacky pink, magenta, blue, and lavender, and at night, God help us, thousands of permanent lights on the buildings emphasize the colors. Had Christopher Columbus been confronted by such a spectacle when he sailed into this harbor for the first time, I have no doubt he would have turned his small armada around, never to return.

Flew down here yesterday, leaving behind a typical New Hampshire snow and ice storm. Shortly after eight this morning a limo picked me up at the hotel and drove me down to the wharf, where I boarded the Carnival cruise ship *Fantasy*, which had just docked an hour earlier. In the reception area I was greeted by representatives of Water Resources International, a Phoenix-based firm that provides equipment capable of improving the quality of water we consume at home and business. The company's top salespeople, along with their spouses, were being rewarded for their performance with a five-day cruise that included my speaking to them on the secrets of success after their Nassau docking.

They were already gathered in the ship's theater when I arrived. Unlike most business gatherings, this group was comfortably dressed in T-shirts, bathing suits, slacks, and shorts of various lengths, yet they were as attentive and receptive as any group I have ever addressed. As usual, following my speech I conducted a question-and-answer session, giving everyone present free rein to ask about any of my books, my life, or any subject that might be of interest to them.

Riding back to the Crystal Palace many hours later, after posing for pictures with just about every couple on the ship, I was mentally reviewing the questions that had been asked of me. One theme, as usual, had prevailed. Although this was a group of highly successful producers, they were *still* seeking answers on how to deal with life, how to cope with the constant fear of failure, how to handle rebuffs from customers and the world around them, and how to be happy—in other words, *how to conquer life.* Everyone, it seems, needs to be reminded again and again that we must all learn to live just one day at a time, as Sir William Osler pointed out so effectively with his example of living each day in day-tight compartments. Another remarkable human, the poet Goethe, offered a similar approach to dealing with life but from another direction when he wrote, "Take life too seriously and what is it worth? If the morning wakes us to no new joys, if the evening brings us not the hope of new pleasures, is it worthwhile to dress and undress? Does the sun shine on me today that I may reflect on yesterday? Or that I may endeavor to foresee and to control what can neither be foreseen nor controlled . . . the destiny of tomorrow?"

December 8

It's difficult to realize that ten years have passed since I made my first appearance before the congregation of Reverend Jack Boland's Church of Today in Warren, Michigan. That first engagement, so far as I was concerned at the time, was just another speaking date that had been booked by my lecture agent Cheryl Miller, although the actual presentation turned out to be quite different from any I had ever done before.

Instead of my usual one-hour speech, Jack presented me to his flock at both the nine- and the eleven-o'clock services, and after his introduction we sat very relaxed on two rather tall chairs while he proceeded to interview me, David Susskind–style, about my books, my philosophy of life, my own rocky road, and what I had been doing for the past year. The chemistry between us was great, and both sessions went very well.

During the following year I was presented with the first Napoleon Hill Gold Medal for Literary Achievement at the Conrad Hilton in Chicago, and among the large crowd attending the award ceremonies was Reverend Jack with several of his friends from the church who had all flown down to Chicago especially for the occasion.

After the ceremony, feeling very proud and elated, my hand shaking finally brought me to Jack's table. Following some friendly banter and my thanking them for coming, I turned to Jack and said, "We had fun together, sitting and rapping in front of the congregation, didn't we?"

"We sure did," he said, smiling.

"I'd like to do that every year. Ushering in the Christmas season as we did was a special experience for me, Jack."

"Og," he replied slowly, "we'd certainly like to have you every year."

"Well," I said (and in my enthusiasm I got completely carried away), "let's do it every first Sunday in December—and I'll tell you what, I won't even charge you a fee! How's that?"

Jack's eyes opened wide, but he quickly extended his hand and said, before I could change my mind, "That's a deal!" And it has been a deal ever since.

Yesterday, as in other years, I sat at a large table in the church and autographed my books—this year for five and a half hours—eleven hundred books, they tell me! Then, this morning, in the newly completed lovely huge sanctuary, we did both services as always, and I closed each by reading a touching Christmas story titled "The Christmas Collie" by Ted Paul, accompanied by Christmas carols on the organ. It was a common sight to see tears running down many cheeks in the congregation. Mine too.

After the second service I autographed for another couple of hours. Very often when individuals pass through the line and chat with me as I am signing, they will leave me precious written messages that I am always told to "read later." One message simply read, "Og, thanks for helping us to realize our potential."

I wonder how many birds die in cages believing that the cage's ceiling is the real sky?

December 11

I am sipping a soft drink in the first-class section of a Boeing 727 as it heads toward the Manchester, New

Hampshire, airport. It will land before midnight and with luck I should be home by 1:30 A.M.

Spoke in the Scottish Rite Auditorium, in Fort Wayne, Indiana, this noon. Good audience. Sitting here, as I often do after a visit to an unfamiliar city, I regret that there never seems to be enough time to see the best our nation has to offer.

Fort Wayne, for example, could occupy a visitor for weeks. There is the Embassy Theater with its 1920s architecture, including marble staircases and crystal chandeliers; old Fort Wayne, completely rebuilt from the War of 1812; the Bass Mansion, a nineteenth-century palatial residence with many historical theme rooms; and the Allen County Public Library, one of the top in the nation, housing every federal population census schedule from 1790 to 1910 as well as indexes, family and local histories from the entire United States, and a large collection of military records, passenger lists, and immigration files. There is also the Auburn-Cord Duesenberg Museum, the Diehm Museum of Natural History, the Fort Wayne Firefighters Museum, and a place called the Landing, with gaslights on a thoroughfare that once was headquarters for many businesses along the Wabash and Erie Canal docks and now boasts scores of restored shops and restaurants that, I'm certain, would all be fun to visit.

During my speech I usually touch upon that terrible period in my life when, having lost my wife and daughter, my job, and my home because of my own stupidity and thoughtlessness, I contemplated purchasing a gun in a Cleveland pawnshop and killing myself. After the speech today, as usual I autographed my books for quite a while. One young man, as I was signing his book, leaned forward and said softly, "Og, I've had my gun loaded for a couple of months. Your message today gave me a reason not to use it for one more day. Thank you."

So many times, it seems, we just can't pass out life preservers fast enough.

December 12

This is my sixty-eighth birthday, and I am feeling great. Actually it is my third birthday based on that system I commenced when I reached age sixty-five and called that special day my new date of birth—with a new schedule of twenty-one fresh years ahead. Okay, eighteen to go!

For no explainable reason I started to wonder this afternoon just what was happening in 1923, the year of my birth, and after digging through a few old almanacs and historical timetables I learned plenty.

In that auspicious year the first birth control clinic was opened, *Time* magazine was founded, amateur golfer Bobby Jones won the National Open, and the biggest song hits were "Yes, We Have No Bananas" and "Tea for Two." President Warren Harding died a mysterious death that has never been satisfactorily explained and was succeeded by his vice president, Calvin Coolidge. George Gershwin wrote his *Rhapsody in Blue*, Douglas Fairbanks starred in the silent movie classic *Robin Hood*, Freud completed his epic *The Ego and the Id*, four million German marks were worth a single American dollar, Hitler's attempted coup in a Munich beer garden failed, Schick patented the first electric razor, Jack Dempsey retained his heavyweight title even after his opponent, Luis Firpo, knocked him out of the ring, and 200,000 bigots attended a gathering of the Ku Klux Klan in Kokomo, Indiana. To borrow from Dickens, "It was the best . . . and the worst of times," and of course one can say the same about today. So many of us drift through each day, extending only enough effort to exist in misery and despair. William James, one of America's most distinguished philosophers and psychologists, considered the following remark his most important ever: "Compared to what we ought to be, we are only half awake. Our fires are dampened, our drafts are checked, we are making use of only a small part of our mental and physical resources." Certainly not the way to conquer life.

December 17

Snow has been swirling downward most of the day, soft, feathery stuff that remains light and fluffy in undulating white, powdery blankets on the ground because the temperature is near zero. Several days ago, on an unusually warm afternoon, I strung long strands of tiny white lights around each shrub and evergreen surrounding the foundation of our old place and now, in the darkness, they glisten and glow through the snow that has almost engulfed most of them.

The kitchen has been off-limits most of the day. I need no calendar or the sound of carols to know that Christmas is fast approaching, because Bette has commenced her annual project of baking scores of different and very delicious cookies to share with friends, relatives, and especially our own kids, their wives, and children. Everywhere in the kitchen, on shelves and tabletops, I see open jars of chopped nuts and fruits, cans of Crisco, sticks of butter, old family cookbooks, bags of flour, coconut, chocolate, recipes on tattered old file cards, brown sugar, confectionery sugar, and a delicious fragrance that seems to hover over my aproned lady as she scurries back and forth from the oven with cookie sheets, her hands protected by familiar old potholders. A portable radio sits on one corner of a kitchen counter, and I can hear, just faintly, "I'll Be Home for Christmas."

My world is slowing down. I have delivered my final speech of the year and, other than a few journal entries, I shall do little writing. This is the season when I forget who I am, how old I am, and all my plans for next year. This is when I wrap presents, open Christmas cards, and frequently get down on my knees in gratitude for the greatest gift I ever received—the gift of life.

December 19

Even the most optimistic individual, blessed with faith and serenity and filled with a positive mental attitude, might be tempted to believe the world is disintegrating after a week's exposure to the daily newspapers and television news.

The Soviet Union, mighty bear and tough opponent, is on its knees. General Motors is restructuring its organization and closing several huge plants. Mighty IBM is doing the same as it begins to dissect itself in order to save itself. Salvation Army kettle collections, the backbone of their Christmas fund-raising efforts, are far behind last year's total, although they anticipate feeding as many as twenty-five percent more hungry individuals during this approaching holiday. Things are so tough that someone actually stole the kettle containing contributions today from outside a department store in Portsmouth, New Hamsphire.

What is happening to us? One homeless person in six was denied shelter this year, and one in five could not be fed. Also, it is estimated that we have as many as three million homeless wandering the streets, and the number of school kids who are now receiving free or subsidized lunches has increased by an astounding twelve percent in the past year.

Perhaps the correct response to many of our concerns over daily events that shock and alarm us rests in the words of Thomas Fuller, a seventeenth-century English divine: "Thou must content thyself to see the world imperfect as it is. Thou wilt never have any quiet if thou vexest thyself because thou canst not bring mankind to that exact notion of things and rule of life which thou hast formed in thy own mind."

Good advice.

December 22

This first day of winter has always seemed very special to me. It's the time for slippers, a good book, and an extra log on the fireplace as we try to hibernate, when we can, despite so many interruptions from the outside world.

Headlined as the winter solstice, meaning "the sun stood still," this is not only the shortest day of the year but the day when the earth's axis tilts directly away from the sun so that our supply of sunlight, here in the Northern Hemisphere, is at its lowest ebb. However, commencing tomorrow, each day will be a little brighter, warmer, and longer as our tiny globe slowly tilts back toward that huge, blazing ball that sustains us.

Coincidentally or not, the first spring seed catalogs arrived in the mail this morning, and soon the same agonizing but wonderful decisions will once again confront Bette and me as we ponder the many new seed introductions along with our old favorite varieties of corn, tomatoes, string beans, peppers, and cucumbers.

As a kid I truly hated having to work in my father's garden, but now I'd much rather be transplanting tomato seedlings in our tiny plot of land, my old clothes covered with mud, than walk out on a stage to the applause of a thousand or two. I need constantly to remind myself that when I'm behind the podium, I am planting other kinds of seeds that hopefully will also produce a joyful harvest.

December 25

Somewhere during this festive morning, as our living room filled with wrapping paper torn from gift boxes and the sounds of our grandchildren's laughter blended with Christmas carols from our stereo, I momentarily recalled another Christmas, twenty-three years ago.

In the 1968 Christmas issue of the magazine I edited, *Success Unlimited*, I ran a short piece I had written entitled "A Letter to Two Sons," describing the previous year's Christmas. The public reaction was astounding to me. Newspapers phoned, from just about every part of the country, asking permission to print my piece on Christmas Day, and then Chicago's leading radio station, WGN, phoned and asked if they could broadcast a reading of the letter on Christmas morning.

We had just purchased our first home, a new one, in Arlington Heights, northwest of Chicago. I had managed to borrow $2,500 from my credit union for the down payment. When we moved into the house, we had very little furniture. In fact there was nothing in our living room except a Christmas tree and an inexpensive stereo console that Bette and I had charged at Sears.

And so, on Christmas morning, my wife and our two young sons, along with Bette's mother and father, gathered in the vacant living room to hear "A Letter to Two Sons" on the radio, still ranking as one of the great thrills of my life, even to this day. My first book, *The Greatest Salesman in the World*, had been published just weeks earlier, and little did any of us know how that tiny volume was going to change our lives.

As if it all just happened yesterday, I can still hear the mellow voice of announcer John Mallow, backed by Christmas music, reading:

A Letter to Two Sons

Dear Dana and Matthew,

It's Christmas Eve, and I have retreated to the room which your mother calls Dad's Word Factory.

For the last few hours, in my own fumbling way, I have tried to help your mother wrap your Christmas toys, and they have now been placed under our tree to await your morning onslaught. Funny, but each year I tease mother about the care with which she wraps each package, for we know how little boys handle pretty ribbons and paper, but she still treats each gift as if it contained gold bars, and maybe they do hold something just as valuable—our love for both of you.

When I finished my duties downstairs, I came up to your room and stood between your beds, barely able to see your faces in the soft glow of the night-light. From below I could hear, just faintly, Christmas carols from the kitchen radio.

Suddenly, and without realizing it, I was on my knees—driven there, I guess, by my doubts and fears that I'm not the father I should be. Now, I don't expect either of you to understand this letter, and the odds are great that you will never see it, but I wonder if we have given you the gifts that really count.

Have we taught you to count your blessings, not only so that you will appreciate what you have but so that you will want to do something for those who have not?

Have we taught you to be color-blind, so that you can look at a black, yellow, red, or brown child and see only a friend?

Have we taught you to love your country and to remember the thousands of other boys who gave their lives so that you can sleep in warmth and freedom?

Have we taught you to respect the laws and to understand that if you do not agree with them, you work to change them but you never disobey them?

Have we taught you to pray—and to pray only for guidance, because God can help you solve any problem if you let Him?

Have we taught you never to quit in anything you do, for if you persist, you will eventually win?

Have we taught you to share—not only your possessions but also yourself, without any thought of acknowledgment or publicity?

Have we taught you that the world is really a beautiful place, filled with beautiful people, in spite of what you see on television?

Have we taught you that you can be anything you want to be—if you are willing to pay the price to reach your goals?

And most important, have we taught you how to love? I know you both tell us that you love us, and we tell you that we love you, but it's easy for us to love each other. What we hope is that you learn to love everyone—and that is the hardest job you will ever have—until you learn the secret, and the secret is so simple. All you must remember is that hate grows out of fear. If you are afraid someone is going to beat you in a fight, you immediately begin to hate him. When you grow older, if you are afraid someone is going to steal your job, your girl, or your business, you immediately begin to hate. Without that fear there will never be hate, and without hate it is easy to love.

Our toughest task, then, your mother's and mine, is to help both of you to grow up without fear—and this we promise to do with every bit of our ability. Every child is a miracle, so you are both miracles—and there is no room for fear or hate in a miracle.

I prayed before I left your darkened room—and I was there so long that my eyes had become adjusted to the faint light and I could see both your faces. Because of this special night I could only look at you, my boys, and think of another tiny boy who slept on this night for the first time, nearly two thousand years ago. He was not as warm as you, his bed was not as comfortable as yours, and his poor mother and father were frightened and alone in a strange town.

Yet I wouldn't be here in your room tonight, and thinking these thoughts, if it had not been for that small boy—and I cannot help but wonder what His dad was thinking as he looked down on His sleeping face. If it is not sacrilegious, I want you both to know that I envy that other father, for he gave his son the gifts I hope we can give to you.

One more thing. Children forget quickly, so you don't even talk about Grandpa Teddy anymore. You say "He's dead" when someone asks you or mentions his name. But the last time we saw Grandpa Teddy was as we were driving away from his house two years ago. Just as we were leaving, he leaned in our car window and said to me, "Drive carefully, you've got mighty precious cargo in the back."

Only later, after he was gone from us, did I remember his remark—and now I think of it again and remember all my boyhood Christmases when, no matter how tough the times, there was always a gift under the Christmas tree for his boys.

You are both, indeed, my precious cargo—and I pray to God that He helps me to guide you to manhood and

that He allows me the luxury of hanging around long
enough to see you reach it.

Merry Christmas, my sons,

Dad

The boys have reached manhood and now they both
have their own families, and they are all here, in our old
farm, to celebrate Christmas with us.

1992

I will govern my life and thoughts as if the whole world were to see the one and to read the other.

SENECA

I am constantly reminding others, in my speeches, interviews, and writings, to remember to count their blessings . . . to be grateful for the things they have. In glancing through this morning's paper, with all its tragedies and troubles, it occurred to me that we should also be grateful for the things we do not have. Each of us, if we try, can compile a fairly accurate list of our blessings, but it would probably do us all a world of good if we made a list of our "do not haves." Overdue bills, leaky roofs, cancer, heart trouble, a marriage that's not working, kids who don't visit us, mice in the cellar, high cholesterol, a terrible golf swing, smoking and drinking faults, impatience with others, the AIDS virus, too much lawn to mow. Of course each of our lists would be unique, like our fingerprints, but maybe we really should start thinking about listing what we don't have. Might make us appreciate, all the more, what we do have.

Yesterday's drenching rains and temperatures in the midfifties eliminated all traces of snow on the ground and then, in late afternoon, high winds roared in from Canada as the temperature plummeted. This morning the winds are still screeching and moaning, and the temperature on our kitchen thermometer reads 8 degrees, so I'm sure the windchill factor must be 30 or 40 below.

The rising sun, reflected on the newly frozen surface of ice on our pond, Little Walden, has cast a bright, warm glow into my studio and all the other rooms with southern exposure. There is truly no place in the world I would rather be at this very moment than right here, at my desk, with my old typewriter and a warm fire in the fireplace while the lady I love works upstairs in her sewing room on another outfit for one of our grandchildren.

Today's *Manchester Union-Leader* contained ten full pages showing homes being auctioned after foreclosures, each little ad not beginning to tell the story of heartbreak and shattered dreams behind its tiny house photo and descriptive copy beneath.

Sadly we live in a world of ups and downs, and today's laughter can turn quickly into tomorrow's tears. We must learn, and never forget, that wise bit of wisdom passed down to us by some unknown voice of the past who said that a smooth sea never made a skillful mariner, neither do uninterrupted prosperity and success qualify us for usefulness and happiness. The storms of adversity, like those of the ocean, rouse the faculties and excite the invention, prudence, skill, and fortitude of the voyager. The martyrs of ancient times, in bracing their minds to outward calamities, acquired a loftiness of purpose and a moral heroism worth a lifetime of softness and security.

January 17

I see that a truck driver living north of us in Laconia has just won our local lottery worth about four million bucks. This means that after taxes he will receive approximately $160,000 per year for the next twenty years. He said he was going to spoil his two granddaughters with some of the money by sending them on a "little trip to Walt Disney World."

However, when he was asked if he planned to accompany them to Florida, he replied, "No, I'm too old for that."

How sad. The man is fifty-seven! "Too old for that???"

Years do not make sages, they only make old men . . . some even before their time.

January 23

Completed the seventh chapter of *The Twelfth Angel* this afternoon after filling my wastebasket several times with rejected pages during the past few days. I just couldn't come up with a proper ending for the chapter. I'd write something and it would feel fine, so I'd get up and walk away for a break, thinking I'd licked the problem. Then, usually hours later while doing some simple chore around the house, I would stop, shake my head, go back to the studio, tear up the final two or three pages, and try again. And again. And again. I'm not quite certain what never being satisfied with one's writing indicates. Insecurity? A foolish drive for perfection? Unwillingness perhaps to let go and move on into unfamiliar territory? I don't know.

I remember years ago, for a summer, I lectured to some writing classes in Phoenix at the Arizona Biltmore Hotel, and in my opening session with each new class I would hold up the final typescript of my book *The Christ Commission*. I would tell the eager group of would-be writers of all ages that the typescript contained 332 pages and then inform them that I rewrote that particular book nine times before I was satisfied with it. By rewriting I didn't mean that I merely changed a word or a phrase or two on a page here and there. I actually retyped the entire book nine times and made hundreds of changes with each retyping, a process that required nine additional months after the book was first completed. The point I was hoping to make was that while they might complete a story or a novel and feel very proud of themselves and let it go at that, hoping they could sell it somewhere, the true professional, when he or she finishes a work, commences a polishing process on page one and slowly grinds through the entire book, not once but again and again until it is as good as he or she can make it.

All of us, no matter what we are doing, probably face similar challenges often in the course of a day or a week. We complete a difficult task and walk away from it. It is done. Finished. But was it done to the very best of our ability, or are we settling for mediocrity? When we settle for mediocrity in the small things, we usually end up settling for mediocrity in the big things, including our own success, peace of mind, and way of life. It doesn't have to be that way. We can make a difference in our tomorrows, provided we deliver nothing but the very best we can do, every day!

January 24

The one-hour videotape of my speech "The Greatest Secrets of Success" has one characteristic that, so far as I know, is not on any other videotapes sold in this country, whether they be movies, travelogues, or lectures. When the package was being designed a year or so ago, I had asked if it was possible for my personal autograph to be part of each tape, believing that if it could be done, the sales of the tape would certainly benefit from this uncommon feature.

Well, we finally worked it all out with the production company. I would sign special white labels, each measuring approximately three-quarters of an inch by six inches, which would be affixed to the spine of each video before the company shrink-wrapped the package.

Yesterday I received twelve thousand blank labels, twelve to each sheet of heavy white paper stock. Last night an hour or so before dinner I brought my labels and a green felt-tip pen out to the long kitchen table so that I could visit with Bette while I suffered through the monotony of signing my name again and again. Not too far into my autographing, the freezing rain that had been falling for several hours finally worked its deviltry and our electrical power went out. Bette, my country girl forever, soon had a small oil lamp and four candles glowing brightly on the kitchen table, so I sat there, still autographing, autographing, autographing, in the shadow of a flickering but lovely row of flames. Autographing by candlelight. A first for me. Paul Revere is undoubtedly smiling.

Our tiny state is going through its quadrennial trauma as we prepare for the February 18th first-in-the-nation presidential primary. Since New Hampshire is currently mired in something very close to a depression, with unemployment approaching double digits and real estate prices tumbling daily, the citizenry is not too happy with our nation's leaders. This obvious discontent has attracted scores of so-called candidates with backgrounds so varied that I would truly love to have one-on-one discussions with several to ask them exactly what qualifications they believe they possess that would enable them to lead a nation.

Republican voters will have their choice from among twenty-five candidates, including our incumbent president, George Bush, while the Democrats, if there are any in the state, will be able to choose from thirty-six. Thirty-six!!

There are not many areas in New Hampshire where the population is large enough to provide any candidate with a large crowd to hear his message, so we may be the only place left in the nation where one may walk into a hardware store, diner, or local bank and, as part of a group of five, get a ten-minute lecture on good government by a leading presidential contender.

I think most of our unphony, down-to-earth citizenry are already turned off by all the sound and fury and wishes that every politician would depart on United Airlines Flight 850 that leaves Manchester Airport for Chicago's O'Hare every day at 10:16 A.M.

I know I do.

January 30

A small package containing a videotape and letter arrived from my good friend Reverend Jack Boland yesterday. Since the Church of Today had already sent me several video copies of my first-Sunday-in-December appearance with him, I was puzzled. The accompanying letter was addressed to both Bette and me, and when we read it, both of us knew something was terribly wrong.

The videotape was of a sermon Jack had delivered recently called "Living the Spiritual Life," and Jack's letter asked us to view it and then phone him. Since he was with members of his church on a cruise in Hawaii, his letter instructed us to phone the church and they would know how to reach him. The last foreboding paragraph in his letter stated that he assured us the purpose of the enclosed videotape was not to enhance our spiritual life or change us one bit. Instead it all had to do with him!

We viewed the tape. It was one of the best sermons we had ever heard Jack preach. He emphasized that the holy spirit is the immortal part of us and it will never die. I immediately phoned the church and was given a hotel number and room number to call in Hawaii. Jack answered the phone, amazed that it was us since, at that very moment, he was holding a file card with my phone number in his hand and was just about to call us. He asked if Bette was also on the line, and she greeted him. Then he said, as he had said so often in the past, that he loved us both very much and we were only two of sixteen close friends he was contacting to let us know that apparently the chemotherapy treatments he had been taking for several months, which we all thought were working, had not worked. His lymphoma was back and was spreading through all the soft tissue of his body. The doctors figured that he had between three and six months.

Jack Boland was not seeking our sympathy. He sounded upbeat and told us how grateful to God he was for all the good years he had enjoyed. He said he was treating every day as if it was the best day of his life and he repeated that he wanted us to know he loved us both. He sounded calm and serene. Obviously the great man who had taught so many how to live also knew how to get ready to die.

During the remainder of this day I couldn't get Jack out of my mind. I tackled several unpleasant chores that I normally would have put off for another time. What other time?

February 3

I have known for over a month that the official publication date of my sequel to *The Greatest Miracle in the World*, titled *The Return of the Ragpicker*, would be March 1st.

Despite thirteen previous books, published over a period of twenty-five years, with total sales in all editions and twenty languages approaching thirty million copies, I still continue to act as nervously as an expectant father while anxiously waiting for the new book's debut in the nation's bookstores.

A box containing several copies of the new book arrived this morning. I spent a long time examining it thoroughly, stroking the smooth jacket and even reading a chapter or two. Not bad. Not bad at all. Please, God, let the public like it.

I'm not certain there will be much of a publishing industry at all, as we know it today, by the twenty-first century if some of the findings made by the American Booksellers Association in a recent study are accurate, and they undoubtedly are. The study revealed that *no one* purchased any kind of a book, even a paperback, in sixty percent of United States households during the twelve months ending March 1991. Also, only four percent of the books sold were in the categories of technical, educational, scientific, art, poetry, or literature! And the largest buying group for all books were those past the age of sixty-five!

The signs are obvious. A hundred years ago we sat by the fireplace and read books. They were almost our only source of knowledge and entertainment. They were our windows to the world. Even fifty years ago, with movies and radio vying for our attention, books were still our teachers, our entertainers, our companions. That world has all but vanished, and our hours are now filled to overflowing with television, computers, mobile phones, newsletters, compressed newspapers, CDs, Nintendo games, and an occasional so-called blockbuster book filled with trashy sex, stomach-turning violence, and more trashy sex. Sadly we have no time for Melville or Carlyle or Emerson or Thoreau or Defoe or Swift or Eiseley, for there are so many talk shows we must watch that would cause our grandparents to flee the house in shock. Culturally we are not evolving into a better world, so, more and more, it falls upon each of us to do everything possible to preserve and uplift our own little day-by-day universe.

Approximately fifty thousand new books are published each year. I doubt if more than ten percent of them show any profit. The rest eventually end up being dumped, remaindered for a dime on the dollar. Of course, the fact that 50,000 books are published does not begin to tell the whole story. There were probably 300,000 other books written and rejected by publishers last year, yet every year a brave new group sits down to write and dares to dream of success, and I salute every one of them.

I've been noticing another trend in book publishing: long subtitles on the book jackets, sort of an instant commercial for the book as it bares its glossy cover in the bookstore. This is especially evident in the "self-help and recovery" category, this spring, with titles and subtitles such as, *The One-Hour Orgasm: A New Approach to Achieving Maximum Sexual Pleasure; Country Bound! Trade Your Business Suit Blues for Blue Jean Dreams; Were You Born for Each Other? Finding and Keeping the Love of Your Life; Together on a Tightrope: How to Maintain Balance in Your Relationship When Life Has You Off Balance; Winning with People: Building Your Personal Board of Directors to Help You Succeed; Come Here/Go Away: Stop Running from the Love You Want*; and my favorite—listed under the category of Contemporary Affairs in *Publishers Weekly*—*Accidental Empires: How the Boys of Silicon Valley Make Their Millions, Battle Foreign Competition, and Still Can't Get a Date.*

Thoreau's *Walden*, Faulkner's *Sanctuary*, Ferber's *Giant*, and Joyce's *Ulysses* would have a tough time against that kind of noisy competition.

February 5

In Las Vegas again. This time for the Photo Marketing Association's sixty-eighth annual convention and trade show, with over twenty-three thousand attending from around the world.

I was part of a three-man program today, billed as a "super-seminar." The other two presenters were Stanley Marcus, cofounder of Neiman-Marcus, and Gerald Meyers, former CEO of American Motors. For my session, scheduled for six P.M. in the Broadway Ballroom at Bally's, the room was filled to capacity, thank God. Speech went well, audience very receptive, even a standing ovation, which I was told was the only one all day.

Back upstairs in my room on the sixteenth floor, after the speech, I sat near the huge window and gazed out over the gaudy city, trying to relax and come down from the usual "high" that occurs during my talks.

As I stared down at the miles of multicolored neon, animated electronic billboards, and thousands of lights on the Maxim Casino, Bourbon Street Hotel and Casino, Stardust (with its huge sign proclaiming that SINATRA IS COMING!), Frontier Holiday Casino, Flamingo Hilton, Barbary Coast, and the Mirage, I tried to relate that glowing image of fun and frolic and promises of treasure unlimited to some grim statistics that I had recently learned about the state.

Nevada's state health officer has been putting forth a great deal of his time and effort to introduce programs in the state's school systems that would educate young children on the countless benefits of good health and the sorry consequences of unhealthy activities.

Hopefully the programs will be successful because, sadly, behind the tinsel and trumpets of Las Vegas and Reno, the state of Nevada is the unhealthiest state west of the Mississippi. It ranks first among all states in suicides and percentage of population still smoking, second in lung cancer, liver disease, and deaths from all causes prior to the age of sixty-five.

A horrifying eighty percent of all Nevada's deaths are attributed to unhealthy lifestyles such as smoking or even driving without one's safety belt fastened, and of those hospitalized in the state, in 1990, more than sixty percent of all hospital charges went to treat ailments produced by careless and usually stupid living habits.

There are a lot of tears and heartaches out on the desert, beyond the incandescent glow of all those "happy" lights.

February 17

I was the keynote speaker at the Pointe at South Mountain in Phoenix yesterday afternoon, talking to the executives and sales representatives of Hill-Rom, an old Indiana firm that has manufactured fine hospital furniture for over seven decades.

Having breakfast in my room yesterday morning, and slowly turning the pages of the Sunday newspaper, the thought suddenly occurred to me that no motivational speaker should allow himself or herself to be exposed to the latest news for at least a day before any scheduled speech. For many months now the happenings around the world on any given day would cause even the most jubilant optimist to sob in pain. Consumer confidence at a seventeen-year low. General Motors preparing to close several plants and lay off thousands. Mortgage foreclosures comprising more than half the real estate ads. Health care costing far more than most seniors could afford. Gun-related robberies at an all-time high. Drug traffic increasing so fast that one politician called the effort to halt it no more than "holding a bucket under a waterfall." The Arab-Israeli situation a festering wound that threatens more major calamities. China selling high-tech weapons to third-world dictators. Millions of Russian people standing in line for hours for small food portions. North Korea producing plutonium for their future nuclear weapons. Job-support groups for the nation's unemployed proliferating around the country.

The profile of my Hill-Rom audience concerned me. Their average age was forty to forty-five, their educational background was a minimum of bachelor's with some master's degrees, and their average income exceeded $140,000. Not your usual audience seeking some sage advice on how to become a "success," but my good friend Jim Reed, one of Hill-Rom's best, assured me that I would do just fine. I guess I did. Attentive audience, standing ovation, and a long line to get my autograph in the new book, which Hill-Rom had bought for each person attending.

During my flight home today I had one of the strangest, yet funniest experiences I have ever had in all my years of speaking. My United flight landed at Dulles Airport, in Washington, where I was to change planes for the final leg of my journey to Manchester.

At the Dulles airport I went to the proper gate for my flight and handed my ticket to the smiling woman behind the United counter. When she saw my name, she suddenly smiled, tilted her head slightly, and asked, "Is it really you?"

"It's me," I said, not knowing what else to say.

"Mr. Mandino, I just love your books. I think I have all of them. Would you honor me with an autograph?"

"Of course," I replied, and she handed me a blank boarding pass.

"I'm Judi, with an *i*," she said, and I signed the card, "To Judi, with love, Og Mandino."

She wished me a happy flight. Later we boarded the plane, and I took my seat in first class. Then I opened my attaché case, grabbed a legal pad, and began making notes for the next chapter of *The Twelfth Angel*. Suddenly I looked up, and there was my ticket lady, on the plane, carrying a clipboard. When she spied me, she smiled and came over, saying, "Mr. Mandino, didn't I read that you have a new book coming out soon?"

"Well, yes," I replied, "it's in the bookstores this week."

"What's the book's title?" she asked, her pen poised over her clipboard.

"It's called *The Return of the Ragpicker*, and it's published by Bantam."

"Thank you," she said. "Now, you have a good flight."

Then she turned back toward me and asked, "Do you mind if I tell everyone?"

"Of course not," I replied, assuming she meant that she'd tell friends and relatives.

Instead Judi-with-an-*i* picked up the microphone at the front of the plane and said, "Ladies and gentlemen. Will you all please take your seats because we are preparing to taxi away from the gate, and we can't depart until all of you are seated. By the way, you might be interested to learn that the world-famous author Og Mandino is on board this plane today and he has a new book out, titled

The Return of the Ragpicker, published by Bantam. Yes, he is on the flight, but I won't tell you where he's sitting. Now, all of you have a good flight!"

And with that, Judi-with-an-*i* walked out of my life.

Later, when I told the story to Bette, she smiled and said, "But darling, when she finished, you never did hear that old man back in coach who looked around and said, 'Who the hell is *he?*' "

February 19

I read the ad three times before I could accept what I was seeing. The ad featured a 900 telephone number where, for $1.95 per minute, one could phone and listen to Pope John Paul II deliver his daily message from the Vatican and, like the "other" kind of 900 numbers, one could dial any time of the day or night.

I have visions of Jesus searching for a high crop of ground so that his voice would carry to the throng who had gathered close to hear him. I'm not sure we have made any progress at all since that time. We certainly won't hear any messages with more power even if we climb as close to heaven as Mount Kilimanjaro and use our cellular phones.

John Paul for $1.95 a minute???

February 22

I have been sitting here in my room at the Courtyard Marriott in Warren, Michigan. Tomorrow's appearance at the Church of Today had been arranged by my publisher several weeks ago as a virtual all-day autograph party for my new book. Plans also called for my appearance at both the nine- and eleven-o'clock services, and as we do each year to usher in the Christmas season, Reverend Jack Boland and I were scheduled to chat for thirty minutes in front of the congregation, certainly plugging the new book whenever possible.

However, a week ago I was called by people on Jack's staff and informed that he was in the hospital. Last Sunday he had been wheeled into the church, where he said his farewell to a shocked congregation before being returned to the hospital for still more treatments.

I have kept my promise to Jack and come to Warren anyway. Tomorrow, I have been informed, I will still be a part of both services and be interviewed before the congregation by associate minister Michael Murphy in place of my old buddy. And I was still expected to autograph my books after both services. I am sitting here now, in the twilight, dreading tomorrow, but I did see Jack this afternoon on my way from the Detroit airport to the hotel. Gloria Willkie, a special friend who always volunteers to drive Bette and me when we come here, had picked me up at the airport and as we drove along, she casually mentioned that Harper Hospital, where Jack was a patient, was on the way. Yes, she replied to my silent pleading glance, she would stop at the hospital and I could run in to see Jack. I did. Knocked gently on his door, opened it slowly, and caught him sitting up in bed with a spoonful of food in his mouth and a silly white hat on his head to cover his new baldness caused by chemotherapy. The wonderful look of surprise on his face made the entire trip worthwhile. I moved close to the bed, leaned over, and gently kissed his cheek. He smiled and nodded. I didn't stay very long and told him I'd sure miss him tomorrow. He shook his head and said that he was certain that it would be the most memorable appearance I had ever made at the church. Now, that's a man of faith!

My day at the church went far better than I had expected. Crowds at both the nine- and eleven-o'clock services were huge, and at the eleven every seat all the way back to the highest in the balcony was filled by an estimated gathering of 1,600, a record.

My chats with Reverend Michael Murphy, at both services, went very well. After approximately ten minutes "on stage" with Michael, at the nine-o'clock service there was a loud crackling sound followed by a familiar voice on some sort of loudspeaker system. Surprise! Jack Boland was calling from the hospital, welcoming me and telling his people that he hoped to be back working within a few weeks following new treatments. A long, long, long shot, but he's a fighter, and we both believe in miracles. We'll see.

I autographed my new book after both services—for a total of more than four hours. At one time the line was so long that it extended through the lobby, down several halls, and curled back so that there were layers of people—the longest line, I was told, that had ever been seen at the church. Estimates are that I signed somewhere between four and six hundred books.

This has been a very sad time for me. I have been watching a good friend die, but he is doing it with so much grace and guts that he is acting as if he has already had a glimpse of the other side and it does not frighten or trouble him at all.

Not until one can face death with faith and a smile, I am learning, can one really know how to conquer life.

February 25

Snow is falling gently while a Boston radio station is reporting that the Red Sox have opened their spring training camp in Winterhaven, Florida. Even the temptingly soft carpet of fallen leaves and pine needles in the woods behind our house has now added a fluffy comforter of white, and the tall blueberry bushes, with their branches of dark scarlet, stand out vividly against the snow beneath.

I plan to spend the entire day in my studio, answering mail and doing a bit of writing, so I am wearing my most comfortable slippers. Still, as I watched four squirrels feed on the cornflower seeds I had dropped on the ground for them yesterday, I noticed that the bird feeder above was almost empty, so I slipped my rubbers over my slippers, threw on an old jacket, crunched through the snow, and refilled the feeder. Chickadees, bluejays, and an occasional dove have relied on us throughout the winter, and we haven't let them down. Occasionally an adventurous squirrel will clamber up the square four-by-four post, leap out to the bird feeder, hang on for dear life as the feeder sways back and forth, and then finally stick his little snout into one of the openings and gorge himself. I suppose we should try to keep them from encroaching on the dining birds, but they look so damn cute swinging on that feeder that we just let them do their thing.

There are still some heaps of fallen pine and oak branches stacked in the woods by Bobby Compton, our landscaper, and his helpers. The piles have been covered with plastic to keep them somewhat dry, and one day soon, while there is still snow on the ground, the boys will return and set them on fire, standing by to be sure that only the wood piles burn.

February 29

Last night was a first for me, and at my age anything that can be classified as a "first" in my life is worth cherishing.

Many months ago Amway's Lewis International Group booked me for a speech in Asheville, North Carolina, for the evening of February 28th. Months after the booking was made, they phoned the woman who handles all my speech bookings, Cheryl Miller, and asked her if Og would be willing to give his speech *twice* that night. It seemed they had booked one of the auditoriums in Asheville's civic center for their convention gatherings, but after the announcement was made that I would be the feature speaker, they quickly sold out that auditorium. However, there was also another, smaller auditorium in the civic center, so they booked that one as well once Cheryl had replied that the old man would be willing to try to give two talks in the same evening, even though there was some risk that he might run out of gas before it was all over.

It was the kind of night that speakers dream about. There were tremendous standing ovations in both auditoriums when I was introduced, silent and very attentive audiences while I was speaking, and more cheers and standing ovations when I finished each speech.

Between the two appearances I was taken to one of the lobbies where they were selling copies of my new book. Apparently only two hundred had been ordered, and they were all sold and autographed by me even before the second speech commenced at ten-thirty P.M.

At the airport, waiting to board my plane this morning, I sat in the tiny restaurant and glanced through some of the local travel literature I had picked up in the hotel lobby. As I was flipping pages, I learned, to my regret, that Asheville was the boyhood home of Thomas Wolfe, whose work had greatly influenced me in my younger years. Once again I had flown into a town, done my thing, and departed in such haste that what I had not seen and enjoyed was my loss. In Asheville, besides Wolfe's boyhood home, there was the Grove Park Inn, built completely of boulders taken from Sunset Mountain; Biltmore Estate and Biltmore Village, including the largest private home in America, a 250-room French Renaissance chateau built by George W. Vanderbilt in 1895; a fabulous antique car museum; the Riverside Cemetery, where O. Henry is buried; Carl Sandburg's 263-acre farm, where the talented man spent his later years; and Great Smoky Mountains National Park.

When Bette saw just one of the brochures describing the many fascinating shops at Biltmore Village, she suggested that maybe in the fall we should just throw a couple of suitcases into our car and hit the road for Asheville, the kind of trip we haven't gone on in years. I like the idea. I'm always telling my audiences that they should live each day as if it is their last, but sometimes I forget to follow my own advice.

March 1

Although my new book has been in the stores for at least two weeks, this is the official publication date for *The Return of the Ragpicker*. After ten grinding promotional tours during the past twenty years, I'm glad I'm not touring the nation to promote this one. No nine interviews a day, in city after city, until one wakes in the morning and has absolutely no idea where he is. I did go to radio station WKNE in Keene and, thanks to my good friend, Jim Adams, general manager, was able to record a twenty-one-second spot, which the publisher will use in thirty-second commercials on network radio. Other than that no hype is planned. My newest offspring will have to make it on its own. We'll see.

Yesterday was Leap Year Day, thanks to Julius Caesar, whose astronomers discovered, back in 46 B.C., that the calendar they were using was not quite correct because it was taking our old planet almost a quarter of a day more than the 365 they were showing on their calendars in order to circle our sun. And so, every fourth year's February was assigned an extra or twenty-ninth day, but that didn't end the problem, because the calendar years were now running almost twelve minutes too long. So, in the sixteenth century ten days were chopped off the calendar in a valiant attempt to catch up with things. That caused riots in many parts of the civilized world, initiated by those who were concerned that some mysterious power was subtracting ten days from their lives. We still haven't corrected things completely. Somewhere down the road, in a thousand years or two, we're going to have to knock off another day. I have no idea what good that information will ever do me.

March 5

The Church of Today's minister, and my friend, Jack Boland, died late last night. Our phone rang just after midnight with the sad news. Since today would have been my dad's birthday, I took a short walk in the woods this morning, and in the stillness of the deeper part of the forest I said a short prayer and wished Dad a happy birthday. Then I asked him to look up my friend Jack and help the newcomer if he would, as a favor to me. I'll miss Jack very much. He was everything that one would want in a clergyman . . . and a friend.

March 6

Old friends from our Scottsdale days, John and Maxine Hammond, are dropping in for the weekend. Bette needed some brown-and-serve bread sticks, so I drove to one of our few local stores to get them. On the way home a pheasant came swooping down in front of my Grand Wagoneer, and I heard a horrible thud. I also felt it in the steering wheel. I pulled over to the side of the road as soon as I could and got out. Dead and almost completely embedded in what had been my right headlight was the beautiful bird. It took all my strength to remove the remains from the interior of the headlight. The frame around the headlight was also broken from the impact. I have no idea what made the lovely thing fly in front of my approaching vehicle.

To continue my difficult day with Mother Nature, I went down to our cellar when I got home to see if we had trapped any mice or squirrels in our special Havahart trap, which captures the little guys but doesn't harm them. In the trap, looking frightened and very tiny, was a mouse. I brought the trap upstairs to show Bette, then put it in my Jeep, drove up to the corner of our street, set the trap on snow-covered pine needles, and slowly opened its tiny side door. The mouse dashed out of the trap, hesitated, turned, and looked up at me (a silent thank-you maybe?), then ran off into the woods. Life. So fragile. So damn uncertain.

March 9

Not many days after we had moved into this old place, in the fall of '89, there was a knock on the front door. A muscular, nice-looking guy standing there with a big smile said, "Excuse me, sir, I'm the assistant fire chief in this little town and I just heard that Og Mandino has moved here. I'm also associated with Amway, so I've read just about all of Mr. Mandino's books. Is he really here?"

I was dressed at the time in an old T-shirt and older blue jeans and had not bothered to shave that day, since all I was doing was opening moving cartons.

"I'm Og Mandino," I said.

"My God, my God, what a miracle! You moving to our small town. Wow!" He pumped my hand up and down and said, "My name is Barry Frosch, sir, and I'm a great fan."

I invited him in for coffee, showed him through the house, and told him of our plans to give the old place a complete face-lift. As I recall, since my studio was pretty much set up for work already, I did give him an autographed book.

Barry dropped in often during the next year or so, always careful to bow out quickly if he saw that I was writing.

Then one morning in October 1990 there was another knock on our door. A stranger, rugged and young, was standing there, his eyes red as if he had been crying. "Sir," he said, shifting nervously from foot to foot, "I've come to ask a special favor of you. Barry Frosch's young daughter, Heidi, was killed in an auto accident last night. Her car just slid off the road and hit a pole. Barry and his wife, Sandy, are in shock, but they both think so much of you that I thought you might want to let me take you back to their house so that you can comfort them and ease their pain a little."

Even though I know I looked terrible, I didn't hesitate. "Let's go," I said.

Fifteen minutes later I was sitting in Barry and Sandy's living room, Barry's head buried on my left shoulder and Sandy's on my right. I did what I could as each held tightly to one of my hands.

Six months or so ago Barry and Sandy dropped in one day to see what we had done to the old place, and they were like two little kids being taken through toyland.

This morning we heard the terrible news. Barry and Sandy, on their way home yesterday from a church service in Augusta, Maine, were both killed in a head-on collision only fifteen minutes from their home!

Once again, as I have so often in my life, I sought refuge in the words of my beloved mother. Back when I was very young, she would take me with her to every wake within a couple of miles of our house, because she seemed to know everyone. In the 1930s, of course, funeral homes were rarely used, especially by the poor, so the deceased was usually on display in the family's living room. My mother, with me in tow, would immediately embrace the bereaved relatives after we had entered the mourners' house, and of course many tears were shed. But not by my mother. She would speak softly and lovingly to all those crying and say, "You really should wipe away your tears and cry no more, because where Robert is now, I know he wouldn't change places with any of us."

After hearing the terrible news this morning, I sat at this desk for a long time, recalling my mother's advice. Yes, Barry and Sandy are gone. But would they come back, would they leave heaven, if they could? Knowing how unselfish and giving they both were, I concluded that they would probably even walk out of paradise if they had an option. One major reason. There is a Barry junior, age eleven.

March 10

The weather bureau has just announced that this has been the warmest winter since they started keeping records almost a hundred years ago. Also, here in New Hampshire we've had just about half of the normal snow accumulation, and this morning I heard the first plaintive cry of a phoebe—*fee-bee, fee-bee, fee-bee*—from deep in the woods. Another messenger with the good news that spring is getting closer every day, but as usual it is tiptoeing in on muddy dirt roads and dark gray skies.

Longfellow, a New Englander who endured many silent springs, once wrote, "If spring came but once in a century, instead of once a year, or burst forth with the sound of an earthquake, and not in silence, what wonder and expectation there would be in all hearts to behold the miraculous change. But now the silent succession suggests nothing but necessity. To most, only the cessation of the miracle would be miraculous and the perpetual exercise of God's power seems less wonderful than its withdrawal would be."

March 12

Attended our annual town meeting this evening. What a wonderful old tradition. Less than two hundred citizens gathered in the junior high school gymnasium at seven o'clock and approved or denied twenty or so proposals involving the town, after voting for town officers two days ago.

With a moderator on the tiny stage, flanked by the town's three selectmen at tables on one side and the town clerk keeping notes on the other side, each proposed item that would have increased the town's budget, during this painful recession, found tough going.

We turned down the request by the fire department for $110,000 to purchase a new Class A pumper fire truck, authorized the withdrawal of $19,200 from the capital reserve fund to purchase a four-door Ford Explorer for the police department, anguished over but okayed a request to withdraw $88,000 from the Solid Waste Capital Reserve Fund to commence construction of our own transfer and recycling station, nixed the request for $80,000 to reevaluate all the property in town, and gave many citizens their moment in the spotlight as they paraded to the front of the gymnasium and said their piece into an inadequate microphone.

We have heard for years that our vote and our voice doesn't count, and that has been one of the explanations as to why fewer and fewer of our citizens are going to the polls. It was a thrill tonight to actually watch one's vote in action, yet I couldn't help wondering why, in a town of almost three thousand, less than two hundred bothered to show up.

The malaise of helplessness spreading across our land will eventually prove our undoing unless we wake up.

There was a note under our door when Bette and I arrived home, from a friend of Barry and Sandy's. The note said that there would be a memorial service for them at two P.M. on the fourteenth at the Congregational church in a nearby town, and an afternoon service would be held, primarily for all their Amway friends. The note also asked if I would say a few words at the service, and if so, I was to phone the friend, who was staying at our downtown inn. I phoned and said I would be honored.

March 14

Barry and Sandy were buried, side by side, in Maplewood Cemetery this morning, not too far from the lot that Bette and I purchased a year or so ago.

The memorial service in the afternoon had a full church, and we all said our "farewell" to two special people who are now where they should be—with God.

March 18

I guess it never stops being a thrill. Casually leafing through my just-received March 16th issue of *Publishers Weekly* while eating lunch, I see that *The Return of the Ragpicker* has moved into the tenth spot under the magazine's listing of hardcover religious best-sellers. When I think of the thousands of newly published books, all fighting for their little spot in the sun, I continue to remind myself, often—very often—how fortunate I have been.

Samuel Johnson, that old British lexicographer and conversationalist, as well as author, once said, "Life affords no higher pleasure than that of surmounting difficulties, passing from one step of success to another, forming new wishes, and seeing them gratified. He that labors in any great or laudable undertaking has his fatigues first supported by hope, and afterwards rewarded by joy."

Mr. Johnson, I know, spoke from experience.

March 20

My calendar is telling me that this is the first day of spring. However, every New Englander knows that even though this may be the vernal equinox—spring to the astronomers—it doesn't necessarily follow that today our crocuses and daffodils are bursting through the soil and the lawns are turning green.

It has been snowing most of the day, following a night when the temperature got down to five above zero. This morning I caressed the top of my golf clubs lovingly as I brought the rubbish out to the garage. It is not getting dark now until after six in the evening, so one feels that, snow or no snow, spring cannot be very far down the road. In the meantime, since I am not able to dig in the flower garden or play a round of golf, I shall sit at this old typewriter and try to earn my keep. I am now working on chapter 10 of my new book, *The Twelfth Angel*. It still seems to be writing itself, and I think that's a good sign.

March 26

We have acquired three nocturnal visitors, large raccoons who amble out of the woods behind our house late in the evening and munch on the sunflower seeds that have fallen to the ground from our bird feeder. We have turned the outside light on, expecting to startle them and send them packing, but they just glance in the direction of the house for a brief time and then go back to their feeding. I know they deserve to live as well as all the birds and squirrels that we feed, except that these three big guys can play havoc with our summer garden if they continue to drop in on us. I'll figure out something before June.

The ice is melting on our pond as the temperature today climbed close to fifty degrees. Still everything is brown and wet and uninviting. One daffodil or crocus shooting up anywhere would change the mood.

The Twelfth Angel is coming along in fine style. I'm now on chapter 11, and with luck I should be finished within a month.

Cheryl just booked me to speak to the Executive Breakfast Club at the Drury Lane Theater in Oak Brook, Illinois. The date is what intrigues me, since it's May 21st of next year! Fourteen months away! I'll be there! God willing?

April 1

In the past twenty years or so I imagine I've appeared on at least twelve hundred radio and television programs, but today was a first. Bette was also a guest with me on Manchester Channel 9's new program *The Cathy Burnham Show*. We taped the show this morning, before a live audience, and it will be shown at five P.M. on the ninth.

Driving down to Manchester, I could sense that Bette was a little tense, but her responses, once we were taping, were bright and sharp, and she seemed completely in control.

Driving home, I asked her if she would be willing to do it again sometime, and she responded, "Anytime!"

How many times in our life have we been afraid to tackle a tough job or project, believing that we just didn't have enough talent or brains or guts to succeed, and then once we have forced ourselves to try—and successfully completed the challenge—we look back at what we have done, finally realizing that our greatest enemy, the one who urged us not even to try because we would certainly fail, was none other than ourselves.

April 3

I have flown more than 300,000 miles in the past year and thought I was truly a world traveler until a tiny news clipping helped me to put everything in perspective.

It seems that the Optical Astronomy Observatories in Tucson have just announced that they believe they have discovered a black hole that is several million times the mass of the sun. Where is it? In a "nearby" galaxy. How nearby? Well, they estimate that it is 2.3 million light-years away. It has been many years since my high school science classes, so I had to check in our encyclopedias to be reminded that light travels approximately 6 trillion miles in a single light-year.

Now, if I multiply that 6 trillion miles per each light-year by 2.3 million light-years, I will know how far away that black hole is.

I give up. My adding machine doesn't have that many spaces, and I do realize at last that I haven't really traveled very far on God's map.

April 7

This was an important day in our lives. In the morning we drove down to the bank and paid off our mortgage on this home and land that Bette and I have grown to love so much. Tonight, for the first time in our long married life, we will be sleeping in a house that we own completely.

This afternoon, with our attorney's guidance, we signed our newly drawn-up wills, durable powers of attorney, and living wills. How easy it was to keep putting off such things, but we finally got off our duffs, and hopefully our actions will make things a lot easier for our sons and their families when we are gone. I understand that six out of ten Americans still die without a will, leaving nothing but problems to those they love instead of a little joy and some happy memories. How sad.

April 9

Spoke in Atlanta last night, at the Westin Peachtree Hotel. They tell me there were seventeen hundred people in the Peachtree Ballroom when I walked out on stage at slightly after seven P.M. Great audience!

Afterward, sitting at a table next to the stage, I autographed books for nearly three hours, but my greatest thrill and happiest portion of the evening was reserved for the very end of my autographing session. Suddenly, as I was signing books, I realized that the line had changed from adults to what now seemed a group of teenagers, some wearing baseball hats backward, fluorescent T-shirts, and torn jeans; and the books they presented to be autographed, all paperbacks, had already received plenty of wear. Each of the kids, after the book was signed, asked for a hug, and of course I stood, hugged each, and then sat again. After four or five had passed through the line, I asked, "Is this a group from some organization?" and the pretty little girl standing next to me told me that they were all in a drug recovery program and loved my book *The Greatest Miracle in the World.* Many of them passed me notes to be read later, and one young man presented me with a gray medal he had been wearing around his neck, inscribed, CLEAN AND SOBER, 30 DAYS. He had earned it, he said, thanks to my books, and he wanted me to have it. Back in my room I spread out the many messages the kids had left me and read them, often through tear-filled eyes.

This afternoon, when Bette picked me up at the airport, we headed for home as quickly as possible, sat in our family room sharply at five in the afternoon, and watched ourselves on *The Cathy Burnham Show* on television. My original opinion of the taping was correct: Bette was great.

April 12

This was going to be a weekend of outside chores, including many of the initial steps one takes to prepare the landscape for six months of enjoyment. I had purchased aluminum sulfate and peat moss to spread around my blueberry plants, both the wild and the cultivated ones, and I planned to pick up most of the dead fallen limbs that were strewn beneath the pines. If I had any extra time, I would also fertilize the lawns.

Drove Bette to the airport this morning. She was going to spend the next ten days in Arizona with our children, and I would join her next week after my speech in Camp Hill, Pennsylvania. Well, I saw Bette off okay, but by the time I had returned home, a light snow was falling. Later in the day it turned to a combination of rain and snow, and icy sleet fell for almost six hours. Scratch all outside duties, answer fan mail, and get back to the book, with a break, of course, to watch the Masters Golf Tournament.

April 16

They tell me that there were more than a thousand people in the audience at the Penn Harris Convention Center in Camp Hill, Pennsylvania, when I walked out on the stage almost four hours ago. I autographed books for more than two hours following my talk and I'm now back in my room at the hotel, savoring the precious peace and quiet.

This is another very special part of our country that I love, and I'm sure that I could spend several weeks in southern Pennsylvania, with Bette, just being tourists and relishing every moment of our visit.

What a marvelous variety of attractions only short

drives from here: Three Mile Island; the Rockville Bridge over the Susquehanna River, largest stone-arch bridge in the world; Hershey's Chocolate World (where I would be happy to spend a week); Indian Echo Caverns; Ike Eisenhower's only permanent home; the battlefields of Gettysburg; Amish buggies on the back roads of Lancaster County; the *Pirate of the Susquehanna* riverboat; and the golden domed state capitol in Harrisburg.

Pennsylvania was, and always will be, Benjamin Franklin country, above all. Among that great man's writing, my favorite has always been his self-written gravestone epitaph:

The Body
of
Benjamin Franklin, Printer
(Like the cover of an old book, Its contents torn out,
And stripped of its lettering and gilding,)
Lies here food for worms,
Yet the work itself shall not be lost,
For it will (as he believes) appear once more
In a new and more beautiful Edition
Corrected and Amended
By
The Author

April 17

I am sitting at Gate A-7 in the Harrisburg, Pennsylvania, airport, waiting for the boarding announcement and trying to fight off the usual letdown that seems always to follow a speech. I see in *The Patriot*, Harrisburg's morning newspaper, that drug trafficking, once pretty much a big-city activity, is now infecting most of small-town America.

Not far from here, in the nearby town of Carlisle, citizens have organized into a small army of volunteers who will patrol their Memorial Park area in pairs, armed only with a flashlight and a radio, to attempt to put a stop to the open-air peddling of drugs in their community.

Two earlier residents of Carlisle, Molly Pitcher, who carried water to Revolutionary War artillerymen when her gunner husband was wounded, and Jim Thorpe, great Indian athlete and Olympic champion, are probably both turning over in their graves.

It is getting very rough out here, but we cannot turn our back on the threats to our country and our very way of life. If we do, if we allow the monsters to pollute our world with fear and crime and dope, we will have only ourselves to blame. I'm pretty sure we still outnumber them. Now we've got to organize in some fashion and declare war before we see America gradually destroyed and our dreams buried.

April 21

I imagine that at least one radio station in every city with a population of half a million or more proudly boasts that they have a "traffic-copter" which will guide commuters around all the morning and afternoon traffic problems on our choked highways. Yet in the hundred or so large cities that I have visited during the past couple of decades I've never been able to understand what any of these gentlemen are saying as they fly over the highways and byways. They yell into their microphones, speak at least four hundred words a minute, and seem to have a language of their own—something between a guttural German and exaggerated pig Latin.

Are all these stations playing a hoax on us? Do they all

possess the very same recording, made in the early eighties perhaps, that they just keep playing over and over during the morning and afternoon drive time? If they are, who would know?

April 26

As I write these words, I am in my hotel room at the Hyatt Regency looking down on San Antonio's famed River Walk.

Yesterday I spoke to more than five hundred mostly female skin consultants and managers of Rita Davenport's fast-growing Arbonne International, and last night I attended the company's awards ceremony and closed their evening with a few hopefully inspiring words. Since Rita and I have been good friends for more than twenty years, I worked very hard at giving that special lady her money's worth and then some.

The River Walk is a special landmark, unique to San Antonio, extending for a mile and a half or so along the San Antonio River but below the busy downtown streets. It is lined with lush cypress and palm trees, colored umbrellas and hundreds of shops, galleries, hotels, and sidewalk cafés where one can sip a margarita on the rocks while watching countless river taxis glide slowly beneath old stone bridges as the sound of mariachi bands hovers in the air.

The Alamo is quite near the River Walk. I still remember my surprise the first time I saw that beloved American landmark, which is now almost completely hidden by modern buildings. It seems so tiny, this very special place where Jim Bowie and Davy Crockett and 187 other brave men resisted General Santa Ana's hordes of soldiers for a dozen days before the final American was slain.

Are there any such Americans, call them patriots if you

will, walking around today? I'm not so sure anymore. Wonder how many could repeat the words of Daniel Webster, and *mean* them:

> I was born an American; I live an American; I shall die an American; and I intend to perform the duties incumbent upon me in that character to the end of my career. I mean to do this with absolute disregard of personal consequences. What are the personal consequences? What is the individual man, with all the good or evil that may betide him, in comparison with the good or evil which may befall a great country, and in the midst of great transactions which concern that country's fate? Let the consequences be what they will, no man can suffer too much, and no man can fall too soon, if he suffer or if he fall, in the defense of the liberties and constitution of his country.

April 28

Suffering from a small case of culture shock. After a couple of great days in what has been not so jokingly called Mexico's northernmost city, San Antonio, I accompanied Bette on a leisurely scenic drive, northeast across New Hampshire, to the town of Hanover, home of Dartmouth College, where Bette had been scheduled for a series of allergy tests at the Dartmouth-Hitchcock Medical Center in nearby Lebanon.

We had time, so I went out of my way to take a walk on Dartmouth's campus, with its spired red-bricked buildings covered with ivy. I suddenly remembered a boy named David Tyler, who was attending Dartmouth after he graduated in my 1940 class at Natick High in Massachusetts. Oh, how I had envied him. I couldn't possibly imagine how wealthy his parents must be in order to be able to afford to send him to ultra-exclusive Dartmouth.

Now it was fifty-two years later and I was finally on the campus of my dreams, watching sloppily dressed kids rushing to classes and missing all the smiles and laughter and music I had just left behind in San Antonio.

May 5

Bette and I joined W. Clement Stone and his wife, Jessie, last night at Chicago's Mid-American Club to celebrate Mr. Stone's ninetieth birthday at a black-tie dinner that included former president Nixon.

Since Chicago will always be our "second home," we arrived two days early so that we could be pampered at the Ritz-Carlton Hotel on Chicago's Magnificent Mile, and once again were fortunate to secure the same twentieth-floor suite where we have spent many happy moments in the past few years, usually while Christmas shopping at Water Tower Place.

On our first free evening, Bette and I hired a horse and buggy and, holding hands under our cozy blanket, clip-clopped our way around downtown Chicago, recalling some of our earlier days in the big city when we were struggling so hard to crawl out of debt and "become somebody."

As we were riding past the CBS studios on N. McClurg Court, Bette reminded me of my television appearance there, live, on *The Lee Phillips Show*, way back when I was promoting my book *The Greatest Miracle in the World*. Bette also reminded me that our son Matt's grammar school class watched the program in their classroom, and then their assignment was to write to Mr. Mandino and tell him what they thought of his television appearance, all very much to our son's embarrassment.

At the Ritz how wonderful it was to phone room service and to hear a friendly voice say, "Good morning, Mr. Mandino, how can we serve you?" No wonder this very special hotel keeps winning the coveted AAA Five Diamonds Award, year after year.

Three decades ago, long before I had ever written my first book, I was a salesman for W. Clement Stone's insurance company. Each year the first week in May was called Presidential Birthday Week, and we all went the extra mile to sell as many policies as we could to show Mr. Stone how much we respected him. Corny, perhaps, but it worked. In 1961, on that special week, I sold 113 introductory policies, and now here I was, thirty-one years later, holding Bette close while we both looked down on Chicago's millions of lights. Happy Birthday, Mr. Stone! You helped make all our dreams come true.

May 16

Drove down to Nashua on this bright Saturday morning and autographed books for two hours at the Reflections Bookshop. Denise Crompton, the store's owner, wrote a warm letter of invitation, and I think I surprised her when I responded that I would come. Although we have been back in New Hampshire more than two years, the fact that I am living here is still known by very few, and I hope it stays that way. The poet Robert Lowell once said that solitude is as needful to the imagination as society is wholesome for the character.

May 21

Looked out to see a solitary raccoon dining on the seed droppings from our bird feeder in the backyard. I opened the back kitchen door and stepped noisily out on the deck. Didn't frighten him. He looked up at me, cocked his pointed face complete with the familiar black mask across his eyes, and then went back to his feeding. I stepped off the deck and walked slowly toward him. He glanced up at me once, when I was less than ten feet away, sat up on his hind legs as if to taunt me, and then turned and strolled leisurely between two blueberry bushes back into the pines.

Bette and I have decided, with some sadness, that this will be the final week that our bird feeder will be available to all our feathered neighbors. They will now be on their own, which they should be, until late October, when their available menu in the woods and fields will have been all but eliminated by frost. At that time we will let them all know that the welcome mat is out again at the Mandinos', and they will be free to come eat whenever and as often as they wish, through the winter. That also includes our friend the squirrels, both gray and red, chipmunks, and, yes, even my new friend, the bold raccoon.

May 24

At noon yesterday in Philadelphia I spoke at the National Sales and Service Conference of the United Consumer Club in the large ballroom of the Wyndham Franklin Plaza Hotel. Notre Dame's football coach, Lou Holtz, had spoken to the group earlier in the day, and I was certain he'd be a tough act to follow, but everything worked out just fine.

Like every other large city, Philadelphia has its share of

traffic jams, noise, dirt, and pollution. Although I love that city, Liberty Bell and all, I couldn't wait to get back to my special haven in the woods, and I seem to miss it, more and more, each time I leave.

The United Consumer people had handed out pads of notepaper to everyone attending my speech. The pages were light blue, lined, with my smiling mug in the background of each page. I can't wait to hear Bette's comments when she sees them.

May 25

In the spirit of three-day weekends, where Mondays become all sorts of holidays, this is supposed to be Memorial Day. It's a legal holiday, the banks are closed, and Paula will not be driving down our dirt road to plunk our mail in the mailbox.

I see that the annual parade in Manhattan that once enthralled hundreds of thousands of patriotic Americans did not take place this year. They said there was "not enough interest."

May 27

Boasting a coat of translucent green with white markings and red wings, the Japanese beetle, not much larger than a dime, is one of the farmers' most feared enemies in the eastern part of our country. Native to Japan, where its population is held in check by many parasites, the little rascal somehow made its way to this country in 1917, probably in grub form hidden in the root balls of live plants shipped from Japan. In any event the voracious little monster spread swiftly, from Riverton, New Jersey, where it was first discovered, and by now the entire country east of the Mississippi suffers millions of dollars of damage each year as adult beetles feed upon the leaves and flowers of hundreds of varieties of plants, very often completely defoliating them.

Last year, after living so many years in Arizona, I was not aware of these little monsters until they had almost eaten every leaf off our beloved birch trees on the front lawn as well as the roses.

This year I'm ready for them. I purchased six of the latest and best Japanese beetle traps, called TRECE, and hung them on their special metal-rod stands, in the orchard, the flower garden, near the vegetable garden, and even on the lawn close to the pretty birches that had taken such a beating last year.

Let them come! They are in for one hell of a surprise this year!

May 30

No matter what the nation is doing, this day is my Memorial Day. Filled with so many memories. Flowers. Cemeteries. Parades. This was also the day when my father commenced his gardening activities for the year, and although I hated it, I was forced to participate.

How natural, then, that after all these years this should be the day when I start our garden. Planted six Supersonic Tomatoes, which promise to be large, red, and meaty and produce in seventy-nine days. Also early bell-type Midway sweet peppers, two rows of early Sunglow sweet corn, a row of Golden Butterwax beans, one row of long Tendergreen beans, and a row of Blue Lake 274 green beans.

Had much more to do, but the old body was growing weary. Still it's a beginning, and for the next month or so both Bette and I will be adding several more rows of vegetables and salad greens.

There is something almost sacred about working a garden. The peace that settles on one is difficult to describe, although Alex Smith, the old Scottish poet, tried when he wrote, "My garden, with its silence and the pulses of fragrance that come and go in the airy undulations, affects me like sweet music. Care stops at the gates, and gazes at me wistfully through the bars. Among my flowers and plants and trees, nature takes me into her own hands, and I breathe as freely as the first man."

June 2

Wrote the final sentence on the last page of the new book, *The Twelfth Angel*, yesterday, and I am already suffering through the usual withdrawal pains. As I have done with all its predecessors, the typescript has been read and re-read, perhaps a dozen times in the past month, and when a page has been scarred with more than half a dozen corrections and changes from my red felt-tip pen, it is always retyped. This process goes on and on until I am finally able to convince myself that I couldn't improve it very much more no matter how long I worked on it.

I feel very good about the book. As usual, during the past months I have grown to love and respect my main character, young Timothy Noble, who had no athletic ability and was tiny for his age. He was drafted last by the Angel Little League team, and the book is hopefully a sensitive narration of his struggles through the season to get his first base hit. Just one! The ending, if I have succeeded, will touch the reader at many depths and will probably be called "a typical Mandino ending."

I could not have written the book without the help of

my son, Matt. He not only played many years of Little League but later, while in college, coached several championship teams. Whenever I got myself into a jam reading Little League rules or playing the game properly, I would be on the phone to Matt, and he would patiently take me through the correct process.

I am a lucky father.

June 4

Having been an Army Air Corps private, stationed in Atlantic City during the winter months of 1943, I can still feel the biting winds off the roaring Atlantic as we marched and drilled up and down Atlantic City's famous boardwalk.

Oh, how the times they have changed! I see that the city police are now riding up and down the same boardwalk, on their twenty-one-gear mountain bikes, writing traffic tickets for bicyclists, who are not allowed on the boardwalk after ten in the morning. One of their first arrests involved a seventeen-year-old at Arctic Avenue who had eight bags of heroin in his possession.

Gambling casinos along the boardwalk have made the oceanfront a neon imitation of Oz, but if one walks two or three blocks away from the water, one is still confronted with hunger, poverty, and every possible sort of crime. On second thought perhaps things don't really change at all. They just get progressively worse as our level of tolerance increases. Still, as Pascal once wrote, with all the miseries surrounding us, threatening our destruction, we still have an instinct that we cannot repress, which elevates us above our sorrows. And, I add, gives us hope of a better tomorrow. Without that hope, for many life wouldn't be worth living.

June 9

Across the road from our house is an old, weather-beaten shack that Bette and I love just the way it is. Our youngest, Matt, took to the old building from his first visit, so now we lovingly refer to the old structure as Matt's Shack.

In the shack I keep many tools since our vegetable garden is close by. At the back of the shack is a single nine-pane window of glass, dusty, dirty, and covered with several cobwebs. I walked into the shack to get a rake this morning and saw a strange sight—three yellow butterflies and a bumblebee, all flying at the dingy window, again and again, unable, I guess, to understand why they were being prevented from continuing their flight when they could plainly see the pond and the trees just beyond the window.

I stood and watched for several minutes until I just couldn't stand seeing the poor creatures suffer any longer. I moved close to the window, reached across, and gently clasped both wings of one of the butterflies, then walked out the door and away from the shack for perhaps ten yards before releasing the lovely thing, which immediately climbed high above me, heading north. I returned to the shack and this time took one butterfly between the first two fingers of my left hand and the other butterfly between the first two of my right hand. Outside, I released them both and they, too, headed north.

Back to the shack. The huge black-and-orange bumblebee, enraged and frustrated, was still flying noisily again and again at the windowpanes. I put on my heavy leather garden gloves, grasped the big guy as gently as I could, and walked him outside, raising my hand high above my head before releasing the noisy devil.

All writers have rather far-fetched imaginations, I guess, but I couldn't help concocting a little playlet in which one of the freed butterflies turned to the other after I had released them and asked, "Who was that who freed us?" and the other replied, "I'm not sure, but I think it was God."

June 11

It is shortly after dawn and I am flying to Mexico City from the city of León. In Mexico City I shall board a plane for Newark, make a change in Newark, and arrive in Manchester around ten this evening. Long day, considering I requested a wake-up call for four-fifteen A.M.

I spoke yesterday morning at the Fiesta Americana in León to more than five hundred businesspeople of León and surrounding towns. Their organization's Spanish name is "LaCamara de la Industrial del Calzado del Estado de Guanajuato." León, a city with more than a million population, has been for many years a major force in the world's shoe industry, but in recent years has felt strong encroachment by the Chinese and other Asian countries. Now the hundreds of shoe stores in the city are on their knees for lack of business and the firms that build shoe-manufacturing machinery have very little smoke rising from their chimneys.

The group was very quiet and attentive as I spoke to them with the aid of an instantaneous interpreter, who did a marvelous job. Mexican audiences in years gone past have usually been smiling, happy groups, but this bunch looked like they were listening to a funeral mass. Still, when I finished, they delivered a long and standing ovation, and I spent another hour responding to their written questions, which were translated for me. Then an hour of autographing, followed by an interview with the local newspapers plus a small television segment for a local station.

At the León airport my ego received a tremendous boost. When I handed my ticket to the person behind the ticket counter, he looked at the name, frowned, and then asked softly, "Señor Og Mandino, the writer?"

I nodded my head, at which point the clerk turned and yelled to those behind the other Continental ticket counters, in English, "Hey, everyone, this is Señor Og Mandino, Señor Og Mandino!"

I shook hands with all the Continental personnel present as well as several tourists during the next few minutes. Boarded the plane a very proud man.

June 13

Perhaps ten feet or so into our pine woods, behind the house, the lovely genus of orchid called the lady's slipper has appeared in force, forming a single file across the open area of woods for perhaps a hundred yards. What a special time in the year when these pink, rare beauties flaunt their dainty but unusual shape that resembles a shoe, a lady's slipper. They will be with us for only a few short days, these special gifts from God. None are ever plucked for any of our vases. They will spend what little time they have swaying gently above the pine needles, loved and protected.

June 18

Spoke to more than sixteen hundred people last night at the O'Hare Exposition Center, west of Chicago. During the question-and-answer session that followed my speech, I was asked why Chicago was my favorite city, as I had stated earlier during my speech. The answer was easy. I told the crowd that I had arrived in that great city in 1963 with Bette and our young son, Dana, with all our belongings in the trunk and on top of our car. I was about to commence a job as a bulletin writer in the sales promotion department of W. Clement Stone's Combined Insurance Company at a salary of ten thousand dollars per year!

Thirteen years later I retired from the presidency of W. Clement Stone's magazine, *Success Unlimited*, with three best-sellers under my belt and the announcement that I was going to spend the rest of my life writing, speaking, and playing golf.

Sixteen years after my retirement I'm still doing what I said I would be doing and, at the tender age of sixty-eight and a half, I believe I am beginning to reach my full potential at last.

June 21

Father's Day! Since my piece "A Letter to Two Sons" had enjoyed such a great reception in *Success Unlimited* magazine as well as on the radio on Christmas Day, I wrote a second piece, titled "Father's Day," and ran it in our June 1969 issue. Same reception from my readers, and radio station WGN once again had their great announcer, John Mallow, read the piece on Father's Day morning. I still have a recording of his radio rendition, and when I play it, the years always seem to fade away.

FATHER'S DAY

It was like hundreds of other predawn Sunday mornings stretching backward through the years.

At the first mutterings from the hybrid radio and alarm clock, I awoke and flipped the off button before it disturbed anyone. I slipped quietly to the window and watched for a few moments as the June moon reluctantly retreated behind the trees. It was going to be a warm day.

I showered, shaved, and dressed in my favorite golf outfit, the Arnold Palmer shirt with matching slacks that had set me back thirty bucks at the pro shop, and tiptoed downstairs to the kitchen.

While the water was boiling for my cup of Maxim, I moved quietly out into the garage, stepped carefully between the four bicycles and two automobiles, pushed up the hanging door, and moved my golf cart out into the driveway. When the guys came by, I'd be ready. If we were lucky, maybe we could tee off today before nine and we'd be home by two-thirty or so.

I downed my orange juice and two One-A-Day vitamin pills and sat with my coffee and doughnut. I had at least twenty minutes to kill before I would hear the single toot from the station wagon carrying the rest of the foursome.

As I sipped my coffee, I watched two robins playing tag in our locust tree. Then I heard the sound of bare feet upstairs. My watch read six-fifteen. Who was up? Then I heard a second set of feet. Could both boys be having bathroom call at the same time?

After a few moments of silence my mind returned to

the match coming up. I hadn't broken eighty all year, but today was going to be different. I had straightened out that hook on the last few holes last week and now I was ready. I looked at my watch again. Ten more minutes.

I sat facing away from the hall that leads from the up-stairs stairway so I didn't see them come up behind me. But I heard them, my two sons. In unison they said, "Happy Father's Day, Dad." Then I was embraced as only a twelve-year-old and a six-year-old can manhan-dle you, and each kissed my cheek.

Matt, the youngest, was holding a white envelope on which he had scrawled "Dad." He handed it to me with all the pride he usually reserved for an "A" school pa-per. I opened the envelope and carefully removed the card, which read, "To the greatest Dad in the world." It was signed with the same scrawl, "Love, Matt."

Then Dana, my twelve-year-old, obviously feeling a little too grown-up for such sentimental foolishness, handed me his envelope. His card was exactly like Matt's: "To the greatest Dad in the world." Matt, before his older brother could shush him, said, "We bought them with our own money, Dad."

I thanked and kissed them both and then suggested that they get back to bed since it was still very early, but they wouldn't hear of it. They had planned to see me before I left, and now that they were up, they were go-ing to stay up. Soon they were at the table devouring large bowls of the latest vitamin-enriched cereal.

As I watched the two of them, a strange feeling came over me. Perhaps it was just early-morning mist flowing through the screen door, but Dana seemed to be aging before my eyes. Or perhaps it was just the first time I had actually looked at him in a long time. He was hand-some and luckily for him was getting to look more and more like his mother. Gosh, he had grown up, and between my long hours at the office and my weekends on the golf course, I hadn't noticed the change in him. The horrible thought suddenly hit me that he would have a draft number in six years and would be more or less out of my life in ten years, war or no war.

Then I looked at Matt. He was already in the first grade. It was only yesterday, wasn't it, that I had paced the floor outside the delivery room until I heard his first yell? What happened to those six years? He glanced up from his bowl, and all I could see were those big brown eyes. For the first time I noticed how red his hair was getting, almost the shade of his grandmother's hair, which he had never seen.

Matt frowned at my staring. "What's the matter, Dad, don't you like the cards?"

I assured him they were great and then I heard the horn. The guys were here. I rose, gave them another hug, and headed toward the garage. They followed me. When I reached the driveway, Matt said, "Play a good game" and Dana said, "I hope you win."

I waved and walked down the driveway toward the awaiting car. Bob got out of the driver's side to open the back gate in the station wagon for my clubs. I said "good morning" and then a few other words. Bob frowned, nodded, and got back in the car. He gunned the motor and roared off.

I stood there in my Arnold Palmer shirt and my pants to match, hardly understanding what I had done. Watching me from the garage, as puzzled as I was, stood my two pajama-clad boys.

Finally Matt came running down the driveway and leaped into my arms. I buried my face in his small chest until he pushed my head back and asked, "Daddy, why are you crying?"

What could I say to him?

How could I tell him that my tears were for all those

hours I had wasted on all the projects and jobs and golf courses that would still be there long after my two little men became big men and left me forever?

July 4

In my long life I have watched fireworks from many grandstands and parked cars, but none was as unusual as last night.

Bette's mother, Rita, has now been at the Catholic Medical Center in Manchester a total of fifty days as she recovers, very slowly, from a triple bypass. Almost every day Bette has driven the fifty-plus miles to the hospital with her dad, who has several health problems of his own, to visit with "Nana." By now most of the nurses and attendants greet Bette and "Gramps" warmly as old friends, so it didn't even surprise me when we were all invited to come at dusk last night and sit in the lounge on the fifth floor with Nana to view the fireworks, which were being set off from a city park no more than two blocks away.

Matt and his expecting wife, Lori, flew in from their Scottsdale home to spend a week with us, so they came along to the hospital, where we all took turns holding Nana's hand as we watched a spectacular display of glowing rockets and arching balls of flame explode in a shower of every possible color. Most of the time, however, Gramps sat close to his lady, holding and stroking her hand gently. When it was over, with tears in his eyes he said huskily to Bette and me, "Thanks for letting me watch the fireworks with my girl."

July 6

More than half the cities and towns in our nation are now operating in the red. They are broke, according to the National League of Cities.

And how are we as individuals doing? Just as poorly. Figures from the Federal Reserve, released last week, inform us that our total consumer debt stands at more than $720 billion, and I guess if we hang on long enough, our credit cards will destroy all of us. We now owe, through our plastic alone, almost $250 billion. Billion!! We also borrowed $23 billion on the hard-earned equity in our homes, and most of that money was used to pay off other debts.

Charles Bridges, a wise old English minister, once wrote, " 'Out of debt, out of danger,' is like many other proverbs, full of wisdom; but the word danger does not sufficiently express all that the warning demands because a state of debt and embarrassment is a state of positive misery, and the sufferer is as one haunted by an evil spirit, and his heart can know neither rest nor peace till it is cast out."

Were we better off when we had no credit cards, when we had to have the money to pay for most things before we acquired them? Are we better off than our parents and grandparents only because of the personal debts we've all racked up, debts that wreak mortal havoc with so many lives when the paychecks needed to repay the debt cease coming?

July 8

Played a round of golf with my son, Matt, at the local golf course. Watching him swing, so gracefully and effortlessly, I kept remembering how tiny he was when I first put a small golf club in his hands and dropped a few balls on the grass. Where have the years gone? He will be a father sometime in November.

July 9

Just when we were all beginning to wonder whether summer would ever come and stay for more than a few hours, after a night of heavy rain the temperature has been climbing all day and is now above eighty. From early morning the westerly winds have turned even old pine trees into swaying palms, a perfect day for us to hang, at the corner of our house very near our deck, the Woodstock Georgian chimes that Matt and Lori brought us, and now, even above the moaning wind, one can hear musical patterns borrowed from ancient chants.

The earliest corn I planted is now close to two feet tall, string beans look like they're ready to bloom, tomato plants are in bud, and even the lettuce looks promising. The one major error I have committed in my garden during the past two years here is that I didn't thin the plants out enough, didn't give them room to grow. This year I have, and the difference is so noticeable.

Walked around our place this afternoon. Sat on a boulder and watched the deep ripples in our pond. If the temperature holds in the eighties, we should be picking blueberries in a week or so. Can't wait.

July 11

I doubt that there is anything more difficult than performing before a group of one's peers, but thank God it is over and I don't think I made a fool of myself. Flew down here to Orlando yesterday, and at five this evening I was the keynote speaker to the National Speakers Association. More than twelve hundred professional speakers and people involved in other aspects of our profession, such as agents and meeting planners, crowded into the main ballroom at the Peabody Hotel for the annual convention's opening ceremonies, which were followed by my remarks.

When I was finished, I bowed, thanked the crowd for being so nice, and walked down off the stage. A large group immediately gathered around me with hugs and flashbulbs popping for almost an hour, and when Ed Scannell, our association president, finally rescued me, he said softly as we were walking through the lobby, "Og, I've never seen a speaker treated like that before in all my years in the business. Do they always gather around like that for autographs and hugs?"

I nodded my head and grinned—sheepishly.

"Had to see it to believe it." Ed sighed.

Way back in 1975, only a few years after Walt Disney had waved his magic wand over square miles of mud and swamp to produce Walt Disney World, Bette and I had driven from our home in Illinois, with our two young sons, for a week's vacation with Donald Duck and Mickey Mouse in Orlando. Now one needs a month and a truly fat wallet to see all the attractions in the area: Sea World, Universal Studios, Alligatorland, Cypress Gardens, Reptile World, EPCOT™ Center, the Disney-MGM Theme Park, Adventure Island, Busch Gardens, the Kennedy Space Center, and Silver Springs, not to mention a trip to a very special restaurant called Arabian Nights, in the small town of Kissimmee, which seats over one thousand and presents a show featuring eighty horses, including a mystical unicorn, Arabian dancing horses of the desert, and even a quarter-horse square dance.

Makes one want to remain a kid forever.

July 15

I see that many old pilots, navigators, bombardiers, and gunners, all members of the U.S. Army Air Force, have returned to England to celebrate the fiftieth anniversary of the first Eighth Air Force arrivals in the spring of 1942.

With my newly trained air crew I arrived in England, a twenty-one-year-old lieutenant with my bombardier wings shining so brightly on my jacket, in the summer of '44, concerned that the war might be over before I flew my first mission. D day had already occurred, and our armies were advancing rapidly into France. As it all turned out, there were many frightening moments during my thirty combat missions over Germany when I would have been very pleased to have had the war end immediately.

I wonder what has happened to my old airfield, the 445th bomb group's base, in the little town of Tibenham. Is it now part of somebody's farm, choked with tract homes, or just buried under weeds and brambles?

More than half a million of America's young men and women served in England sometime during the war. At least fifty thousand died fighting the Nazis, and the bodies of many of them still remain in foreign soil. God bless every one of them. We'll never again see such a magnificent sight or hear such a frightening, awesome sound, thank God, as an entire bomb group of thirty-six taxiing B-24 Liberators, waiting for the flare signaling their takeoff, each plane finally thundering down the runway with all four engines roaring. I am so proud to have been a tiny part of that great effort.

July 17

It is almost midnight and I am in my pajamas sitting at the desk in my huge room at the Red Lion Riverside Hotel in Boise, Idaho. Outside my window balcony the Boise River is making gurgling sounds as it slips by in the bright moonlight.

Tomorrow evening, at a banquet in the main ballroom, I'll address many of the top producers of Aim International, who have gathered from many nations to celebrate their tenth anniversary of marketing a variety of increasingly popular health foods, such as Barleygreen and Just Carrots.

July 19

The speech for Aim International went very well last night. Since their top distributors from many nations attended, it was a different experience, after the speech, to autograph copies of my books printed in English, French, and Spanish. More important perhaps, on a truly personal basis, the more I kept hearing about their products, the more I became intrigued. Barleygreen, developed by Japanese scientist Dr. Hagiwara, is barley powder made by a special patented juicing and air-drying process to preserve the nutritive value of the young barley plant, so often mentioned in the Bible. The powder, mixed with small amounts of brown rice and kelp, is now available in packet form, and one has only to dissolve a packet in six ounces of cold water to enjoy a unique "salad in a glass."

Same with Just Carrots. Each packet contains the nutrients found in one pound of raw carrots with its much-needed supply of beta-carotene, which has finally been recognized as an important substance our body easily converts to vitamin A.

I'll begin tomorrow. A drink of Barleygreen soon after I arise and another of Just Carrots in the middle of the afternoon. We'll see if I notice any difference in a couple of months.

This was a rare occurrence for me. I have spoken to hundreds of company conventions in the past fifteen years, but never before have I personally embraced, for my own personal use, any of the companies' products.

July 21

For the fifth consecutive month *The Return of the Ragpicker* is on *Publishers Weekly*'s list of ten religious best-sellers, nationally. I am very pleased, of course, but for the life of me I do not understand why *Ragpicker* is considered a religious book. There is no dogma, no biblical quotations, no reference even to God unless it is in someone's opening words in a conversation.

With rubbish of the basest sort making it to best-seller lists these days, perhaps my writing is considered "religious" just because I use no four-letter words—except *love*.

July 23

We stocked our pond with forty-eight goldfish this morning. A dozen of them were four to six inches in length and the rest were tiny things. The larger ones formed an immediate school and kept close to each other as they circled the area, again and again, where they had been dropped into the water. The smaller ones headed for the deeper parts of the pool. I hope all of them can adjust and be happy in their new home. Bette and I welcome them with love and promise to be good stepparents.

July 26

Thanks to my books, my past keeps catching up with me. In *The Return of the Ragpicker* I wrote about how, on each Patriot's Day—always April 19th when I was a kid—my mother and father would take me to watch the runners in the Boston Marathon as they raced by. Through the years one developed favorites, and ours was a man named Johnny Kelley. Kelley, now in his eighties, is still running marathons, bless his heart.

I received a letter this week from a lady who had read *Ragpicker* and was writing to tell me that her dad was a friend of Johnny Kelley's. She then went on to inform me that her father was Archie San Romani, a great miler who had represented our nation in the 1936 Olympics. Her phone number was enclosed, and I did something I rarely do: I called her.

After she was finally convinced that she was talking to Og Mandino, I unloaded my surprise. I told her that when I was eleven and twelve years old, I constantly dreamed of being a great runner someday. Next to our home, in Natick, Massachusetts, was an abandoned nursery, and day after day I would run those dirt roads, working on my speed and endurance. Back then I was not called Og. I was the son of an Italian immigrant father and a first-generation Irish mother, had been baptized Augustine Anthony Mandino and that's what the kids called me, usually accompanied by giggles. Since I dreamed of being a famous runner, I adopted, as all kids do, an adult hero. Who else? There was only one famous American runner with an Italian name—Archie San Romani. And so, on those lonely nursery roads I was Archie San Romani, winning track meet after track meet and medal after medal. Dreams.

Archie San Romani finished fourth in the 1936 Olympics in the 1,500-meter run, but that didn't change my feelings about him at all. He was a very special man who had overcome the terrible adversity of almost losing one of his legs after being hit by an automobile as a child, and the world record he set for the 2,000-meter run endured for twenty-five years.

Talking on the phone, his daughter surprised me with the news that although Archie was not well, he was still alive and lived near her. I asked her to give him a big hug for me and to thank him for his inspiration. During my senior year at Natick High, in one track meet in 1940, I managed to win the 100-yard dash, the 220-yard dash, and the quarter-mile, a feat that no one at that school has accomplished since. Thank you, Archie.

July 28

Spent the entire day alone. Bette was up before dawn and on the way to the hospital in Manchester, where her mother was scheduled to go under the surgeon's knife for the fourth time in eleven weeks, this time in an effort to transfer veins from other parts of the body to her left leg, which has been gradually losing all its circulation. I have much new respect for my gutsy mother-in-law. A triple bypass, followed by a second entry days later when things had not healed as planned, followed by a tracheotomy, followed by a transfer of some veins from her upper right thigh to her lower right leg that was losing all circulation, followed by the same procedure today in the left leg. Today's major problem, however, was that Nana just didn't have many veins left that were long enough for the transfer, or large enough.

I have just heard from Bette. She and her seventy-nine-year-old father have been at the hospital since seven this morning. It is now nine-thirty in the evening and she called from her car phone to tell me that they were on the way home. Her mother's operation had taken more than thirteen hours, and the surgeon who had commenced the procedure early this morning had to ask for assistance late this afternoon, as he was near exhaustion. Nana, according to Bette, is now back in her intensive-care room, still with her two feet, although there is no guarantee that amputation, due to lack of circulation, may not still be ahead for the brave lady.

So what did I do with this day all alone? Household chores. Some enjoyable, some not. I sprayed each room, along the baseboards, with a pest-control liquid. Then I planted three short rows of lettuce—our late-September and final supply if Jack Frost doesn't ambush us early. I fed the new goldfish that were stocked in our pond last week and finally I picked blueberries with my blueberry can hanging from my belt, at the waist, just as my blueberry cans hung from my belt fifty years ago.

Actually it was a little boy picking those blueberries today, wedged solidly among the branches so that he could reach the higher berries, with a backdrop of pine trees behind just as it was in the 1930s, on our little farm only about two hours' drive south of here—two hours and half a century.

It was truly a day of memories, and I guess I needed it—just to be reminded how lucky I am to still be able to drop freshly picked blueberries, by the handful, into a shiny tin can.

The older I get, the more convinced I become that the only true method of conquering life is to embrace each day, no matter what problems one has, with all the love and gusto and gratitude that one can muster. Then take a deep breath of that air that even the richest person who died yesterday cannot savor today . . . take that breath, look up, thank God for the gift of a new day, and live it . . . with few, if any, frowns plus a basketful of smiles.

It was almost dark before I fed my new neighbors, the goldfish, this evening. They are not adjusting very well to the pond. So far I have found three of the larger ones floating on the surface, dead. The others, at least the larger ones, seem to gather under some sort of leafy vegetation that has sprouted on one edge of the pond. I tossed in the fish food, as near to them as possible, but they made no move toward it. Then I waited in the rain for perhaps five minutes, but they just were not interested.

A line from Thoreau suddenly began running through my mind—"Who hears the fish when they cry?" I wonder. The world is getting so noisy that we scarcely hear our neighbors when *they* cry. We must listen more attentively. We cannot keep our helping hands buried deep in our pockets any longer. Who hears the fish . . . ?

August 1

The entire month of July has come and gone without a single day hitting the ninety-degree mark, a record that has only been matched eight times in this century. Farmers are already complaining that this is the worst hay-growing season in memory, and I can notice it in my own small garden patch, where the corn is still not much higher than my belt line and yet it has already sprouted its tassels on top. Lord only knows what the corn will look

like when picked. Whatever happened to "tall as an ele-
phant's eye"?

Amazing how a few degrees less in temperature can affect so many lives and businesses. Public Service of New
Hampshire just announced that its early figures indicated
we had used six percent less electricity in the past couple
of months; air conditioner sales are nil as well as new
swimming pool installations.

Bird migrations south have already commenced, always
the opening downbeat to fall's grand entry. Dragonflies
and warblers are heading below the Mason-Dixon Line,
and soon we'll be getting our bird feeder cleaned up to
hang in its usual place in our backyard for the winter.

Still, the rainbow of perennials continues to make our
garden a very special place. Daylilies of orange, yellow,
and crimson, rising high above clumps of pale yellow and
green hostas while astilbes of pink and white vie with
deep red and white phlox for one's attention. Every day, it
seems, another miracle of nature catches our eye—yellow
sedum, lavender Nepeta, dark blue veronica, silver
artemisia—a new surprise each morning. Does autumn
have to come? Yes, sigh all the budding fall chrysanthemums, we deserve our day too.

August 3

They removed Nana's left leg, just below the knee, this
morning. Despite valiant medical efforts, the vein trans-
plants didn't work as they had on the other leg.

I commenced my new book today. Working title is *The
Spellbinder*. It's one I've been itching to write for several
years and has been sold to Fawcett. The world of public
speaking remains a mystery to the average individual, although the odds are great that he or she has listened to at

least one speech delivered by a paid professional during the past twelve months.

On every day and evening of the week, in hotel ballrooms and motel business conference rooms, auditoriums, and theaters, from coast to coast, thousands of conventions and seminars take place. Almost every one of them employs one or more speaking professionals, either for a keynote address, a "warm up the troops" kickoff for a special sales campaign, or as an expert on some facet of business such as time management or closing a sale. Two years ago a group of meeting planners estimated that there were at least a million convention or seminar programs in the nation during the course of a year that required the talents of one or more paid speakers.

Both those who plan and arrange conventions and seminars as well as the thousands who deliver speeches and lectures are extremely well organized with their own associations and publications. A very big business it is, yet the average citizen, even one who attends several conventions or seminars each year, knows very little about this fascinating industry.

There have been scores of nonfiction books written on how to prepare and deliver a speech, but so far as I can discover, there has never been a fictional book where the focus is on a public speaker—until now.

Our oldest son, Dana, his wife, Carole, and their two children, Danielle and Ryan, flew across the country from their Arizona home to spend the past week with us. Between hospital visits to see Nana, they took my Jeep Grand Wagoneer and spent a couple of days at Lake Winnipesaukee with another couple at Old Orchard Beach, so now the two grandchildren are boasting that they have seen both the Pacific and Atlantic oceans.

Yesterday, their last day with us, was spent mostly playing on the beach of white sand that I had prepared for them on the west side of Little Walden. The kids also enjoyed frolicking in my newly purchased inflatable rubber boats with their mom and dad. God, how they are growing!

Late this afternoon, after we had driven them to the Manchester airport and kissed them good-bye, I walked across the street toward our little beach. Not until I was standing close to the water did I notice that, in the sand, in huge block letters, someone had written "THANK YOU!" I walked back to the house very slowly, fighting back the tears.

As Dana said at the airport while he was hugging us, "There is just never enough time." Time has become a most sought-after jewel in this world of stand-up lunches, dashes for airports, and early-morning meetings. It seems we have no time for the things that really matter, such as family, a good book, a day in the hammock. We will never conquer this life, never greet the dawn with joy and anticipation, until we have learned to make a portion of every day our own personal treasure. As Thoreau warned us, there is little use in ushering in our days with a prayer if they are then consecrated to merely turning a few more pennies. As that special man once wrote, "If I shall sell both my forenoons and afternoons to society, as most appear to do, I am sure that for me there would be nothing left worth living for. I trust that I shall never thus sell my birthright for a mess of pottage."

I'm going for a walk. In the woods.

August 27

Now that the threat from the Soviet bear has faded away, the world should be striding forward into a new era of prosperity, joy, laughter, peace, and quiet.

Spend thirty minutes watching the nightly news on television, and all you can ask yourself is what happened. A million or more are now starving in Somalia. A typhoon has just destroyed more than ninety percent of the buildings on the small territory of Guam, leaving thousands homeless. In Yugoslavia the Serbs and the Croatians are savagely attacking one another both night and day, and our Census Bureau has just announced that more than two million people joined the ranks of poverty last year. We now have, in what was our special nation, unlike any other, almost thirty-six million people living below the poverty level.

I had to do a little digging to learn what was considered the current poverty level. For a family of four, $13,924. For a single person, alone, $6,932.

President Bush is trailing in the public-opinion polls, primarily because the areas he would normally expect support from, the suburbs, are turning away from him. With good reason. Those earning among the top five percent in 1989 have seen their income fall almost five percent, double the decline suffered by the lowest-earning fifth of families.

Here in New England it is beginning to look like the most frightening period since the Depression. Homes, lovely homes, are being foreclosed on every street.

I walked out to the flower garden at twilight and sat myself on a rock. Just a slight breeze whistled through the maple trees, which are already beginning to lose their golden leaves. I don't know how long I sat there, feeling so damn helpless, wondering what I could do to help change the mood of the land. What could I say, or write, that might help? I know my books are doing some good. Letters from readers have doubled or more in the past few months. "How to conquer life" doesn't even seem appropriate to our terrible situation. Probably should be more like "How to survive in a world filled with tears."

August 28

I see that someone has mustered up enough courage, and money, to produce a movie dealing with the authentic genius Stephen Hawking and his masterful work *A Brief History of Time*. Hawking's books, describing the creation of black holes in the universe when stars collapse in on themselves, attracted millions of readers such as myself who tried very hard to understand this special person's insight and explanation of stellar activity.

Most amazing is not Hawking's already-classic book but the man himself, for he is completely paralyzed and can only communicate with the world by tapping letters of the alphabet into a special voice-synthesizing machine.

What a rare miracle! Here is a man, stricken with amyotrophic lateral sclerosis, which we all know as Lou Gehrig's disease, a man who cannot feed or wash or dress himself and yet is still able to reach out to teach us things about our universe we never dreamed.

How does one explain such a human? How many, sentenced to his terrible confinement, would have merely given up and wished themselves dead? What secret spark enabled this unique man to explore a world that the average human does not even know exists? Is that spark in all of us, waiting to be ignited? The mystery of life is not an inch closer to a solution than it was when Greek philosophers claimed that earth was a disk, covered by a dome of sky.

September 2

The Omni Shoreham Hotel, in our nation's capital, is one of our country's great treasures. Now over sixty years old, the hotel has history vibrating in the stones that one can feel even when merely walking through the lobby. Every inaugural ball has been held there since Franklin Roosevelt's first. If some, or maybe all, of the hotel rooms could only talk! Harry Truman held his private poker games in D-106 while his chauffeur and limo waited outside. When King Saud of Saudi Arabia arrived for a visit, years ago, he was accompanied by thirty-two limousines and scores of armed guards, but the hotel management handled them as they do everything else, with grace and class. President Quezon of the Philippines used the entire "B" wing of the Omni Shoreham as his permanent residence during World War II; Ike brought Mamie to the Shoreham Terrace the night before he announced his availability as the Republican candidate for president; and John F. Kennedy courted Jacqueline in the famous Blue Room, which boasted, in years gone by, such entertainers as Rudy Vallee, Judy Garland, Frank Sinatra, Lena Horne, and Maurice Chevalier.

I spoke last night in the glowing Regency ballroom. The people representing Excellency In Action had been in Washington for nine weeks selling tickets to our event, and the room was filled to capacity—2,350!

In the book I am now writing, *The Spellbinder*, my fictional crusty old agent, Bart Manning, attends a speakers' national convention to scout out new speaking talent. For several months I have been trying to decide what hotel would make the best setting for the convention that Bart attends, but now my search is over. It will be here, at the Omni Shoreham.

Early this morning, after several phone calls to hotel management, I was met by Kevin Kober, senior sales manager of the establishment, and given a lengthy tour of the place. As Kevin pointed out the hotel's features and landmarks, I made notes as swiftly as possible. Kevin assured me that the Omni Shoreham would be delighted to be the sight of my fictitious convention and that if I had any questions in the future, as I was writing the book, I was free to phone as often as necessary.

I have one regret. Kevin said that the hotel had a haunted room, but he forgot to show it to me, and I forgot to remind him. Damn!

September 5

Back in the early sixties, when I was trying to put my life back together after losing everything that was important to me because of my drinking, I remember a cross-country drive in my old Ford Falcon, destination Los Angeles, ultimate goal of probably half of America back then.

Not any longer. The Los Angeles county coroner's office investigated 263 possible homicides in August alone as more than 200 gangs take to the streets, night after night, senselessly killing one another and anyone in their path. I wonder how tough it's going to get out there now that the state has had to take a deep breath and adopt a budget that cuts away at every department, including law enforcement.

I also wonder how many members of the L.A. gangs are among the thirty million nationwide who cannot read, a situation that is costing us more than $225 billion a year in lost productivity. Where are we heading? What will this nation look like in fifty years?

September 7

Labor Day is upon us, and most New Englanders are still wondering what happened to summer. Only three or four times did the thermometer flirt with ninety degrees in this southern portion of New Hampshire, and my old and trusty Vornado fan, which ran almost constantly here in the studio last summer, was only on a single day.

Never liked Labor Day as a kid. It meant that my dad was home, and as much as I loved him, this was always the commencement of harvesting our garden, which included me in the long list of assigned chores. Labor Day also meant that school was about to begin for another year. Another year? Dear God, would it ever end? I didn't know then that everything ends, sooner or later.

Wish I were in the fourth grade again.

September 9

I am writing these words in my hotel room at the Hyatt-Regency Hotel in Scottsdale, no more than two miles from the lovely home where we spent fourteen happy years before moving to New Hampshire. Three years ago, on my first trip back to this area after moving, I had to drive by our old home, just to look, just to be sure that it was getting the same tender loving care that we always gave it. It was, and after passing the place I hurried away before memories engulfed me.

Bette always packs my suitcase for me, thank God, and when I hung my clothes up, soon after arriving last night, a yellow sheet of paper fell out of my white "speaking" shirt. . . .

Good day!
Don't forget to button down your collar.
. . . break a leg!

Love ya tons,
Betsie

Spoke to sales representatives of the MetPath Clinical Laboratory this afternoon. After taking my bows, at the conclusion of my speech I was so tempted to step back to the microphone and make one additional point. Before each sales representative was a blank pad and pen, for taking notes, I assume. And yet, as I delivered my speech and looked around the room, no one was writing. No one! Do they all have great memories, or, God help me, was I not saying anything worth preserving on paper?

September 13

Almost a warm, lush summer day, with the temperature over eighty, as we roll downhill toward winter. The pines behind our house are noisy with the chirps of chipmunks and drones from hundreds of crickets. Japanese beetles are still tumbling into my traps, and the perennial flower garden is even more lush and colorful than it was in August.

New Hampshire natives are preparing for our annual invasion of "leaf-peepers," that horde of motorcoach-traveling tourists from everywhere with cameras around their old necks and "fanny packs" containing their money wrapped tightly around their waists. Good thing our old road is a dead end.

September 20

Chrysler is in the process of recalling more than four thousand of their new midsize LH cars—to replace a defective five-cent washer that could foul up the steering system.

"Never neglect the little things in life" should be very high on anyone's list of rules to live by, and yet, in this age of haste and waste that has engulfed all of us, that simple but powerful principle is usually ignored.

Years ago a good friend of the famous lyricist Oscar Hammerstein II flew him over New York Harbor in an open-cockpit two-seater, to give him a different perspective of that great metropolis. As the tiny plane circled and banked, lower and lower, directly above the Statue of Liberty, Hammerstein stared down at the top of Liberty's crowned head in awe. Every braid and curl on the top of the lady's head was cut and polished as smoothly as the rest of her entire body and garments.

And yet . . . and yet . . . when August Bartholdi completed that magnificent structure, rising more than three hundred feet above New York Harbor, in 1886, the airplane had not yet been invented. No one, so far as the great craftsman knew, would ever see the top of this statue, except an adventurous seagull or two, so there really was no need to carefully carve and polish every detail on the top of her head, was there?

The little things, more often than we realize, make the difference between success and failure.

September 22

My friends the moose have come out of the woods in great numbers and are being seen, even on busy highways, as their mating season commences. Apparently, as usual, the most powerful males have most of the available females on a short string, so the young bucks are scrambling for any kind of attention they can get. One giant eight-hundred-pounder wandered into a Manchester residential neighborhood yesterday, and it took police almost four hours to coax the big guy back into the woods.

Even a moose needs someone to love.

September 25

Fortunately we have only about five more weeks to suffer through a presidential campaign that will probably rank with the worst of the past, and that's saying something, when it comes to charges and countercharges that the two candidates are firing at each other.

Before Election Day arrives, both President Bush and Governor Clinton will be spattered with mud, deservedly so, I'm beginning to believe.

The president continues to affirm that he knew nothing of the arrangements that led to the Iran-Contra scandal while, almost daily, another individual involved with the plans to sell arms to Iran in exchange for the release of American hostages comes forth to affirm that Bush was not only present at many of the meetings but was also an advocate of going ahead with the ugly deal.

Governor Clinton, on the other hand, is having his own tussle with his past. He maintains that his avoidance of the draft for the Vietnam War was purely by chance. Others who claim they know the details insist that several strings were pulled to see that Clinton did not have to become a soldier in the U.S. Armed Forces.

I wonder why, in a nation that continues to produce scores of corporate and academic leaders, both men and women, smart enough, capable enough, and moral enough to lead our nation, we continue to move mediocrity, immorality, stupidity, and just plain ineptness into our White House.

An old eighteenth-century Irish politician, Daniel O'Connell, once wrote, "Nothing is politically right which is morally wrong."

September 26

Spoke at the old and very special Embassy Theatre in Fort Wayne, Indiana, this afternoon, to the annual state convention of the Indiana Realtors. Everything suddenly becomes very worthwhile when someone comes up, after a speech, with tear-filled eyes and says that they needed to hear the things I said. Everyone has golden moments, or at least they should have, and I'm beginning to believe that mine are the times when someone tearfully expresses thanks for changing or saving their life. Although I can't swim, sometimes I think I'm still a pretty good lifeguard.

September 28

A morning filled with peace and joy at what I was doing. With a brisk breeze blowing, the temperature in the low sixties, but the sun shining brightly, I planted six Honeysuckle Magnifica beneath the black pipe arch that separates our flower garden from the fruit orchard beyond. These vines, with purple-tinged leaves, will wind their way around the pipes for more than a dozen feet into the air and from early spring through summer will produce hundreds of red and yellow flowers that look more like some strange species one would discover in the desert.

Then, along the front of the low stone wall across from our house, the wall that frames our old red wagon, I planted six Blue Rug juniper, approximately two feet apart from one another. These small plants will spread to form an almost-silvery-blue carpet along the stones. After they were all in the ground, I covered the area with a bale of brownish-red peat moss and watered everything.

To cap off a wonderful day, I went out just as night was falling to cover our tomato plants since the news had mentioned possible frost. As I was spreading an old bedsheet across several plants, a sudden movement in our pond caught my eye—a great blue heron! He extended his long, thin legs and stepped up on the grass. Then, as I spoke to him, he turned toward me and stared in my direction, across the pond. I moved closer to my visitor, but instead of becoming frightened he merely walked several feet along the water's edge and then turned to study me again, his long neck tilted and his head cocked. I spoke to him again. He walked several more feet. For at least ten minutes we continued this one-sided conversation before that special creature of God gave me one final glance, lifted his giant wings, and flew off above the pines.

Honeysuckle Magnifica, Blue Rug juniper, and a great blue heron. Days don't come much better than that.

September 30

Now they're telling us that all that milk we have consumed, since infancy, was unnecessary. Some very big names in medicine, such as Benjamin Spock; Frank Oski, director of pediatrics at Johns Hopkins University; and the Physicians Committee for Responsible Medicine announced that there was absolutely no reason to drink cow's milk at any time in our life, since it was designed for calves, not humans.

Several months ago the American Academy of Pediatrics

hinted that whole milk might produce iron deficiency in infants, and there has been talk that juvenile diabetes might be triggered by cow's milk for those genetically prone to the disease.

One by one all my childhood staples are being taken away, and I don't like it a damn bit. I love cereal. I eat it every morning. I buy every new shredded flake produced—but now I'm truly confused. What am I supposed to pour over my fat-free, cholesterol-free Special K?

October 1

Having lived for so many years in metropolitan areas such as Chicago and Phoenix, it is easy to assume that since I now live in a tiny rural town in New Hampshire, there's nothing to do, away from home, except to drive around and look at trees and ponds. A free newspaper that I picked up at our village store, titled *Autumn in New Hampshire*, contained a page headed WHAT'S HAPPENING THIS MONTH? and I was totally amazed at the variety of events available.

There was a bridal fair at Keene State College, the Twenty-sixth Annual Fall Foliage Festival at Loon Mountain, an art show at Laconia's downtown mall, a Shaker Harvest Festival, Apple Harvest Day, the Fifteenth Annual Craft Quilt Show at Cannon Mountain, a fall bus trip to Hancock Shaker Village, an Antique Identification Day at Strawberry Banke, the Opera Nazionale Italian performing *Rigoletto* at Dartmouth College, George Winston in concert at Portsmouth's Music Hall, an Annual Ciderfest, a Chili Cook-Off at Portsmouth's Prescott Park, the Indianapolis Ballet at Manchester's Palace Theatre, an Oktoberfest at the Mill at Loon Mountain, a road race and health fair, a Shaker chair-taping workshop, soprano Faith Esham at the

University of New Hampshire, a Fall Architecture Symposium, *The Mikado* at the Music Hall in Portsmouth, the musical *Forty-second Street* at Manchester's Palace Theatre, plus scores of Halloween parties, including pumpkin carvings and old-house hauntings.

For this day alone, October 1st, I could go to the Deerfield Fair, or the New England Sled Dog Club Race in Auburn, or listen to Philip Walker lecture on Christopher Columbus at the Manchester Institute of Fine Arts. Even better, I can put on a heavy sweater and take a long walk and let the outside world just move on without me.

October 2

Speakers, even we old professionals, tend to repeat the same speech, time and time again, once we find a combination of words and ideas that appeal to an audience. The trial-and-error method of putting together a winning speech often takes years, and after we become comfortable with the flow of words, it is very difficult to make any changes. It's much easier, as someone said, to get a new audience than it is to write a new speech.

Well, after many years of giving the same comfortable talk to hundreds of groups, I delivered a new speech last night as promised. Howard Caesar, senior minister at the Unity Church of Christianity in Houston, is a special friend, and through the years I believe I have given at least six speeches in Houston sponsored by Howard and his church. When my agent, Cheryl, booked me, several months ago, to appear there again, I phoned Howard and promised him I would write a new speech for his people so that all those who purchased tickets would not feel cheated and claim that they had heard me say the same things only last year. Howard was kind enough to assure me that his people wouldn't mind at all if I gave the same talk as last year, but I told him I had plenty of time to work on a new one and it was long overdue anyway.

Well, we had a full house last night in Houston and the audience was great. I'm pretty certain they enjoyed the new talk, and during the question-and-answer period that followed the speech, one young lady stood and thanked me for my talk because she said she needed to hear the things I had said. She also congratulated me for having the courage to dare to say the things I had said instead of delivering a sugarcoated message and telling everyone how great they were when they knew in their hearts that each had room, much room, for improvement. She also asked if she could get a copy of the poem I had read.

Toward the end of my talk one of the points I made was that people should never do anything in their lives that they would have to apologize for doing to those they love. Then I shared with them an old poem, author unknown, that I had been carrying around for my own benefit, for many years:

The Face in the Glass

When you get what you want in your struggle for self
And the world makes you king for a day,
Just go to a mirror and look at yourself
And see what *that* face has to say
For it isn't your father or mother or wife
Whose judgment upon you must pass,
The person whose verdict counts most in your life
Is the one staring back from the glass.
Some people might think you're a straight-shootin' chum
And call you a great gal or guy
But the face in the glass says you're only a bum
If you can't look it straight in the eye

That's the one you must please, never mind all the rest,
That's the one with you clear to the end,
And you know you have passed your most dangerous test
If the face in the glass is your friend.
You may fool the whole world down the pathway of years
And get pats on the back as you pass,
But your final reward will be heartache and tears
If you've cheated the face in the glass.

Driving me to the airport this morning, Howard asked me if I would come back again in a year, so we've made a tentative date for the fall of '93.

October 3

For many years from the midseventies through most of the eighties, I collected checks signed by celebrities and famous people. It was fun, and I was really into the hobby so long as the checks were averaging around a hundred dollars each, but as the prices in this specialized area of autograph collecting continued to soar, I finally moved on to other vices (although I still look at my little group of treasures every now and then).

Among my small collection are checks signed by Aaron Burr, Thomas Edison, Theodore Roosevelt, Charles Steinmetz, Al Smith, Zane Grey, Ty Cobb, and Elbert Hubbard. One that I'm certain has increased considerably in value in the past several weeks is No. 477 of an Oswego bank check made out for *Twenty Dollars* and payable to *Self*, dated *Nov. 27, 1840* and signed *J. Fenimore Cooper*. During the past week the film made from Cooper's classic *The Last of the Mohicans* grossed almost $10 million at the box office, leading all other movies for the second straight week.

Several months of my early years were spent in bed

fighting serious onsets of bronchitis, and I still treasure the countless hours of thrills and joys spent with Cooper's marvelous characters, such as Long Tom Coffin, Natty Bumppo, Harvey Birch and Uncas, the last of the Mohicans. They will never die and I'll never part with Mr. Cooper's personal check.

October 6

Spent most of the morning catching up on my mail and had probably answered forty or so letters before I was stopped dead in my tracks. Ty Boyd, from Charlotte, North Carolina, is an old friend, and I had the honor of serving on the National Speakers Association board in 1979–80 when Ty was our association president. Ty was writing to congratulate me for the job I had done at the national convention in Orlando, back in July, and then he went on to relate how, on a trip to Hawaii in April 1991, he had read my book *A Better Way to Live* and was so struck by my "rules to live by" that he had decided to write a special message to his six children. After he had finished it, the piece had remained in his notebook for several months before he came across it again and realized its message was something that could wait no longer; it had to be shared with his six wonderful, grown children, and after he had shared it with them, he thought I should also have a copy, closing his letter with "See what you do to people, Mandino?"

After reading his powerful piece I immediately phoned him and was fortunate enough to catch him home. I told him that I was keeping a journal and that I hoped to publish it someday and asked his permission to include his message in the book. He agreed. Said he would be honored. But not half as honored as I am to include such a loving and touching piece in one of my daily entries.

THOUGHTS ON BEING YOUR OWN PERSON

A Message to Anne, Tempe, Mimi, Robert, Eliot and Molly Boyd.

I have just read Og Mandino's *A Better Way to Live*. That book contains some wonderful, simple truths that, if practiced, will make us all more whole and real and happy and fulfilled and cherished and successful.

I hope someday you'll read this book. The "secrets" it contains are for each of us to discover. Today would be a great day to start.

One of Og's rules deals with how important our family is in our lives and how the most important thing we can do for our children is to provide them with the right kind of example and continue to love them no matter what occurs in their lives because the greatest success we can possibly achieve is having a loving family with which to share our lives.

And so I want to say some things to you. Your success and happiness are so important to me. There is a time for dependence and a time for independence. It is time for you to know that love means "letting go" as parents. This is my attempt to give you my blessings, love, and support in this Declaration of Independence.

I have sought my own success so hard that I've had too little time for you. I am sorry for that. I haven't taken those times we've had available and done my share in loving you back. Goodness knows, you have loved me without judging. I must learn more and better ways. I hope you'll help me.

I've been too quick at times to criticize, often not taking the time to listen to your reasons for doing, for living your lives your way. There is usually another way than "my way." And it may be a whole lot better than my thinking. And it may not. But you need to make your own decisions. They are not mine to make. We made rules, and moralized and guided you when you were younger, but now it's time for me to relinquish the decision maker's role. You are your own person. You have a good mind. You can and will prosper by your own decisions.

I will still give you my counsel. But only if you ask. (This is going to be very tough for a "teller." Just help me to learn this difficult rule.) I'll fail. Have patience. Know that I respect you. You are a wonderful part of the world. You have *everything* you need to be an independent, successful, happy person. You don't need to drag along any mental garbage I may choose to try loading on your back.

I will be a good role model for you. Here's another tough assignment. I have failed you often. I can never be the guy you give me credit for being. But I can try. If you can, forgive me my past; it can't be changed. But my future is in my hands just as yours is in your hands. I will do all I can to live up to your expectations. I will love and care for your wonderful mother. I will be a good community citizen. I will try to leave our world better for having been here. I will allow you the dignity you deserve. We can still all grow together. It's time for adult-to-adult relationships, however. Your ship is now under way in your trip through life and it has a good captain. The sea will not always be smooth. You will have tough decisions. You'll fail. You'll laugh and cry. But, you have what it takes to be a good captain. Persevere. Keep on. You can be and do about anything you really want to do. Anything.

I release you from all those many tapes that play in your heads of *should*s, *ought*s, *that's bad*, all the things that Daddy said that now keep you from reaching your potential. For the most part I said and did those things in honesty and in my best judgment. I may not have been right at times. We both may have learned better. At any rate, I hope you'll keep the good guidelines until you've found better ones. But keep looking!

If I've said or done hurting things, I'm sorry. I would never mean to hurt or injure you. I hope any hurt was minimal and, if you were hurt, that the lesson was sound. Know that I am your biggest supporter and can think of no reason why I would ever not be very proud of you and our family. My goodness, we do have so much love and reasons to be happy and proud.

I will work on being a better parent, a better husband, and a better person. We all must do that. It's an evolutionary journey. Let's help each other. I will ask when I know I need your help. But please help me if I seem lost along the way. And I will do the same. Person-to-person.

Now, go out and be the best **you** you can be. I hope you won't always choose to take the easy road. Work hard at being a total person. Give life your best shot. Whatever you do, wherever you find yourself, no matter the circumstance, know that you have everything you need to be a special citizen of this world. You have all the intelligence you'll ever need. (Don't confuse this with knowledge. We must continue to learn every day of our lives.) But you are intelligent. You have the physical and emotional health, the citizenship and opportunities that are envied worldwide. And you are loved! Have fun along the way. I'll be watching. And cheering for *you*!

Love,
Dad

October 8

I doubt that there has ever been a longer or more varied exhibition of sugar maple colors than we have enjoyed this fall. One must be extra careful while driving on New Hampshire's highways these days since the flaming scarlet and lustrous gold leaves are causing even our natives to stop their cars by the side of the road, get out of their vehicles, and stare at Mother Nature's handiwork as if they had never seen her do her fall ballet before.

October 19

The season's first light sprinkling of snow fell this morning, and to celebrate the occasion Bette and I hoisted our new L. L. Bean bird feeder, with its twelve individual feeding stations, on the old gray four-by-four post in our backyard. In less than an hour blue jays, squirrels, chipmunks, sparrows, and black-capped chickadees were all feeding voraciously from the feeder and the seed I had sprinkled on the ground beneath.

With only three weeks to go in this sorry presidential campaign, I see that Democratic candidate Clinton continues to insist that he wants the "rich" to pay their "fair share." I will never understand why, in this so-called land of golden opportunity, one must pay a penalty for making a success of one's life. Those who have worked or studied additional long hours as they struggled and sacrificed to accomplish their goals almost always must pay a penalty in additional taxes for their success. Why?

October 22

Have finally completed reviewing the copy-edited manuscript of *The Twelfth Angel*, which my friend and editor at Fawcett Books, Susan Randol, returned to me a few days ago. There were perhaps a dozen or so editorial changes involving a word or two or a phrase or sentence, usually questioning whether those words or thoughts were necessary to the advancement of the story. I accepted perhaps half the suggested changes or omissions and with a green felt-tip pen printed "thanks" next to them while next to the rest I merely printed "stet," that tough old printer's command, so used and abused by those of us in the writing business, meaning "let it stand!"

Punctuation, however, specifically commas, are another matter with me. Fawcett's copy editor had inserted scores of commas where I had none and removed many that had been placed by me so carefully and lovingly. After printing "stet!" for probably a hundred times, I stopped at the top of page 72 and decided to hell with it! I had gone through this same situation in the past, with copy editors at my other publishers, and allowed myself to get all upset until I finally realized one day that it didn't really matter all that much and that I should stop being so pigheaded and proud about the matter.

Accordingly, I inserted a note to Susan telling her that she was free to use all the damn commas that her copy editor wanted to use and I doubted it would do very much harm to my "style" or my book.

As I packaged the manuscript to return to Susan, I remembered something that John Steinbeck had once said when a friend of his, upon reading a just completed chapter of *The Grapes of Wrath*, told John that his punctuation was terrible and his spelling was worse. Steinbeck smiled and nodded and said that he didn't worry very much about either of those skills. He knew his publisher had a roomful of college kids who got paid (1936) forty dollars a week to correct spelling and punctuation but he doubted if any of them could have written *Of Mice and Men*.

October 25

It didn't even have a name when I was a kid, but now Alzheimer's disease strikes a terrible note of fear into everyone whose hair has started to turn and whose stride has shortened. I read recently that more than four million Americans are probably suffering from this frightening form of mental disability, and I know I tremble, more than a little, whenever my memory fails me, if only for a brief period of time. "Is this the beginning?" I always ask myself and then try very hard to put the fear out of my mind.

Unfortunately there are still no credible tests to diagnose Alzheimer's disease in those of us who are living. Apparently only by analyzing our brain tissue after we are dead can it be verified that we did indeed have the dreaded disease. Meanwhile there are so many symptoms causing confusion or loss of memory, not related to Alzheimer's, that are a result of conditions such as depression and drug reactions that are treatable.

As of now we are helpless to prevent the advance of the disease from its early stages of occasional forgetfulness to frightening periods of uncontrolled dementia. What concerns me most is that we can suffer for up to twenty years or more with the disease, getting progressively worse each year, before we are finally rescued by death. And, of course, since we still have no idea what causes Alzheimer's, we have absolutely no idea how to prevent or cure it.

I can think of no more terrible living hell than to have a loving spouse giving round-the-clock care, day after day and year after year, to an Alzheimer's patient. This is a torture that would test anyone's love to the limit and far beyond. I'd put a bullet through my head before ever letting Bette or my children endure that kind of hell.

And each day I pray that somewhere, in some laboratory, someone looks into his or her microscope and among the mysterious world of cells and nerve fibers and plagues discovers the key that will alter millions of lives through the next millennium.

October 27

Close to noon, after working for a couple of hours on the second chapter of *The Spellbinder*, I rose from my desk and, as I do often, looked out one of the southern-exposure windows facing our old dirt road and our pond, Little Walden, beyond.

On the eastern side of the pond there is approximately twenty feet of grass that is bordered by huge boulders that were excavated when the pond was dug. Suddenly, from between two of the larger boulders, something tiny and black and very swift darted across the grass, down the embankment, across the grass, and into the water. Within minutes it emerged, raced up the embankment, across the grass, and disappeared between the boulders. Soon it reappeared, ran down to the water, and leaped in again. And again it emerged, dripping water, raced up the bank, across the grass, and disappeared.

I called to Bette, who was in the kitchen, and when the tiny animal appeared for the third time, she was quick to identify our visitor—a wild mink who was probably feeding his or her young in some sort of domicile beyond the stones with whatever he or she was fishing out of our pond.

A couple of hours later, by the sheerest of coincidences, I happened to look out toward our backyard, where our bird feeder is located, and there was our wild mink again, standing just outside the window, watching with great interest while bluejays, chipmunks, and a dove or two ate heartily of the grain I had scattered on the ground. Then, as if this just wasn't his kind of crowd, he turned and trudged slowly into the woods.

Our little friend with long, jet-black fur looked like he would be fun to pet, but after a little research I think I'll pass on the opportunity if it's ever presented to me. Apparently wild mink have ferocious dispositions, and with their gleaming green eyes and snapping jaws they are to be avoided since, when frightened, they discharge a horrible liquid from their anal glands that would make any skunk odor seem like the fragrance of a rose garden. Independent little cusses too. As soon as they are able, they leave their parents and their birthplace and go alone in search of a territory they can call their own.

Sounds like an American pioneer before he learned to look to Washington to solve all his problems.

November 3

Earlier this evening I spoke at the famed Meyerhoff Symphony Hall in Baltimore to a near-capacity crowd despite a horrendous rainstorm that had commenced earlier in the day. Although the speech was well received, I'm pretty sure I'll remember this trip because of two seemingly insignificant incidents that happened soon after my arrival in the city.

After I had checked in at the Marriott Inner Harbor Hotel and hung my clothes up, I decided to take a walk, at least around the block, in what was, at the time, only a light rainfall. I turned left, after leaving the hotel, and had probably gone no more than a short block when there they were, two street people lying in the middle of the sidewalk, covered with two tattered blankets that provided no protection from the rain, passing back and forth a bottle of wine in a paper bag. There was no avoiding them, and as I walked past, the one holding the wine bottle raised it in my direction and said hoarsely, "I bid you good afternoon, sir."

After a good fast walk of several blocks I returned to the hotel. I had just passed through the front door and entered the lobby when I saw her, a street lady, dressed in the most god-awful outfit—short skirt, long woolen stockings, dingy white sneakers, a woolen cap pulled down over her ears, and a large blue plastic bag hanging from her shoulder. She was standing, out of sight of all hotel personnel, next to a large rack that held scores of folders and brochures describing the various attractions of the Baltimore area. I stopped, before I got too close to the rack, because the old gal seemed to be carrying on an animated conversation with some invisible person by her side as she angrily waved one of the brochures from the rack.

"You've never taken me to the National Aquarium," she was shouting. "You always promise, but you never do!"

"Okay," she shrilled angrily as she reached for the rack again, "how about the Baltimore Zoo? They've even got a hippo. I've never seen one. Want to go there?"

Now she cocked her head as if she was listening attentively. Then she nodded and said, "I know, I know, you always want to go to the Babe Ruth Museum. Not me. I hate baseball. You know that."

I walked through the lobby very slowly, went up to my

room, sat in a very comfortable chair right next to the window, and silently thanked God for my life.

I believe that I have still so much to accomplish. That knowledge alone is all I ever need in order to deal with any problems of the day without turning away from them. Life, I am positive, is like any other of our possessions. It derives its value from use. Anyone can conquer it by living with a purpose and a goal, even if that goal is no more than to give another a little hope for tomorrow.

November 4

We have now elected the man who will lead our nation for the next four years, Bill Clinton, although he did not receive even half the popular vote and there is strong uneasiness about his presidency in many quarters, including my own studio.

Undoubtedly soon after he takes office, he will touch as many buttons as he can to reduce our level of unemployment, but many will judge the man and his selected gathering of experts on how he eventually deals with the exploding national deficit, which threatens to destroy us.

Before Clinton completes his first term, in 1996, we will have reached that terrifying milestone when we are paying more interest on our debt than is being collected from every citizen in taxes. If our deficit runs away from us and we commence printing money as fast as we can, we will face the same nightmare that so many other countries, such as Germany, have endured in this century. Inflation can ruin a lifetime of careful and often painful saving. When bread is selling for a hundred dollars a loaf, all our sacrifice, all our life's efforts for that matter, becomes completely worthless.

I hope that the deficit problem is high on Mr. Clinton's

list of "things to deal with." The time bomb is ticking loudly.

November 8

For the second straight night our temperature dipped into the twenties, and this morning there was a thin sheet of ice on our pond. We are already having almost-daily visits from our friend, Jim Knight, and his UPS truck, as our Christmas orders from many catalogs are being fulfilled.

Nana came home yesterday, almost six months after she entered the hospital back in May. There is now a long ramp in the garage so that Gramps can wheel her up to the first landing, where she mounts the "electric chair" that will carry her up the stairs to their apartment. She is beginning to walk with her artificial leg, and today she actually made it up the steps in the garage without help. For the next three nights, like last night, she will have a home-care assistant who will be in the apartment, through the night, should she need assistance in any way.

Spoke to Nana a little while ago, and she seems despondent. There is so much she wants to do, but she's still not very mobile, so she's frustrated, but I shall never forget the gutsy fight this lady made to overcome almost impossible odds.

November 11

Our youngest son, Matt, called a couple of hours ago to tell us that we are grandparents once again. Matt and Lori's first child, a boy, who will be christened William Augustine Mandino, arrived at two P.M. Arizona time, and both mother and baby—and dad—are doing well. Matt says they will not be calling their boy Bill or Willie. He will be Will and he wanted to make sure we got the message. Okay, Matt.

This is also Veterans Day, which, during those long-ago years when I was growing up, was called Armistice Day. I remember how my dad would stop whatever he was doing for one minute, at eleven in the morning, to celebrate the signing of the Armistice with Germany in 1918. The eleventh hour of the eleventh day of the eleventh month of the year. Memories.

They are still reading the names of those killed in Vietnam, reading them aloud, as they stand vigil by the long and striking wall in our nation's capital. By the time they finish, they will have read more than fifty thousand names.

During my war, World War II, we lost more than 400,000 Americans, but no one is reading *their* names. How quickly we forget.

November 19

My old boss and dear friend, W. Clement Stone, was constantly telling others to learn to seek the good in every adversity. If there is a single good that has come out of the agonizing recession our nation has suffered in the past year or so, it is the discovery by merchants and manufacturers, from those who sell bread, milk, and sliced meats to those who manufacture hundred-thousand-dollar automobiles, that the customer is truly king and needs to be treated accordingly in order for that old cash register to keep ringing.

Living out in the country as we do, Bette and I have learned to do a good deal of our shopping, especially around Christmas, through the catalogs that arrive daily. She opened a package this morning containing some

Christmas-gift items she had ordered from a San Francisco company called, of all things, Red Rose Collection. The package had obviously been wrapped with great care, to protect the rather fragile items enclosed, and beneath the wrapping paper inside was a handwritten note thanking Bette for her order and hoping she was pleased with her purchases. Then, beneath the final carefully wrapped item was another note, also handwritten, "How did we do? Let us hear from you if you were pleased. Thank you," and the note was signed.

With that kind of care and attention, I'm pretty certain that any future catalog from Red Rose will be looked at and probably ordered from by this household.

Yes, the customer is king again, and those who recognize this fact and act accordingly will reap the benefits while the others who wait on one as if they were doing that person a favor will never understand why they are slipping into chapter 11.

November 26

Thanksgiving Day . . . and we are so grateful that Nana, wheelchair and all, was sitting at our table today next to Gramps, giving thanks.

Holidays always bring me back to my childhood, and I can still remember my beloved mother telling me about the custom followed by so many early New England families of placing five grains of dry corn on each plate at Thanksgiving to remind everyone at the table to count their blessings. During that first terrible winter, she would explain, the original Pilgrims, who had already buried half their group after crossing the Atlantic on the *Mayflower*, had so little food that each survivor received just five little grains of corn.

Few of us in this insane world of confusion and haste even stop to realize and appreciate the many undeserved blessings that have been placed within our reach. Instead, from what I've observed, most of us mistakenly believe that whatever good fortune we have enjoyed is somehow deserved and due us—payment, in a way, just for living. And happiness never seems to accompany that kind of an attitude. Henry Ward Beecher once said that "a proud man is seldom a grateful man for he never thinks he gets as much as he deserves." And therein lies most of our unhappiness.

I'm certain that our lives would never be just a parade of hours filled with remorse, self-pity, and anxiety if we spent just a few moments during each day focusing on the good things we have in our life.

November 28

Fifty years ago this evening 491 people died in Boston's Coconut Grove nightclub fire, most of them from asphyxiation when trapped by exit doors that only opened inward. It will always be one of our nation's worst tragedies.

I remember that night so vividly, not just because of the terrible fire but because it was a milestone in my life. On the following morning of November 29, 1942, I was to report for duty in the Army Air Force at the Boston Armory, so, to celebrate my departure, I had a date the night of the 28th with my favorite girl of the moment, a petite blonde named Dotty Robinson. I was going to say farewell to her in style by doing it at the Coconut Grove.

Although we arrived at the Grove at a fairly early hour, a surly doorman told us at the door that the place was packed and no one else was allowed inside. I remember how terrible I felt, but I finally gathered my immature wits and walked Dotty a short distance to Boylston Street and the Beachcomber, who were glad to have us.

We had a wonderful evening together, drinking and dancing and doing a lot of talking and hand holding and remembering. In 1942 I still had neither an automobile nor a driver's license, so after a lovely evening Dotty and I walked back to the B & W bus terminal in Park Square to catch our bus back to my home, where Dotty was staying for the night, sleeping with my sister, Jackie, so that she could see me go off to war early the following morning. While waiting for our bus we did hear someone in the terminal mention that there had been a fire at the Grove, but we thought little about it. The following morning, still not knowing how close we had come to death, I awoke Dotty, kissed her and Jackie good-bye, and my dad drove me to the train depot to catch my train for Boston and a new life.

I've thought about that close brush with death hundreds of times through the years. Shakespeare wrote that "Heaven from all creatures hides the book of fate." Maybe so, but I certainly would like to see just that one specific page dated November 28, 1942.

December 2

For two weeks now we have been trying to trap a large, bold raccoon who comes out of the woods at night to feast on any bird feed that has spilled from the feeder onto the ground. We decided to really go after this marauder after we found the bird feeder on the ground one morning, torn from its post and smashed, obviously the work of a large animal that did some climbing.

Our friend, Edd Houghton, who does so much great work around this place for us, lent us his large Havahart raccoon trap, designed to catch but not harm the animal, and we set it out at night, close to where the bird feeder had landed, with apples and crackers ladled with peanut butter inside the trap as bait. Each morning, for several days, all our goodies would be missing but the trap's door was still open! We had no idea how this raccoon managed to go into the trap and remove all the food without springing the trip hammer that would lower the door behind him. After losing all our bait for a week or so, we decided to change our tactics. Bette bought some cheesecloth and made a small bag, which she filled with goodies, then we tied it to the back wall of the wire trap, reasoning that when the animal moved softly into the trap to remove the food, he would discover that the food was anchored down and in his efforts to wrestle it free he probably would spring the trap. Ha! Next morning we found Bette's cheesecloth bag, shredded, hanging outside the back of the cage, and all the food was gone.

I had one last desperate card to play. We have a small wire feeder that we usually fill with suet for our birds when winter gets vicious and snow covers the ground. It's built pretty much like a square cage, and Bette filled it with her usual fare of delicacies. I then wired it to the bottom of the back end of the inside of the cage, tightly. Our friend would have to enter the trap as always to get to the food, but when he discovered it was within a metal cage, we hoped he would forget to be gentle and tug and pull at the feeder until all that rocking movement sprung the trap.

Success! When I looked out our kitchen window this morning, the cage was filled with something gray and furry. I hurriedly put on my jacket and ran out into the yard. The raccoon was facing away from the food, toward the trapdoor, which had closed, preventing him from leaving, and as I knelt down, he didn't move at all. I thought that perhaps he was dead. Then his small head, which had been buried between his two front feet, turned in my direction momentarily before he buried it again. I could almost hear him saying, "Well, you've got me. I blew it, but it was fun while it lasted. Should have known that you'd figure out some way of nailing me sooner or later."

I told him not to worry. Later in the day I would take the trap and drive it to a less populated area of our town and release him into the woods, hoping he would never find his way back to us. He never looked up at me as I spoke softly to him, too ashamed at getting caught, I guess, even to acknowledge that the game was over.

December 6

Darkness has fallen over Detroit's Metro Airport. I am on a Northwest Airlines 727, destination Phoenix. Before many hours have passed I will be holding my newest grandson, William Augustine, in my arms. Bette flew west five days ago, and hopefully she will be waiting for me at Sky Harbor Airport.

I have just completed my eleventh annual visit to the Church of Today in Warren, Michigan. I dreaded this trip since it was the first without Jack Boland, and when I walked through the front doors on Saturday, there were tears that I couldn't control running down my cheeks. Later, on Saturday, when the huge Christmas tree in the main lobby was lit, ushering in the season, I turned away, again unable to control my emotions.

After the tree lighting and carol singing, I took my seat behind a table, as I have done for many years, and autographed books for several hours. As usual, many left folded notes for me "to read later." One of the notes read,

"God bless you, sir! I hope and pray that someday I can help as many people to live happy and harmonious lives with others as you have."

This morning, both church services went well with the new minister, and my special contribution this year was the reading of one of the most touching Christmas stories ever written, "Barrington Bunny," from the book *The Way of the Wolf* by Martin Bell. The church added a wonderful and clever new touch this year. Just before I began my reading, ushers walked down each aisle carrying boxes of Kleenex. That very special church will be Jack Boland's greatest monument, and I'm proud to play a small part in their annual calendar of events. Optimist that I am, I did tell them that I'd see them again next December.

I cannot believe that the big guy is no longer among us while I am still walking around enjoying the day.

December 8

My new grandson is as handsome as I knew he would be and he also has a great set of lungs. Holding him for the first time, after arriving in Scottsdale on Sunday, was one of the great thrills of my life. Now we have three great little human beings to spoil—Danielle and Ryan from the Flagstaff contingent of Mandinos, and Will.

Had more fun today than I've had in a long time. Father Matt is working, of course, and Bette had an appointment with a local hairdresser, so little Will's mom, Lori, and Grampa Og took the baby to the mall to be photographed with Santa.

I was wheeling the little guy through the mall, looking about as proud as I could look, when I began to notice people stopping, staring at Lori and me, and then continuing on. Finally I figured out what everyone's problem was. Here's this old man with white hair. On his arm is a lovely young blonde, and the old guy is pushing this tiny infant in a stroller. Could it be?

After I realized what was happening, I had to keep fighting the temptation to reply to each questioning glance with, "Yup, he's mine." Someone once wrote that a man never grows old who keeps a child in his heart—and, I might add, in his stroller.

December 19

Our Christmas tree is up and decorated, Bette's fabulous and growing Snow Village has been laid out in the living room, and we are now either frantically running errands or wrapping presents. Strung the outside lights yesterday, and when we turned everything on after dark, the place glistened and twinkled like some fairyland. I guess we'll never grow up and I do know how much the kids love it.

Matt, Lori, and Will, as well as their white German shepherd, Blanca, will arrive this evening, while Dana and Carole and Ryan and Danielle will be here on the twenty-first.

I might as well cover up this typewriter and forget about using it for a few days while I enjoy our most precious possessions, the love of all our kids.

A very talented eighteenth-century lady once wrote, "God sends Children for another purpose than merely to keep up the race. . . . . to enlarge our hearts; and to make us unselfish and full of kindly sympathies and affections; to give our souls higher aims; to call out all our faculties to extended enterprise and exertion; and to bring round our firesides bright faces, happy smiles and loving, tender hearts."

Thank you, God.

December 20

Actually learned something new today. One task that has always frustrated me was the removal of prices and price tags from various purchases, since most of them seemed to be glued on with some mysterious concoction that will never give way.

I happened to be walking by the sewing room, where Bette is still wrapping gifts, and watched with fascination as she attacked a price tag on a rugged box. She pulled out two inches or so of Scotch tape from her dispenser, applied the tape over the price tag, and then ripped the tape off. Voilà! The price tag was now a blank, and the price had somehow transferred itself to the sticky side of her tape.

When I expressed my wonder, she just shook her head and replied that "everyone" knew how to do that.

December 25

It was a lovely Christmas, with gifts galore for all, but the greatest present for Bette and myself was to have all our family together under this old farmhouse roof.

Charles Dickens once wrote, in the longest sentence I believe I have ever seen,

> How many families whose members have been dispersed and scattered far and wide, in the restless struggle of life, are then reunited, and meet once again in that happy state of companionship and mutual goodwill which is a source of such pure and unalloyed delight, and one so incompatible with the cares and sorrow of the world that the religious belief of the most civilized nations, and the rude traditions of the roughest savages, alike, number it among the first days of a future state of existence, provided for the blest and happy!

"Happy, happy Christmas that can win us back to the delusions of our childish days," Dickens continued, "recall to the old man the pleasures of his youth and transport the traveler back to his own fireside and quiet home!"

December 28

I continue to be amazed at the growth of the health food industry, and I confess that whenever I am in a mall containing a health food store, I visit and spend lots of time browsing, searching for that one magic potion that will supply me with more energy and drive than anyone has a right to have.

Fascinating to me are the mystical-sounding chemical-medical words used to describe the ingredients in some of the magic elixirs offered. For example, you can buy an energy booster with "octacosanol" to improve one's stamina, and you can buy a very special vitamin C tablet that contains "bioflavonoids." Then there is a tablet that includes "glutathione peroxidase" that hopefully will slow down the aging process of your old skin and prevent sun spots, and another tablet to assist the stressed-out individual that contains both "methionine reductase" and "catalase."

I'm always tempted to buy a bottle of each. I did try one bottle of a high-nutrition tablet that fascinated me because it contained Siberian ginseng, damiana, ginger, golomon sea, gotu kola, capsicum, juniper berry, and ma huang. Didn't feel any better or any worse. Maybe it needed a longer trial run.

Received a catalog yesterday containing fifty pages of miracle potions, from products to increase one's sexual desire to tablets for one's prostate gland. There is a pill to halt postnasal drip, another to help us better digest our meals, one to help us kick the terrible habits of smoking and drinking coffee, and a shampoo treatment to halt hair loss, which has arrived in my life too late.

Then there's a capsule made from the roots of yucca plants, a favorite of the Indians of the Southwest for who knows how long. Apparently Indians from that part of our world rarely suffered from some of modern man's most common physical complaints, such as arthritis, high blood pressure, and intestinal disorders, and the red man apparently credits a good deal of his fine health and energy to the yucca root.

Most of the good health offerings are quite expensive. Do they work? Probably some do, while many are just exercises in self-indulgence. I doubt that Sir William Temple would have approved of all these special elixirs when the great seventeenth-century statesman wrote, "The only way for a rich man to be healthy is by exercise and abstinence and to live as if he were poor."

1993

*No life is so hard that one can't make it easier
by the way one accepts it.*

GLASGOW

One of the most important self-motivators I learned from my prime mentor, W. Clement Stone, was "Do it now!" As we roll into a new year, this is the time to think of all the plans we made a year ago that are still sitting on the shelf, gathering dust. Sydney Smith, an eighteenth-century minister, once wrote,

A great deal of talent is lost in the world for want of a little courage. Every day sends to their graves obscure men and women whom timidity prevented from making a first effort; who, if they could have been induced to begin, would in all probability have gone great length in the career of fame. The fact is, that to do anything in the world worth doing, we must not stand back shivering and thinking of the cold and danger, but jump in and scramble through as well as we can. It will not do to be perpetually calculating risks and adjusting nice changes; it did very well before the Flood, when a man could consult his friends upon an intended publication for a hundred and fifty years, and still live to enjoy success afterwards; but at present, a man waits, and doubts, and consults his brother, and his particular friends, till one day he finds he is sixty years old and that he has lost so much time in consulting cousins and friends that he has no time remaining to follow their advice.

"Do it now" still works. It is one of the best ways to conquer life because if it is followed to the letter, there never is any time for alibis or complaining or self-pity.

January 6

Soon after each new year commences, every newspaper and weekly periodical seems to run its own list of those who have departed in the previous year. Our losses were great and many in 1992. Off to better places and already sorely missed are Sam Walton, billionaire and brilliant founder of Wal-Mart stores; Eric Sevareid, vintage newscaster who wrote a marvelous book, many years ago, titled *Not So Wild a Dream* that truly enlarged my dreams to be a writer; Red Barber, who will never be surpassed in describing the action of a baseball game; Bert Parks, who will always be remembered for his masterful handling of the Miss America pageants and whom I once bumped into on West Forty-fourth Street in New York and just kept staring at him, after apologizing, until he turned the corner; Isaac Asimov, master of science fiction who could write a book in a week if he had to; Dana Andrews, whom I will always remember for the great movie *Laura*; Paul Henreid, who in a movie with Bette Davis taught us high school boys how to light two cigarettes in one's mouth at the same time and then hand one gracefully to our date; Lawrence Welk, whom Bette and I danced to, on New Year's Eve, many, many years ago; S. I. Hayakawa, former U.S. senator from California but also the author of a classic for anyone with ambitions to be a good writer or speaker, titled *Language in Thought and Action*. Also Sal Maglie, Peter Allen, Roger Miller, Chuck Connors, Dorothy Kirsten, Mary Wells, and Menachem Begin.

They all knew how to live. They will all be missed.

January 8

Addressed the Toledo Association of Life Underwriters this morning at the lovely Masonic Auditorium in Toledo, Ohio. Great crowd, warm reception!

I had been a little upset when Cheryl, my agent, made a commitment that I'd be in Toledo early enough to attend a dinner being held for several association and municipal dignitaries. Upset, but not for long. On the way to the hotel from the Toledo airport, my nice driver was telling me about an old avid Mandino fan who was disappointed that he would not be able to hear me speak because he was in the hospital and seriously ill and not given much chance to make it. I suggested that we go to the hospital first and, if they would allow it, I'd stick my head in his room and say hello to the old boy, which I did. I remember him saying, after I introduced myself, "I do believe I have died and gone to heaven. I cannot believe Og Mandino would come here to see me."

We chatted for several minutes, and then I leaned over the bed, kissed him on the cheek, and departed. At seven that evening I was picked up at my hotel and driven to Toledo's famous Inverness Country Club, home of so many historical golf tournaments through the years. What a strange and wonderful sensation it was just to walk down their paneled halls and pause before photographs of golfing greats such as Byron Nelson, Sammy Snead, Ralph Guldahl, Jimmy Demaret, and Jack Nicklaus. If there is such a place as heaven for great golfers, I'm sure it is here at Inverness.

As mentioned, the speech went fine, but for me, after Inverness and my new friend, John, at the hospital, the talk was anticlimactic.

January 13

Flight to Newark Airport took only an hour from Manchester, but we circled Newark for almost two and a half hours before we could land. There is something about flying around in dense clouds and getting helplessly jounced around by Mother Nature that gradually begins to wear down the boldest and most courageous individual, and by the time we finally landed I doubt there was anyone on board who wasn't frightened.

Long cab ride into Manhattan, in the rain, before finally checking in at the New York Hilton. For the next two days I'll be involved in the recording of my new book, *The Twelfth Angel.* I am more than a little nervous this evening, a feeling I no longer get preceding a speech. Tomorrow I am scheduled to read the part of Little League coach John Harding as he interacts with other characters, especially the book's hero, diminutive Timothy Noble, and on the following day, also as John Harding, I will read all the narrative material alone.

January 16

I have spent the last two days in New York City, at the Corelli/Jacobs Recording Studio on West Forty-fifth Street, participating in the recording of my new book, *The Twelfth Angel,* which Random House will release simultaneously with the publication of the book.

Leslie Corn, the multitalented woman who heads Arielle Productions, and I have worked together before on audiotapes of six of my previous books for Bantam, so I knew I was in good hands. She had prepared the audio script of my book and sent it to me for approval several weeks ago. Our only problem, she reminded me, was that we still needed to do more editing and cutting, which is always painful to the author, in order for the story to fit into a ninety-minute tape.

I wrote the book as a first-person narrative by a Little League coach, John Harding, and I played Harding's role on the tape backed up by some very talented Broadway people like Bob Sevra, Steve Newman, and Margaret Klenck. Each appeared at the scheduled time yesterday, and we did our scenes together. After lunch Noah Segan, the talented young eleven-year-old who was to play the book's hero, Timothy Noble, appeared, and we read all the scenes together which involved Coach Harding and Timothy. He was perfectly cast for the role and I remember that after one of our scenes I said, "Noah, you are very, very good!" He responded like the old pro that he is and said, "You are very good too, Mr. Mandino!" Noah was indeed wonderful, and the final scene between us was such a tough one yesterday that when we finished, I felt emotionally drained. Noah now plays the young son in the television hit *Grace Under Fire*.

Today was all mine without any actors. For all the necessary moments of transition between one scene and the next, I just sat in my little soundproof booth and, with Leslie's excellent coaching, read all the story narrative until midafternoon, when seven young men arrived from nearby schools, recruited by Leslie, and played the part of our Angel Little League team, cheering and yelling and urging on their fellow players. They were great, and as they were leaving, Leslie handed each one a twenty-five-dollar check, causing a lot of little eyes to open very wide as they exclaimed, "Thank you, thank you!"

After they departed, I had a few more pages of narration to do. The closing pages of *The Twelfth Angel* are quite powerful, and my voice broke several times during the reading. When I had finally finished, I pushed against the heavy soundproof door and stepped out into the main studio, where Leslie was sitting next to our sound engineer, Jerry LaRosa, who had been my engineer on a previous recording. There were tears running down Leslie's cheeks, and when I glanced over at Jerry, his eyes were very red.

I do believe our tape will be a winner!

January 18

Began the long and always painful chore of taking down all the Christmas trappings today. It was such a great holiday, filled with love, plus the gift of Nana's presence after she had survived such a terrible year and the presence of our newest grandson, Will. Happy memories of smiling faces as presents were unwrapped make it all the more difficult to remove silver garlands and glass ornaments, many made by Bette, from our tree.

I wonder what mysterious quality is activated in us that helps us to remember even the tiniest details of Christmas days long ago. That doll, that windup train, that red truck, that teddy bear, that Christmas when one's mother was very sick in bed. Someone once wrote that remembrance is the only paradise out of which we cannot be driven away.

Just a little more than eleven months to next Christmas, although I'm certain that both Bette and I will commence shopping for our gang very soon.

January 20

Just received a wonderful note from my dear friend, Sister Maria Leonor Bernado, writing from her nun's residence, Notre Dame of Bongao, in the Philippines:

Dear Og,

To let you know that as I prepare for New Year I never forget to thank God for the gift of people. I believe He can still inspire you to write books to touch and change the lives of many people. At midnight of Dec. 31, I will ask him to bless you, your family, and your work.

My New Year Wish! May the light of Christmas continue to burn in your heart and consume your life with JOY! Mabuhay! Cheers! Happy 1993! My love and prayers for your family.

Love,

Leonor

January 22

I am at the Houston International Airport, and heading home.

Yesterday evening I was guest speaker at the fifty-second annual banquet of the Cleveland, Texas, Chamber of Commerce.

Cleveland is a small town of seven thousand or so, about an hour's drive north of Houston, and since they have no facility large enough to handle a crowd of any size, the banquet was held in the gym-cafeteria of the Correction Corp. of America, a privately owned and run prison. Last night, behind closed doors, I delivered my speech to a truly "captive" audience, and it was great fun. I doubt that most of the townspeople had ever listened to a motivational speaker before, but they were a good audience, and I was told later that the standing ovation I received was the first ever, for any speaker, at this organization's annual gatherings.

What made this trip so memorable was that my lodging

for both nights was in a log cabin out in the woods, a lovely, cozy, and very comfortable rustic cabin but with no television or telephone. My cabin was one of thirty or so scattered around several small bodies of water called Chain-O-Lakes. It was an eerie feeling stepping out on the porch after dark and hearing the water gently lapping against the rocky shore directly below while all sorts of strange and mysterious sounds came from the dark woods beyond.

Riding through Cleveland on the way to the Houston airport this morning with Michael Heilor, who with his wife owns the Omni Physical Therapy Company in Cleveland, I was amazed to learn that the tiny town boasted eighty-eight churches. I saw many rambling ranch-style houses that Michael valued at around $100,000 that would sell easily, in many parts of the country, for a quarter of a million dollars or more. In the chamber of commerce's annual membership directory I learned that the average house sold for $45,000 in the latest reporting period, that a three-bedroom, two-bath apartment could be rented for $370, and that the town's average household income was $25,000!

What a wonderful place to live and raise a family! William Penn once observed that the country is where one can find the philosopher's garden and his library, in which he reads and contemplates the power, wisdom, and goodness of God. Small-town America, I sure do love you, especially after spending three days in Manhattan last week!

January 27

This is a sad day for our nation. Not only has Sears announced the closing of more than a hundred stores but it is discontinuing its huge catalog, which for many of us, as we were growing up, was one of our few windows to the outside world.

Today, with scores of color-television channels to show our children all the wonders of the universe, it is difficult to remember back to the days when sitting by the coal stove in our kitchen and turning the pages of a Sears catalog occupied us kids for hours on end. Memories. Photos of that Flexible Flyer we dreamed of owning, that new Lou Gehrig first baseman's mitt, and wow(!) . . . look at that Daisy air rifle!

Then, of course, as we advanced into our teens, all young males suddenly discovered the many Sears pages of pretty women dressed in lingerie, who all looked far more enticing than the following generation of *Playboy* and *Penthouse* models. Even after sixty years all those special images from childhood are still vivid and alive. The world will just not be the same without that big semiannual book from Sears, Roebuck.

February 2

Alex Haley's powerful book *Roots* became the most-viewed television epic of all time, and the power of its message holds up today as well as it did when first aired.

Although Haley is no longer among the living, I doubt very much that he is resting peacefully. A son and brother plus two women who claim to be his wife are fighting over Haley's million-dollar estate and most of the author's possessions of value are now being auctioned off to help pay Haley's deep indebtedness, even including his treasured Pulitzer Prize. Scores of other lawsuits are also pending against the estate, and according to Haley's son his dad's funeral expenses still have not been paid.

Alex Haley obviously overextended himself. He lived

with the apparent belief that his vein of gold would run on forever, forgetting or ignoring that ancient warning, "Do not accustom yourself to consider debt only as an inconvenience; you will eventually find it is a calamity."

February 5

Ever since I wrote a tiny book titled *U.S. in a Nutshell* many, many years ago, where I tried to show the reader how to deal with numbers both large and small that we are confronted with daily, I have been attracted to statistics of all sorts.

Our nation's annual budget deficit is now over $300 billion. How can one possibly relate to that figure? We just try to break it down into figures we can comprehend. If we spend a hundred dollars an hour, *every* hour of the day and night, how long would it take to spend $300 billion? More than 342,000 years!

I see that it is now costing the taxpayers $30,000 per year for each prisoner we have behind bars, and we have now passed the record-breaking million mark in prison population. What a terrible waste. Somehow it just doesn't seem fair when we read that we are currently spending only $1,620 per year on the average welfare recipient.

Another "statistic" I stumbled on recently is that the fastest-growing segment of our population is the "over-one-hundred gang," which pleases me greatly. During the past ten years the number of centenarians has doubled, will double again by the year 2000, and fifty years after that the Census Bureau estimates we might have nearly a million senior, senior citizens.

Only one problem with the increase in centenarians. When Uncle Sam devised Social Security for every citizen, way back in the 1930s, our average age at death was sixty-three, and monthly payments were not due us until our sixty-fifth birthday. Social Security cannot possibly continue making payments to so many of us old fogies for thirty-five years or more after we retire when we were only supposed to collect, if at all, for just a short time before they buried us.

February 8

My generation grew up idolizing two people who seemed to glow with the luster of greatness, J. Edgar Hoover and Marlene Dietrich. Now I feel betrayed. Hoover, it turns out, placed illegal and huge wagers through friends, who passed on the cash to mobster Frank Costello. He apparently had another male agent as his lover and he enjoyed dressing in women's dresses and black lace stockings with a wig and false eyelashes.

Dietrich, according to her daughter Maria Riva, had a long list of lovers ranging from John F. Kennedy to Edward R. Murrow and even contends that her mother permitted a lesbian governess to rape her when she was only fifteen. Her final years, almost penniless, were spent in a drugged and drunken stupor.

Longfellow was correct. Time has a doomsday book, on whose pages illustrious names are constantly being recorded. But as often as a new name is written there, an old one disappears. Only a few stand in illuminated characters never to be effaced.

Let Hoover and Dietrich disappear.

February 13

Flew to Portland, Oregon, on the tenth and addressed many of those attending the Fourteenth Annual Office

Systems and Business Expo at the Oregon Convention Center on the morning of the eleventh. The journey back to New Hampshire's Manchester Airport, later in the day, was a little more than I bargained for.

First leg of my journey was to be from Portland to Chicago's O'Hare Airport, where I would transfer for the final leg to Manchester. However, when we were no more than twenty minutes from O'Hare, we were told that most of O'Hare's runway lights were out, for reasons unexplained, and so we were taken to the Detroit airport, where all two hundred of us were shepherded to another gate and put on a plane that was to take us right back to O'Hare, where the runway lights apparently were now shining brightly. By the time I arrived at O'Hare, it was past midnight, and of course I had missed the last flight to Manchester. Since I had been flying first-class, I was told by United Airlines that I would be put up at the Hotel Sofitel, miles away in Rosemont, and so, with only my briefcase and no luggage I took a cab to the hotel, checked in, and climbed wearily into bed.

Arrived back in New Hampshire late yesterday. My luggage was waiting for me at Manchester Airport. Despite all the problems it was still a fun experience, except for the challenge of trying to shave with the tiny fragile plastic razor that was included in the toilet kit I was given by United. I decided just to let the beard grow. It's called roughing it. No complaints. Just a thank-you to God for getting me home.

February 14

I've just opened a large brown envelope while sitting here in my studio, that was presented to me by one of the exhibitors, Bill Nassett, at the Business Expo. His new product is definitely God's answer to anyone who has to use a photocopy machine very often. Bill's unique invention is a thin piece of foam board on which is glued a sheet of clear acetate that can be raised so that things to be photocopied will be held firmly between the board and the acetate. On the board's surface is printed a lined grid in special blue ink that cannot be picked up by any photocopy machine. Using the grid, one can lay out several pieces of paper or photos perfectly aligned for photocopy.

With Bill's invention, called STRAIGHT-jacket, one no longer needs to tape documents directly onto the photocopier glass in order to produce a neat copy with all pieces straight and level. Anyone who has ever had to wrestle with a piece of unruly fax paper to keep it flat on a photocopy machine can truly appreciate this brilliant idea. Now one need only slide the fax paper under the clear acetate, smooth over the acetate with a special provided small cloth to produce static electricity in order to hold the paper in place on the board, and make all the copies needed.

Bill Nassett's STRAIGHT-jacket Company is located in Aumsville, Oregon, and although I've never heard of the place, I'm pretty sure that the world will find it and beat a path to his door.

February 17

One of the big thrills in my life, way back in 1973, was to be notified that my name was to be included in the 1974–75 edition of *Who's Who in America*. Of course, I was thrilled to fill out the necessary biographical sheet and returned it immediately, and although I couldn't afford the price, I just had to own a set of those huge leather volumes with my name and brief bio inside.

Since then I have produced an additional dozen books and managed to earn a few honors of which I am proud, so today when I received notice from Marquis Who's Who that they were putting together the forty-eighth edition of their classic to be published in late 1993, I just couldn't resist filling out a new bio sheet and ordering another set of books—especially when the brochure's heading stated that being listed in *Who's Who in America* was a "distinction limited to three persons in ten thousand."

February 21

Snow has been falling for more than a week, interrupted by scattered hours of sunshine although the temperature has hovered constantly between twenty degrees and zero. I remember once reading that when God wanted to punish New Englanders for our sins, He invented February.

Heat, apparently rising through old boards, caused the snow on the roof to melt and drip down to form a long row of glistening icicles that are hanging down from the dining room roof at least five feet in length, looking almost like crystal organ pipes.

This is perfect weather for me to get seriously into my new book, *The Spellbinder*, and during the past eight or nine days I've made great progress, having completed chapters 5 and 6 as well as rewritten both of them several times. The date of my next speech is March 30th in West Orange, New Jersey, so I intend to keep this old IBM Selectric moaning and groaning every single day and night for the next month. I must, since it appears most of May will be taken up with a cross-country tour to promote *The Twelfth Angel* on radio, television, and in the press. *The Spellbinder* is due at the publishers in July, and I've still got a lot of work ahead.

No signs of any robins yet, announcing an early arrival of spring, and as I look out at the snow, I figure that one more six-inch storm will just about bring the white stuff up to my studio windows. So many of our little feathered friends, as well as squirrels and chipmunks, are helpless during this vicious onslaught, and Bette and I make several trips outside each day to keep the bird feeder filled as well as spread layers of fatty sunflower seeds on the ground to gratify tiny metabolisms. It is absolutely amazing to me how our little chickadees and nuthatches and even the doves survive these frigid nights when the temperature hovers around zero and the wind screams through the pines. I have no idea where they go to protect themselves from freezing to death, but I'm sure glad they come to our house for breakfast, lunch, and dinner.

February 28

Open any newspaper or turn on any television set and one would have to assume that humanity has gone mad. A terrifying bomb blast at the World Trade Center in New York City has left at least five dead and floors of one of the world's tallest buildings in shambles. Fighting for the top spot in the headlines is the slaying of four federal agents when they tried to enter a compound in Waco, Texas, where a guitar-strumming prophet and his followers are waiting for the world to end. We have begun dropping bundles of food, medicine, and clothing to besieged Muslims in the bloody Yugoslavian struggle that had been going on for centuries before the nation was enslaved by Soviet Russia and has commenced again, now that Russia no longer has them under its heel.

Blood, starvation, death everywhere one looks. There were twenty-seven thousand murders in our land of liberty and freedom last year, four times higher than the rate in Canada and eight times higher than Europe.

As Thoreau wrote, "The mass of men lead lives of quiet desperation. What is called resignation is confirmed desperation." We cannot allow ourselves to lose hope. Since man first kept records, our existence has been threatened with every kind of possible horror, yet we survive and grow. Tomorrow, we are certain, will be better. And while we wait, hopefully doing the best that we can, none of us need look very far to find someone who needs a helping hand. What better way to conquer life? Early in the eighteenth century, a far more peaceful time perhaps, English author William Melmoth wrote, "To complain that life has no joys while there is a single creature whom we can relieve by our bounty, assist by our counsels or enliven by our presence, is to lament the loss of that which we possess, and is just as rational as to die of thirst with a cup of water in our hands."

March 1

This week marks *Time* magazine's seventieth anniversary, and to honor the occasion, *Time* purchased a full-page ad in *The Wall Street Journal* listing a few of the events of history that have occurred since their birth in 1923. Well, since my birth was also in the same year, I looked over the events listed with great interest. Since 1923 there have been fourteen presidents, six popes, seven constitutional amendments, sixty-five major earthquakes, 1,207 new Broadway musicals, two states admitted to the union, 120 new nations formed, twenty-five world leaders assassinated, one planet discovered, forty-four heavyweight boxing champions, 156 manned space flights, and more than 360,000 new words added to the *Oxford English Dictionary*.

I can't wait to see what the next seventy will bring us.

March 5

For days now I have put in long hours on this typewriter, and I know I'm making good progress on the book, but I've been ignoring the world outside this studio, this special heaven on earth that has been ours now for over three years.

Snowfall has followed snowfall during the past few weeks, and through the efforts of our friends, Edd Houghton, who comes and shovels us out, and Bill Lang, who plows our long and wide driveway, the snow in many places is now piled more than six feet high.

I bundled up this morning and walked up our quiet dirt road, now snow-packed, to the corner. The old animal pound, which I had written about at length in *The Return of the Ragpicker*, is almost completely covered with only the very tips of some of its lichen-covered blue rocks extruding through the white and glistening snow. The temperature was almost zero, and every sound seemed to carry louder and farther than usual. I could hear the tiny beeping of birds from deep in the woods, limbs crashing to earth somewhere in our pine forest, and even the noisy crunching of my boots on the hard snow was magnified.

On my way back to the house I paused and looked through the jagged silhouettes of our old apple trees that bordered the almost-covered stone wall. Our large flower garden is now under a deep blanket of white, and the tiny stone statue of "Bashful Bette," which Edd had mounted for us atop a large flat chunk of granite in the garden, is almost completely buried by snow except for the little girl's head.

Our pond, Little Walden, just across the road from the flower garden, is also completely hidden from sight beneath the snow, and only the top of the old red wagon that we had purchased in the fall and placed in front of Matt's Shack can be seen above the white stuff.

There is a sense of peace and tranquillity here that is impossible to describe. I stop and look at the old farmhouse that we purchased, now standing very sedate and proud because of all the tender loving care that Bette and I have given it, and just shake my head in wonder. Why are we here? Blaise Pascal, the seventeenth-century mathematician and philosopher, once wrote,

> When I consider the short duration of my life, swallowed up in the eternity before and after, the little space which I fill and even can see, engulfed in the infinite immensity of spaces of which I am ignorant and which know me not, I am frightened and astonished at being here rather than there; for there is no reason why here rather than there, why now rather than then. Who has put me here? By whose order and direction have this place and time been allotted to me?

A huge barred owl sat silently in one of our larger leafless blueberry bushes, staring at me intently. I decided to ignore him, reasoning that if I spoke or made any move in his direction, he would flee. First one I've seen in several months. Have no idea where or how he has managed to survive the tough winter we have endured, but I imagine that his food supply is getting pretty low and he is out hunting. Gorgeous bird. Very dignified-looking. Amazing what a little time spent on a lonely road can do for one's peace of mind. Even the most ordinary of strolls can soothe me until I begin believing I'm living in a fairy tale.

March 8

Just completed what may be the most difficult chapter in the new book, *The Spellbinder*. A contest is being held at a speakers' convention and the winning speaker will receive a quarter of a million dollars in cash providing he agrees to do a dozen television commercials for a frozen-food company. Patrick Donne, the book's hero, is one of the finalists in the contest, and of course the speech he gives must be good enough to win the contest for him.

What I had to do essentially was write a complete speech and it had to be as good for Donne as if I were preparing to give it to a large sales convention next week. I rewrote the chapter seven times before it finally felt right.

There is always a point in every book when I feel the very pinnacle has been reached, through tremendous labor, agony, and tears, and now all the rest of the book is just a nice, downhill glide until the finish line is reached. I'm not quite certain that I'm there at the very top yet, but I'm mighty close. The first eight chapters will probably get reworked and rewritten several times before I'm completely satisfied, but I am making steady progress.

Someone once told me that they enjoyed my books because they were so easy to read. "That's because they're so hard to write," I had to remind him.

John Burroughs, a naturalist who wrote with a magic pen, in an essay once exclaimed,

I heard a reader observe, after finishing one of Robert Louis Stevenson's books, "How well it is written!" I thought it a doubtful compliment. It should have been so well written that the reader would not have been conscious of the writing at all. If we could only get the writing, the craft, out of our stories and essays and poems and make the reader feel he or she was face to face with the real thing! The complete identification of the style with the thought; the complete absorption of the man with his matter, so that the reader shall say, "How good, how real, how true!"—that is the great success. Seek ye the kingdom of truth first, and all things shall be added.

March 9

Fifty feet or so behind our house and beyond our bird-feeder post grow two rhododendron bushes, four blueberry bushes, and several mountain laurel, all huge, in an uneven but somewhat parallel line with our house. This spring I hope to extend that line toward the east with several old-fashioned rosebushes that will, hopefully, provide a magic entranceway into the forest beyond.

I had forgotten how much winter protection rosebushes need here in New Hampshire, and after half my large bed of Simplicity roses succumbed to the cold last year, despite all my tender loving care and protective rose cones, I had them all dug up in the spring and replaced with perennials and a few small arborvitae.

More and more, in recent years, the old-fashioned roses that trace their lineage back a hundred years or more are being rediscovered by rose fanciers and featured by several garden nurseries, replacing, for many, the assembly-line production of common commercial roses that are grown and sold by the tens of thousands. Many of the rose old-timers were great favorites in nineteenth-century Victorian gardens, and although they all but disappeared for several decades, they are now enjoying a great revival because they appear to be easy to grow, fight off pests and disease well, can handle the cold, and grow to vigorous bushes, many more than six feet tall and almost as wide, covered with lovely blossoms.

The more I have been looking at my rose catalogs, the tougher time I am having trying to select the six or eight "old-timers" I want to plant this spring. Even their names are provocative and tantalizing: "Madame Hardy," a damask rose with white double flowers; and "Reine des Violettes," a hybrid perpetual with almost five-inch blooms of lilac-purple that grows to a regal eight feet in height. In my Wayside Gardens catalog, always one of my favorite plant sources, is "Reine Victoria," a bourbon with warm, rose-pink doubles; the "Jacques Cartier," close to a damask with clear pink and fluffy petals; "Blanc Double de Coubert," a rugosa with large, open pure-white almost-double flowers in a bush that will eventually measure six feet by five feet; and the one that will probably be my favorite called "Stanwell Perpetual," a damask with large pink three-inch double flowers that apparently blooms right through the summer and on into October and November, its five-feet-tall plants giving off a pervasive fragrance that must be what it smells like along the path to heaven.

With what is beginning to look like a very difficult May schedule, including two or three weeks on the road to promote *The Twelfth Angel*, I don't know when I'm going to find the time to plant these lovelies, but I'm sure going to order some of them and have a go of it. If they work out well this year, we'll add to the flock next year and the next and the next—please, God!

March 10

In doing some research for *The Spellbinder* this afternoon, I came across a great Victor Hugo quote that was unfamiliar to me. For many years, at every opportunity I get, I have been urging people to make a list of the things they want most to accomplish during the day, in order of their priority. I call my list the "Do It Now!" list, but it really doesn't matter what name you give it. When you actually write down and deal with your goals one by one, you will have taken a giant step toward an eventual better life. It's almost a sure ticket to success. Victor Hugo put it this way:

> He who every morning plans the transactions of the day and follows out that plan, carries a thread that will guide him through the labyrinth of the most busy day. The orderly arrangement of his time is like a ray of light which darts itself through all his occupations. But where no plan is laid, where the disposal of time is surrendered merrily to the chance of incidents, all things lie huddled together in one chaos, which admits of neither distribution nor a review.

As Benjamin Franklin once said, "If you love life, don't squander time because that's what all our lives are made of."

March 13

This weekend shaped up as a real "milk run," as we old air force personnel once called those combat missions where we encountered no enemy fighter planes and little, if any, antiaircraft from the ground. I was originally scheduled to depart Manchester Airport at ten-thirty this morning, fly to Newark, where I would transfer to another Continental flight headed for West Palm Beach, where I was booked to address the top management of the Fruit of the Loom Corporation in their closing convention session at the lovely Ocean Grand Hotel. However, yesterday afternoon I heard a couple of weather reports that warned us of a vicious storm headed east, scheduled to strike our area close to noon. Reasoning that even if I were fortunate enough to get out of Manchester, by the time I landed at Newark International, an hour or so later, no planes would be departing for anywhere, I phoned my travel agent, Nancy, and we changed the flights. I was now scheduled to depart Manchester at six-thirty A.M. instead of ten-thirty, and hopefully I would not only be able to get out of Manchester Airport but also land at and depart from Newark for West Palm Beach before all hell broke loose.

Well, Bette and I awoke at a little after three this morning, and rode for an hour in the dark before arriving at the airport just after five-thirty A.M. only to discover that all Continental flights to Newark had already been canceled.

Fortunately for me the nice young lady at the Continental counter got a lovely glow on her face when she saw my name on the airline ticket and said, "Sir, I love your books. Let me help you."

With that she stepped from behind her counter, hoisted my heavy suitcase, and yelled, "Follow me!" At the United Airlines counter, which I saw was also being manned by an old friend, Dick Biron, she handed my tickets to him, said a few words I couldn't hear, and smilingly said to me, "He'll take care of you."

And so, instead of flying to Newark, I boarded a United Airlines flight, and two and a half hours later landed at Chicago's O'Hare International! Their next flight for West Palm was scheduled for five hours later and it was completely booked, so I was put on standby. If I failed to make that one, I was scheduled for departure on a much later flight that would have put me into West Palm Beach slightly after midnight!

I was the seventh and last standby to get on the plane. Arrived around six-thirty P.M. to be met by a very relieved Pam Berger, Fruit of the Loom meeting planner. We went directly to the hotel, and as soon as I had checked in, I inspected the Royal Poinciana III, where I am scheduled to speak tomorrow morning. I am now in my lovely room, very relieved, as I watch telecasts of what is being called the "storm of the century" batter the entire East Coast. I walk to my window and see that even here, among the wealthy, a very angry Atlantic surf is playing no favorites as it pounds furiously against the lovely white sandy beach not very far from this building.

No one else has a job like mine.

March 14

Speech went very well this morning. Was introduced by Fruit of the Loom's chairman of the board and chief executive officer Bill Farley and got my biggest laugh when I thanked him for his thoughtful touch of having everything in my room monogrammed with *OG*. Ten-second delay before everyone realized that we were staying at the Ocean Grand Hotel and the initials *OG* were on every towel, facecloth, robe, and carpet in the entire hotel.

On the front of the lectern was hung a print of Fruit of the Loom's familiar trademark, and I told the audience that when I was a little boy and my mother would dress me, I would point to the basket-of-fruit trademark and ask her what that meant. Mom always told me that meant I was wearing the very best.

Back to the hotel room to watch television news reports

of what was a vicious storm with already more than a hundred dead, millions of homes without power, and every airport in the East closed down.

Luckily I was able to get through to Bette, and she reported that all was well and that she still had power. The snow, she said, was already higher than our first-floor windows and there are at least three feet of the white stuff on our back deck.

Several weeks ago I made arrangements with my dear friend as well as my attorney, Gabe Perle, to get together with him while I was down here. Gabe practices law in Stamford, Connecticut, but has a winter home close by here in Jupiter. Gabe picked me up around six this evening and drove me to his gorgeous home. As his garage door automatically lifted, he pointed to a golf cart with his bags already on board, parked in the other garage stall. "Eat your heart out, kid." He smiled.

Spent a lovely evening with Gabe, his wife, Pat, daughter, Liz, who is Addison-Wesley's publisher, and several friends of Gabe. Had a fun meal at his club and then he drove me back here.

Hopefully I'll be able to get home tomorrow, although the late television news just showed that Philadelphia International Airport, my first destination, is still closed.

March 15

Boarded my U.S. Air flight early. According to my schedule, I had approximately an hour on the ground in Philadelphia to transfer to my flight for Manchester. Then, after our West Palm Beach flight was loaded, we were informed that there would be a delay of approximately an hour before takeoff for Philadelphia because our flight didn't have a crew! The horrendous storm was playing havoc with personnel schedules as well as airports. That meant that if I arrived an hour later, I would miss my flight for Manchester, and God knows how long I would have to wait, since we were also told that there was only one runway open in Philadelphia.

Then, miracle of miracles! A flight crew appeared from nowhere, and only twenty minutes after the announcement we took off, and I had to run like hell from Terminal C to Terminal B in Philadelphia, but I made it with more than enough time, since that flight was also delayed.

Finally arrived in Manchester at around six-thirty this evening. Loveliest sight I have seen in a long time was my Bette sitting in an airport chair, knitting, waiting for her guy. It was indeed quite a weekend. On the way home we stopped at our favorite Mexican place, Shorty's, in Bedford, and held hands. I had been so damn worried about her, along with Nana and Gramps, and fearful of what might happen if our power went out and we had no water, light, or heat, and of course she was worried about her old guy spending a couple of days on a hard bench or floor in Philly, America's grungiest airport. All is well.

March 16

Outside, it looks like a scene from the movie *Dr. Zhivago*. I tried to videotape all I could of our white wonderland this morning. Our friend Edd and his brother spent more than four hours just shoveling the snow off our back deck, and it is now stacked at least ten feet in height just beyond the deck's railing. Unbelievable. The statue of "Bashful Bette" in our garden is completely buried, and only the very top of the arrow on our five-feet-tall sundial still shows.

The snow has been plowed back on both sides of the road so high that people can see nothing as they ride along, and anyone trying to drive out of their driveway has to creep out very slowly into the main street.

March 19

Don Robinson has coached men's gymnastics at Arizona State University for more than twenty-five years. During those years twenty-three of his athletes have earned All-American status, his teams have finished in the top ten a dozen times, and in 1986 they won the NCAA championship.

Don has been a friend for more than twenty years. While I was still editing *Success Unlimited* magazine, in the early seventies, he visited me in my Chicago office and we developed an instant liking for each other. He also became a raging fan of my first book, *The Greatest Salesman in the World*, and began purchasing hardcover copies by the case. The book was required reading for his athletes, and Don gave copies away by the hundreds through the years.

Don and I have maintained contact with each other for the past quarter century. During the years we lived in Scottsdale, we attended many gymnastics meets at ASU's Activity Center.

I have just received some terrible news. An article in the Phoenix tabloid *New Times*, sent by a friend, is announcing the end of the gymnastics program at Arizona State. The article is aptly titled "The Day Their Dreams Died," and the subhead reads, "The men's gymnasts were truly scholar-athletes. They won championships, earned degrees and stayed out of jail. No wonder ASU killed the program."

Arizona State's athletic director has just announced that

because of budgetary problems the school will be dropping men's gymnastics, men's and women's badminton, and men's and women's archery at the end of the current semester.

I immediately called Coach Robinson, who has already won a battle with prostate cancer in the past year. What I learned was that he was told that if $150,000 could be raised, the gymnastics program would continue for another year. Don sounded angry and weary. I know how much he loved the program and every boy he coached. He was far more than a coach to each of them, and one would only need to spend a few minutes with the kids to realize how they felt about Don. When I hung up, I was angry and frustrated. What to do? Don needed a miracle.

March 22

Bad weekend. Little on my mind except how can I help Don Robinson and his team. By noon today I thought I had things all worked out, so I called him at his office. I asked him how many people could be seated in Gammage Auditorium, that lovely theater on campus designed by Frank Lloyd Wright. Don said that the place would hold approximately three thousand and so I made my offer. My tour to promote *The Twelfth Angel* was scheduled to end, for the most part, on Friday, May 21st, so that I could get home, have a haircut on Saturday, and depart again on Monday for Las Vegas, where I had speeches booked on Tuesday and Wednesday. Bette was coming with me on this jaunt for two reasons. I would be staying at Caesar's Palace for the two speeches, and she loves slot machines. Also, four days after my second speech, on Sunday, May 30th, our newest grandson, William, was going to be christened in Phoenix, and we wouldn't miss that for anything.

Since we would be in Phoenix for Will's christening, I asked Don if he believed he could get Gammage Auditorium for perhaps either the second or third of June. When he asked why, I told him that if he could get the auditorium I was offering my services, gratis. I would come speak for nothing if he thought he could generate enough interest and help so that we could sell out Gammage at fifty bucks a pop. If we did, that would be the hundred and fifty thousand that was needed to keep the gymnastics program alive.

It was very quiet on the phone for several minutes before Don spoke haltingly, trying to find the words to thank me. I told him to call me back once he had news on the auditorium and suggested that Thursday night, the third, would be better, since I was scheduled to be on Phoenix's number-one radio station, KTAR, with Phoenix's leading talk-show host, Pat McMahan, on Wednesday and, along with promoting *The Twelfth Angel*, I was sure we could get in a plug or two about Mandino's appearance at Gammage for such a worthy cause.

March 26

Our first robin was walking around under the bird feeder this morning. Finally, as if it were some experienced mountain climber, it began to climb up the piled-up snow on one side of the feeder. When it reached the top, it just looked around for a short time, decided it didn't like anything it saw, and flew off high above the pines.

Spring began six days ago, but our backyard is still under several feet of white blanket.

March 28

The snow is beginning to melt, and the potholes and frost heaves along most southern New Hampshire roads are now so large and deep that the state's leading newspaper, the *Manchester Union-Leader*, has announced a contest asking its readers to nominate what they believe is the most horrible and treacherous stretch of road in our state.

Our dirt road, of course, is going through its annual settling and spreading, so that one cannot drive much faster than five miles per hour without ruining one's front-end alignment. And when drivers emerge from our enlarged cowpath and turn onto actual paving, there is a pothole at the very base of the hill that is certain to cause them to lose control of their automobile if they are foolish enough to try to drive through it. The town road crew is in for quite a spring, filling and patching, especially, as Bette says, since the guys don't like to do anything that calls for them to get out of their truck.

I can still remember when our daughter-in-law visited us here for our first Christmas in the country. Signs everywhere, of course, warn New Hampshire drivers of FROST HEAVES. Carole, who had spent most of her life in Arizona, had never heard of a frost heave and had absolutely no idea what it was.

March 29

Great news! Coach Don Robinson made all the right contacts at the university and just phoned to tell me that he has booked Gammage Auditorium for Thursday evening, June 3rd. He also informed me that he had taken my advice and contacted a special friend of mine, publicist Pierre O'Rourke, who lives in Scottsdale, to coordinate the entire gymnast fund-raising program from promotion to ticket sales since I remembered what a marvelous job Pierre had done several years ago when he organized a dinner at the Arizona Biltmore for the Seventh Step Foundation, who were sponsoring "Og Mandino Day in Arizona."

We're rolling . . .

March 30

Each year the Academy Awards presentations on television get tackier and tackier. I find it absolutely amazing that these supposedly bright and talented performers find it necessary to rely on file cards in order to recall the names of those they wish to thank, commencing with their parents. Why do we idolize these dumb people?

Next year, on Academy Awards night, I believe we will go bowling.

April 1

April Fool's Day it may be, but what I see falling outside my studio window is not an illusion. It is snowing once again! Last year around this time I was spreading peat moss and manure in the garden prior to it being rototilled with Bobby Compton's muscle and skill. Today I have few options except to sit at this typewriter and continue working on *The Spellbinder*.

Catching up on my mail and the newsmagazines this morning, after breakfast as the snow continued to fall, I was lazily turning the pages of *Time* magazine when I was suddenly confronted by the most touching photograph I have ever seen in my entire lifetime. Half a page in size and in four-color was the graphic depiction of a frail and tiny Sudanese child, crouched, with his head buried in his bony hands, having stumbled on the way to a feeding center. Only a few feet behind, watching the helpless little figure, stood a huge vulture—waiting.

Mankind has no answer to why we allow this kind of misery to continue—to exist at all. We still do not understand that we are truly our brother's keeper. And an old German proverb reminds all of us that the word *alms* has no singular, as if constantly to remind us that a solitary act of charity hardly deserves the name.

April 3

Our values are so messed up that professional athletes can now command ten times the annual salary we pay our president. According to the "Team Marketing Report," a sports-business newsletter, it now costs a family of four, including incidentals such as a hot dog and soda, almost $165 to attend a professional football game. We continue to run our life pursuing that elusive butterfly called happiness, that creature whose wings bear a terrible resemblance to green paper money. Happiness, we insist, is out there somewhere. When we find it, we are positive, we will have conquered life. How sad. We are racing down the wrong path, and ahead lies only tears of regret and failure.

From another time a wise old Roman named Seneca, who had more brains and talent than he had time to use, once wrote,

> True happiness is to understand our duties toward God and man; to enjoy the present without anxious dependence upon the future; not to amuse ourselves with either hopes or fears but to rest satisfied with what we have, which is abundantly sufficient, for he that is so

wants nothing. The great blessings of mankind are within us and within our reach but we shut our eyes and like people in the dark, fall foul of the very thing we search for without finding it. Tranquillity is a certain quality of mind which no condition of fortune can either exalt or depress.

There must be a sound mind to make a happy man; there must be constancy in all conditions, a care for the things of this world but without anxiety; and such an indifference to the bounties of fortune that either with them or without them we may live content. True joy is serene. The seat of it is within and there is no cheerfulness like the resolution of a brave mind not to be elevated or dejected with good or ill fortune. A wise man is content with his lot, whatever it be—without wishing for what he has not.

The old boy truly knew the secret of life and how to deal with it and conquer it. Simplicity itself. *We* control our destiny!

April 6

When we moved, my telephone index file came with me, and although we have now lived in New Hampshire for more than three years, I've never tossed out the long list of phone numbers I no longer needed. I guess it's a little like hating to throw away that old shirt one has worn for untold years.

Anyway, as I was searching in vain for a number that I should have put on an index card recently, I decided to clean out the file, and there was a distinct sadness to it, as if I were tossing out precious parts of my past. Out went the car-towing outfit we used when we lived in Scottsdale, the Phoenix company that had transferred my old Super 8 family movie films to videotape, my golf buddies in Arizona, the Pima Country Club, the man who cleaned our pool, and another who did any repairs on our Scottsdale house that I didn't dare tackle. Out, also, were several pages of Bantam Books phone numbers, since I am now being published by Fawcett Columbine, and the number of a charming Mexican girl, Lupita, who was my translator a dozen years ago when I made many radio and television appearances in Mexico City. The company that kept our lawn mower repaired in Arizona went into the wastebasket along with Umberto's Clam House in Manhattan, the nice young couple who bought our Scottsdale house when we moved here, a San Francisco photographer who took the jacket photos for one of my books, the Stretch and Sew stores that Bette owned in Scottsdale and Phoenix, and Don, my Scottsdale barber.

Don's card was on the top of the pile as I prepared to toss them all in the wastebasket. On a whim I dialed his number, heard that familiar voice, and said, "This is a voice from your past." Without hesitation he said, "Og Mandino!" We talked for perhaps five minutes, and I wished him a Happy Easter, which is coming up on Sunday, and hung up. Then I tossed all the cards in the wastebasket, but the memories will remain in another index file close to my heart.

April 8

We have so many terrible potholes in our old dirt road that I called the town barn yesterday, talked to the right person, and early this morning a truck filled with sand arrived followed by a heavy grader. I made it a point to dash out and thank the men in their machines, and they seemed surprised. "Thank you" is becoming rare in this world.

Today the temperature is flirting with seventy degrees, and although we still have more than half the ground covered with snow, there is that special feeling of spring in the air. Still, there are plenty of little birds gathering around our feeder.

Spent most of this day trying to catch up with my mail. One of the most touching letters was from a woman who wrote that she spent so much time living in the past or worrying about the future that she had a terrible time dealing with the present. Many who write complain of this very same dilemma.

In my reply I wrote at length about the Sir William Osler story, which was still fresh in my mind since I had just recently used its powerful message in *The Spellbinder*.

More than eighty years ago Sir William Osler, a distinguished Canadian physician, was traveling to Europe on a huge ocean liner. One day, while visiting with the ship's captain, a shrill, piercing alarm sounded followed by loud, grinding noises belowdecks. The captain explained that the ship was having a safety drill and the sounds were from the many watertight compartments closing below, so that if water ever leaked into any one area of the ship, it would not affect the rest of the vessel. Even if they hit an iceberg, as the *Titanic* did, he explained, the ship would still remain afloat.

Osler, in his address to the students at Yale, recalled that vivid experience and told his young audience that they, too, were on a great journey and that if they lived each day in a day-tight compartment, their lives would be much safer.

"Touch a button," he told his young audience, "and

hear, at every level of your life, the iron doors shutting out the past. . . . the dead yesterdays. Touch another and shut off, with a metal curtain, the future. . . . the unborn tomorrows. Then you will be safe. . . . safe for today."

None of us, I wrote in my letter, are able to carry yesterday's heavy load into the new day. We must leave it behind and forget it. Same with tomorrow. There is only one future, and that is this day. Yesterday and tomorrow do not exist. This moment, this hour, this day, is our only treasure.

In closing my letter I reminded her that she need not search for her Ragpicker. *She* was her own Ragpicker, and her future was in her hands alone.

April 17

Although official publication date for *The Twelfth Angel* is May 6th, the book should be in most stores by next week, and I will begin to tour on May 5th, I believe, although I don't have my full schedule as yet.

The book's jacket is probably the most powerful and striking jacket I have ever had for any of my books, featuring an oil painting of a small boy in his Little League baseball uniform sitting with his legs folded under him, his chin resting in the palm of his hand, and his huge, tattered fielder's glove in front of him.

I learned from my editor, Susan Randol, that the painter's name is Michael Deas and that he could be reached either in New Orleans or Brooklyn. She gave me both phone numbers, and I caught up with him in New Orleans. I told him I'd like to buy the original oil that he painted of the little boy to present to my son, Matt, who had given me the idea for the book.

Bette and I plan to have the oil framed by our dear

friends at Tatewell Galleries in Hillsboro, and to present it to Matt for Christmas this year, in gratitude for all his help when I was writing about Little League and needed technical advice on some of the game's fine points, which Matt gladly shared with me. I have great hopes for the book. The best is all ahead. . . .

April 19

Hopefully we now have some new neighbors. Three days ago a pair of mallard ducks, male and female, landed on Little Walden and spent more than an hour exploring the length and breadth of it. I had to dive for our encyclopedias to learn that the beautiful one with a glossy-green head and neck, a white ring around its chest, and a purple wing patch bordered by black and white bands was the male, while the female is terribly costumed in a coat of mottled brown.

We expected our visitors to depart for other waters after they had completed their exploring, but the next day there they were, swimming regally along, the male slightly ahead of his lady. Bette and I decided to make our move. She went to a nearby garden and grain store and bought ten pounds of a poultry feed called "lay crumble" that we fed to our duck for years when we lived in Scottsdale. I scattered the ten pounds close to the water's edge, all around the pond, and later in the day our visitors reappeared, began sampling our food, and after each bite they would hurry down to the water and wash the grain down with a long drink.

Today they are still with us, so I went to the store and bought a fifty-pound bag of feed. If we are lucky, perhaps our new friends will hatch their children close by, wherever their nest is, and then we'll have a large family swimming in formation across our lake. Bette has even named the couple—Fred and Wilma.

April 20

Turmoil and violence, death and pain—humanity continues to act more like savages than loving citizens of the world, and we seem to be making little progress toward that promised land where hunger, want, and misery have been banished through our love and caring for one another.

Yesterday we watched in horror on our television sets as more than ninety individuals burned to death in a compound near Waco after holding out against federal authorities for almost two months. Across the ocean human blood covers much of the small territory called Bosnia-Herzegovina, and in Ohio a large federal prison has been taken over by its convicts.

In Washington, D.C., the United States Holocaust Memorial Museum opened to help all of us never forget that terrible scar on all humanity when six million Jews and five million others were put to death. In South Africa the carnage continues as black antiapartheid leader Chris Hani is gunned down outside his home, an event that threatens to trigger another bloodbath throughout that afflicted nation. Everywhere on our planet, it seems, there are tears and sobs and cries of despair and grief. Is this what our world will continue to be?

There was a time when my audiences came to hear me spell out some ideas to help them become more of a success. Now it seems that they want to hear not how to gain more success or wealth but how to deal with the horrors that surround all of us . . . deal with them and yet not lose sight of our goals and dreams. Conquering life once meant climbing to the top of the pyramid, the corporate corner office, the joy of recognition and adulation from the world around us. Now, for many at least, it just seems as if the journey from breakfast to bedtime without the loss of anything or anyone we love is all we dare hope for.

April 21

Spring is truly now upon us, and summer is only the turn of a page away. A ferocious wind has been blowing for most of the day, and with the temperature slightly above seventy degrees the snow has just about vanished and the soggy lawns and flower garden are quickly drying out.

A third duck, male, has appeared on our pond, and the two males have spent most of this day pecking and jumping at each other, creating huge swirls of water rippling across the pond while the female, Wilma, stands calmly on shore and watches the two fight over her. Finally one seemed to get the upper hand after perhaps two hours of vicious fighting, and the loser dived beneath the surface, emerged perhaps forty feet away, and flew off toward the south while the victor—can it be Fred?—waddled toward the lady-in-waiting, who was still standing motionless among the short grass.

I cannot think of anything available to view on television that would be half as entertaining as our new neighbors. There is always a fresh and unexpected surprise for us somewhere on our old grounds, in our pond, or hidden among the pines, which moaned all day today.

April 24

Sometime last spring we stocked our pond with several dozen goldfish. Half of them were perhaps a year or more old, two to three inches in length, and already clothed in lustrous gold. The other half were little guys just about the color of the pollywogs that cavort in great numbers in the water.

Several times during this long winter of ours, with the ice perhaps a foot thick on the pond, which was also covered with several feet of snow, I wondered if the goldfish were surviving down there in the depths of their new neighborhood. Well, they did! This morning I spotted at least eighteen of them swimming together! They were now at least six inches long and were losing their gold coats. Since I had returned them to nature, they apparently were now shedding their gaudy attire and adopting shades that would blend better with the color of the pond and protect them from any hungry, soaring birds. One fish looked very strange. Only his head was gold. The rest had already become a grayish brown.

April 29

Just received, from Coach Don Robinson, a copy of an article that appeared in last Saturday's *Arizona Republic* on our attempt to save the Arizona State men's gymnastic program. His accompanying note mentioned that several papers throughout Arizona have been running pieces on our rescue efforts.

Reading the article gave me an idea. Jimmy Cicero is a very talented Scottsdale composer and entertainer. Last year Jimmy sent me a recording he had made of a song he had written, "The Greatest Miracle in the World Is You," after reading my book *The Greatest Miracle in the World.* Both the music and the lyrics are touching and powerful, and I immediately phoned Jimmy at the time to tell him so.

I thought that to have Jimmy close the program scheduled at Arizona State, after my speech, might make a perfect climax to the evening, so I phoned Pierre O'Rourke, who is handling the promotion and publicity, suggesting that he invite Jimmy to join us. Pierre said he would and told me that they are now selling tickets to the event, at Dillards, Gammage Auditorium, and through doorbell ringing by the gymnastics team and its boosters.

As my little hero in *The Twelfth Angel*, Timothy Noble, said, "Never, never, never give up!"

May 4

Tomorrow the tour to promote *The Twelfth Angel* begins. As near as I can recall, this will be my ninth promotional tour in the past twenty years. Commencing in Boston tomorrow, I shall visit thirteen cities before returning home on Friday, May 21st, only to depart again on the following Monday, this time with Bette, to fly to Las Vegas, where I have two paid speeches scheduled, on back-to-back days. Then we'll fly down to Phoenix for our new grandson, Will's, christening on Sunday. Then I'll collapse.

Through the years I have often been asked what it was like to do one of these insane book-promotional tours that include radio shows, television shows, and bookstore autographings every day and night while dashing from place to place, shaking many hands, signing many books, and smiling a lot.

I'm going to attempt to keep daily journal entries for the entire tour. Because of time and weariness I may not be able to keep it up, day after day, but I'm going to try.

May 5

Flew down to Boston from Manchester this morning on the first leg of my tour. I didn't recognize my waiting driver when she first approached me at Logan Airport, but Sally Carpenter reminded me that she had also been my escort many years ago when I had arrived in Cleveland for a book promotion.

I'm certain there cannot be any more difficult job than to work in the publicity department of a book publisher, where your job is to make arrangements for authors while they are traveling to promote their books. That includes every detail, from reserving a hotel room in each city to scheduling the radio, television, and press interviews as well as drivers to take us from place to place. Luckily for me I happened to get one of the best in the business when my publisher assigned Anna DeGrezia to me. Her attention to detail as well as her real caring made it much easier for this old man.

After a hasty lunch Sally and I drove into the very heart of downtown Boston, where I taped a thirty-minute radio program with Dave Fanef at WODS Radio. Then we fought heavy traffic to North Quincy, where I did an hour on radio, live with Jeanine Graf on her show at WEZE. Jeanine, bless her, is an avid Mandino fan, so she just about turned the entire hour into a wonderful commercial for *The Twelfth Angel*. From there we raced across town in increasingly heavy "going home" traffic to the place where I was to tape "The Bookcase" for Continental Cablevision, which was hosted by Kathy Villare. She, too, was outrageously enthusiastic about the book and reminded me that portions of our interview would also be aired on her morning radio show on WMSX.

At five we arrived at the huge, five-story Charlesbank

Bookshop, which is also Boston University's bookstore. A disappointingly small group was waiting for me in one of their store's meeting rooms, ostensibly to hear me give a talk before I autographed. Apparently things have changed since I made my last tour. Authors are now expected to give a talk or do a reading from their book prior to autographing. I had warned both Anna and my West Coast publicity representative that when I gave a speech, I was paid rather well for it. I would autograph, they had been told, but would not do a thirty-minute sales "pitch" as well. Another requirement I had made was that stores having me for autograph sessions were to run an advertisement in their city's morning papers informing the general public that Mandino would be signing copies of his new book at a specific hour.

The manager of the Charlesbank Bookshop informed me that he had not been told that I was not giving a talk, that I was only autographing. I also learned that no ad had been run in a morning Boston paper, but a mailing had gone out to their customers. Now I had a choice. I could walk out in a huff or give a little talk and then sign the books for the few who had shown up at five in the afternoon in the Reading Room on Level 5.

I greeted the few who had come, talked about the new book, and then offered to answer any questions they asked. It was a fun half hour or so before I sat and signed the seven or eight books that had been purchased and perhaps two dozen copies the store had on hand.

Through the years I have been spoiled with long lines waiting for my books to be signed, but since the store had not informed the general public that I would be there, they got just what they deserved—few sales. I went back to my room hoping that the experience at the bookshop was not an omen for the entire tour, since all the media interviews during the day had been great. If Bette had been with me, she would have said that it was only God's way of keeping me humble.

May 6

This was a different and most unusual day. I did all my interviews on the telephone in my room at Boston's Copley Plaza Hotel, while sitting at the highly polished walnut desk in my stockinged feet.

First there was a ten-minute "pre-interview" with Theresa Laehn at radio station WCAR in Detroit. Then, between eleven and noon, we did an hour live. At twelve-thirty, as scheduled, I was phoned by Betty Webb of the *Mesa, Arizona, Tribune*. At one-thirty, following the detailed schedule that Anna had provided me, I phoned Louise Collins at WHDA Radio in New Town, Pennsylvania. All three interviews went very well. The fourth one, however, had me worried. I was to do fifteen minutes, live, with Mark Elfstrand at WORD Radio, Pittsburgh, between four and four-fifteen. Problem was that my plane was departing Boston's Logan Airport for Pittsburgh at five-thirty, which meant racing across Boston after that interview, the very worst time of day as far as traffic is concerned.

By the time I had completed the one-thirty-to-two program with Louise Collins, I was all packed. I went down to the lobby, found a bell cap, and had him come for my luggage, which he was to hold until a Fifth Avenue limo came to the hotel for me at four-fifteen, as arranged. He was to load my luggage into the limo and ask the driver to wait, telling him that Mr. Mandino would be down as soon as I finished the radio program, at four-fifteen.

I was off the phone exactly on schedule, grabbed my briefcase, and dashed for the elevator. My bell cap was waiting in the lobby, and since I had already talked to the people at the front desk regarding my hurried departure, I just sailed out to the waiting limo and arrived at the airport with twenty minutes to spare.

The flight to Pittsburgh was uneventful, and another waiting driver and limo delivered me to the Westin William Penn, where I am now reviewing tomorrow's schedule. Already I am wishing that I was sitting under the pines in our backyard.

May 7

Every tour day is different. Last night before crawling into bed, I unpacked the clothes I planned to wear today. This morning, after room service brought my breakfast, I called a bell cap for my luggage and checked out of the hotel. I have two interviews plus an autographing scheduled for Pittsburgh before I go to the airport and board a late-afternoon plane for Philadelphia.

Another surprise was in store for me when I stepped out of the hotel. My waiting driver was another old friend who had driven me around on tours in the past, Sandi Kopler. I taped fifteen minutes on WLTJ Radio with Rick Charles and then did an hour, live, on the oldest commercial radio station in our nation, KDKA Radio, where we were deluged by wonderful and very admiring listener phone calls. Not one was phoning with a question. All were calling to thank me for what one or another of my books had done to change their lives for the better.

Naturally I made it a point to remind our listeners several times that I would be autographing copies of *The Twelfth Angel* at Borders Bookstore between noon and one. When Sandi and I arrived at the huge bookstore, there was a long line, and instead of the hour scheduled, I signed books for almost two hours. Sandi then raced me to the airport, where I boarded a plane for Philadelphia, where I was met by Joan Mendel. She drove me to the Ritz-Carlton to check in and then we rode for almost an hour to the Chester County Book Co. in faraway West Chester. Since I had done no radio or television to promote my appearance, we had to rely on their ads and mailing, and I was disappointed at the short line that was waiting to have their books autographed when we arrived. However, as I commenced signing and talking with the nice people, others kept arriving, and as it turned out, I autographed books steadily for the entire scheduled hour. Then, before departing, I signed all copies of the book that hadn't been sold, which should help to move them out in a hurry.

I very much doubt that I will stay in any hotel on this entire tour that will top the elegance, cleanliness, and downright class that I found in my hurried visit at the Philadelphia Ritz-Carlton. Although Chestnut Street, where the Ritz stands proudly, has deteriorated a great deal since its heyday as a class place to shop following World War II, I'd be willing to wager that the blighted areas on Chestnut will soon disappear and the stately ambience of the past, with the Ritz as the flagship, will return.

Finally crawled into bed just before midnight. I phoned home. All is well. Left a request for a wake-up call at four-fifteen. I am being picked up, downstairs, at six-fifteen, God help me!

May 8

Publishers rarely send an author who is on tour to a city for a single appearance. Expenses prohibit it, but obviously my publicist, Anna DeGrezia, and Fawcett-Ballantine knew what they were doing when they sent me to Dayton for an autograph session at Books and Company.

When I arrived at the Dayton airport, I was met by Kathy Tirschek. I loaded my luggage into her trunk and we headed immediately for the bookstore. A long line had already formed by the time we arrived, and I imagine I signed for more than two hours. Store people estimate that I autographed around 200 copies of *The Twelfth Angel* plus at least 350 copies of my other titles.

Autographing books would be a lark if all I did was sign my name. However, almost everyone who approaches the autograph table wants me to stand and give them a hug or pose for a picture, and many have tears in their eyes as they ask me to inscribe special words in their book. Often I am asked to autograph old hardcover copies of my books, and now and then someone will hand me a 1967 first-edition copy of *The Greatest Salesman in the World*, which I am pleased to inform the shocked owner is now worth at least five hundred dollars in the book collectors' market—and that's without my signature.

After the long autograph session, which had pleased the store officials, Kathy drove me back to the airport. I removed my luggage from her trunk and caught my plane for Detroit, where I was met by an old friend from the Church of Today, Alan Semonian, and driven to the Radisson Southfield Plaza, my home base for the next two days. Tomorrow will be a very special day, autographing at the church, even though my old buddy, Reverend Jack Boland, is no longer with us. I'll do my best, Jack.

May 9

Mother's Day. And if I couldn't be home with Bette, the Church of Today with all its memories for me of the past twelve years of visits is certainly the place I want to be. As it turned out, this day will be one I shall never forget.

There are two Sunday services, one at nine and one at eleven. I commenced autographing at least forty minutes before the first service. I was still signing an hour *after* the second service ended. The Church's bookstore finally ran out of books, and I was told that 580 copies of *The Twelfth Angel* had been sold! A miracle.

In midafternoon I was picked up at the hotel by my driver and driven to Borders Bookstore in Birmingham, Michigan, where I signed more than a hundred books. Most memorable of all those in line was a woman, Claudreen Jackson, who is president of the Wayne County Chapter of the Michigan Society for Autistic Citizens. She was pushing her autistic daughter in a wheelchair. They had come to see Og. I rose from my seat, walked around the table, and gently kissed the little one. She smiled at me. It has truly been a good day.

May 10

Following Bette's advice, I prepared several bags of laundry and dry cleaning to be picked up by hotel services this morning. After doing a live fifteen-minute telephone call with Michigan State University's WDBM from my room, primarily to promote my appearance at Jocundry's Book Store in East Lansing this evening, I was picked up by my driver, and in the next six hours we were lucky even to find time for lunch. At eight-thirty, in Detroit, we taped a thirty-minute program with Dr. Lynn Boyle titled *Meet the Guests* on WDTR-FM, then we taped thirty minutes with Colleen Burkcar on WKQU in Southfield, then a fifteen-minute tape with Gayle McNight on WLTI-FM, followed by a brief taping for WJBK-TV, Channel 2, Noon News.

After a hasty hamburger and milk shake I did thirty minutes on WJR's *The Warren Pierce Show*, concluding with another thirty-minute taping of *State Edition* on WDET with Nkenge Zola.

I have taught myself to rate my performance on every appearance in terms of how well I managed to present the book and how I was treated by the host or hostess of the program. This was as close to a perfect day as it can get.

The autograph session at Jocundry's was great. Sold more than a hundred books! I was also handed a copy of the *Lansing State Journal*, which had a nice feature on Mandino.

Most of all, however, I don't believe I shall ever forget a man and woman who were standing in line. She was holding a young boy whose face was somewhat distorted. When she stepped close to the table, she said, "Og, this is our son, Jonathan. He has Down's syndrome, and the doctors tell us he is now bleeding internally. We don't know how long we will have him, but we wanted to bring him here to see you before we lose him."

When I had collected myself, I rose, walked around the table, and took the little guy from his mother's arms. I kissed him gently on his cheek and he smiled up at me. Then he reached up and placed his small palm on the tears that were running down my cheeks. I handed him back to his mother and father and returned to my seat, wondering what God had in store for me next. When I looked up, many in the line had tears in their eyes.

I am now back in my Southfield hotel room. It is almost midnight and I'm pretty exhausted. I must try to catch some sleep. I have requested a wake-up call for three o'clock—less than four hours from now—so that I can have some breakfast and can dress in time to hop in the limo, which is scheduled to pick me up and take me to the airport at five A.M. Destination tomorrow: Houston, one of my favorite cities.

May 11

This was another of those days when I was visiting a city but never stopped long enough to unpack or check into a hotel. I arrived in Houston shortly before noon, and my driver, Clair Draper, rushed me to KTRK-TV, Channel 7, where I did seven or eight minutes live on *Good Morning Houston.* Then we went to the Unity Church, where we taped a segment for KTHX-TV, Channel 20, before I settled down and autographed in the church's bookstore. The church's pastor, Howard Caesar, is an old and dear friend, and it was fun to visit with him again, although there wasn't too much time to gab.

At two I did a live hour with John Downey on his show at KILT, and then we made a long haul out to Conroe, where I autographed books in Hastings Bookstore. After the long drive back from Conroe, Clair dropped me at the airport, and I was soon on Continental Flight #1274 heading for Dallas. A Sunset Limo driver met me at the gate and drove me to the Hotel Adolphus. I'm weary.

May 12

It is almost midnight, and after the hectic day I've had, it is easy to succumb to the temptation of putting off this journal entry until perhaps tomorrow night. But tomorrow is almost as busy as today, and I'll be flying to Denver at ten o'clock at night and doubt I'll be in any better shape than I am right now. So I do it.

First of all, this magnificent Hotel Adolphus is one of

those rare hotels in the heart of a city where one should move leisurely and quietly, enjoying this remarkable place named after its creator, beer baron Adolphus Busch, more than eighty years ago. Its hardwood paneling, marble, and fine antiques, not to mention two great restaurants, don't make it the place to check in to when one is on the run—and I was very definitely on the run today.

Fortunately another old friend, Lenore Markowitz, who has escorted me in years past on similar missions, opened the day by driving me all the way down to Fort Worth to do *Books in Review* on Community Video Cable, a spot on the Southern Baptist TV Network, a radio show titled *Master Control* with Chuck Reis, and then a television show titled *Cope* with Dr. Karen Kayter, which included marvelous phone-ins from listeners. They were so kind and complimentary to me that it almost sounded as if they had been rehearsed, which of course they were not. We then rushed back to Dallas, where I autographed more than a hundred and fifty books for a long line at Taylors Bookstore.

We departed Taylors at a little before two and drove at a leisurely pace out to Denton, where I autographed between four and five-thirty. Then back to Dallas in time to confront a huge line of Mandino fans, God bless them, at Borders Bookstore on Preston Road. I know I signed at least two hundred books for people in line and also signed two hundred other copies of *The Twelfth Angel* for the bookstore, which should assure their fast sale.

I've set my alarm for six. Lenore is picking me up at eight. Picking me up? She just may have to . . .

I am now at the Brown Palace in Denver. It is almost midnight.

To begin our day in Dallas this morning, Lenore rushed me to KRLD Radio, on Metromedia Place, where we did two segments on their *Morning Drive*. Then to Richardson, where we taped *Weekday* with Cindy Dupree on Telecable of Plano before driving to Grand Prairie to tape a *Midday* section on KKDA with Jocelyn Johnson. At one we taped a thirty-minute show titled *Conversations* for Eidos Productions TV at the Irving Public Library before Lenore drove me back to the hotel for a quick afternoon nap. When the operator phoned my room with her four-thirty wake-up call—four-thirty in the afternoon—I could tell she was fighting to keep from laughing out loud. Anyway, Lenore drove me to Arlington, where we taped *Around Arlington* on Arlington Cablevision before we went out to Waldenbooks in Valley View Center, where a great and smiling crowd revived me completely. Sold and signed several hundred books. I couldn't be more pleased by the reception. Those who had already purchased the book and read it, as they passed through the line for an autograph, were filled with praise for my little hero, Timothy Noble. What a great feeling. So many times in the past few days, as I grew weary, I would continue to remind myself that I was doing this for Timothy—not Og Mandino. Timothy is not a character in a book. He lives in my heart. He always will.

Lenore gave me a hug and kiss and left me at the Dallas airport slightly after nine.

This lovely place, the Brown Palace in Denver, has a history as long and as proud as the Adolphus's in Dallas. In my room, resting against the lamp on the desk where I am writing, is a card inscribed, in italics:

To Our Guests

In ancient times there was a prayer for "The Stranger within our gates."

Because this hotel is a human institution to serve people, and not solely a money-making organization, we hope that God will grant you peace and rest while you are under our roof.

May this room be your "second" home. May those you love be near you in thoughts and dreams. Even though we may not get to know you, we hope that you will be comfortable and happy as if you were in your own house.

May the business that brought you our way prosper. May every call you make and every message you receive add to your joy. When you leave, may your journey be safe.

We are all travelers. From "birth to death" we travel between the eternities. May these days be pleasant for you, profitable for society, helpful for those you meet and a joy to those who know and love you best.

I went to sleep remembering how my beloved mother would pray over me before she tucked me in. Is it so strange for an old man to think such thoughts and hope she is proud of me?

May 14

Had a leisurely breakfast in my room, slowly turning the pages of *USA Today* as if I were at home and then dressing at my own pace. My driver, Mary Stobie, picked me up just before ten and drove me to the Denver Public Library, where we taped a program called *Between the Lines* hosted by Susan Valoskovic. Set off to the side, out of camera range, were a dozen or so folding chairs, each occupied by an elderly woman. Susan told me that they never allowed audiences, but because they thought my appearance and words might be helpful, they had invited a dozen homeless women who were being attended to by a local organization. After we completed taping, I walked over and said hello to the ladies, and one surprised me by standing and raising her arms toward me. I hugged her and kissed her wrinkled cheek while she kept mumbling, "Thank you . . . thank you."

Came back to my room here at the Brown Palace and did a one-hour live interview over the telephone with George Tanner of KFLR in Phoenix, which had many great calls from people telling me how the books had affected their lives.

Then Mary and I made the long but scenic ride to Colorado Springs, home of the Air Force Academy, where I taped a fifteen-minute program titled *Cover to Cover*, hosted by Alexa Grumko. We taped at McKinzey-White, a large and wonderful bookstore, and when we finished, I was led to a table and a long line of patiently waiting nice people, where I signed copies of *The Twelfth Angel* for almost three hours.

I fell asleep in the car on the way back to Denver.

May 15

Up soon after five this morning, had breakfast, showered, shaved, and finished packing so that I had checked out by seven and was picked up by Mary soon after. Flew United #785 from Denver and arrived in Salt Lake City, a very special place in my heart, slightly before ten. No hotel check-in here. Just two long autograph sessions at the Deseret Book Store on South State and the Deseret Book Store in Orem.

I was stationed in this lovely city in 1943 waiting for the Army Air Corps to assign this new bombardier to a crew. The first love of my life was a very pretty Mormon girl I met here at a dance, and I dated her until I was shipped off to Casper, Wyoming, to meet and train with my B-24 Liberator crew.

Years later, after I had written *The Greatest Salesman in the World*, President N. Eldon Tanner of the Mormon Church contacted me at my office in Chicago, where I was functioning as the editor of W. Clement Stone's magazine *Success Unlimited*. President Tanner wanted permission from me to quote from my book in a speech he was scheduled to give to an insurance group. I gave it, of course, with my love.

Several years later, while touring to promote another of my books, I found myself in Salt Lake one afternoon with several hours on my hands, so I boldly decided to phone President Tanner at the Church. When I identified myself, they put me right through to the great man, and he asked, "Og, where are you?"

I told him that I was at the Hotel Utah, and he proceeded to give me directions on how to come to his office, which was not very far away. For more than an hour we sat and visited, and I'll never forget our conversation. I remember discussing the events of the past several months and wondering just what was going to happen to our nation, when President Tanner reached over, a twinkle in his eye, patted me gently on my arm, and said, "Don't worry, Og. The country will be okay. We Mormons are here!"

The store manager at the South State Street store was an old friend from other autographings, Boyd Wayne. Was great to see him, and the line waiting for books to be signed seemed to have no end. Perhaps an hour into my signing, a woman, probably in her early sixties, leaned over as she handed me her book and said, "Write something in there that will help me, Og. I buried my man two days ago after forty years of happy living."

I didn't know what to say or write, so I stood, walked around the table, took her in my arms, and whispered in her ear, "You understand, of course, that this hug is not from Og—it's from *him*."

She ran out of the store sobbing. The store clerk, standing by to assist me, said she knew the lady and would take care of her book. I autographed it, using her first name, which the clerk gave me—with my love.

Mary and I then made the long drive to Orem, a ride I have probably made a half dozen times over the years. It was worth it. Huge crowds at the store. I probably signed more than a thousand books in Utah.

I arrived in Phoenix at eight-thirty this evening and am now in my room at the Arizona Biltmore, another place with great memories. On March 3, 1990, in this hotel's great ballroom, I was honored at a very special black-tie function—on "Og Mandino Day."

Can't wait for tomorrow. Although I'll be autographing at Houle's Books on East Camelback between one and three, I'll then get to see our new grandson, William, who is now six months old.

May 16

Sunday in the Valley of the Sun. Spent fourteen happy and productive years here before moving back to New England, so I walked around the lush green grounds of the Biltmore wishing I could still identify the desert birds through the sounds they were making as they flitted from palm tree to palm tree.

There was a rather disappointingly small crowd waiting at Houle's Books when I arrived, but I was introduced to a charming lady, Marsha Blake, who had flown in from Newport Beach, California, with a large shopping bag filled with my books. She said she was in no hurry, that she would just sit nearby and wait until I had attended to the rather short line. However, the short line didn't completely vanish for well over an hour. A peculiar phenomenon of the autographing bit is that people don't always arrive early and wait in line. Often they will time things so that they walk into the store after you have already commenced autographing, and that is exactly what happened at Houle's.

I guess I signed well over a hundred books before I could take care of those in Marsha's bag, and not until I was leaving was I told by the store manager that he had been fearful no one would show up. When I asked why, he said that the Phoenix Suns, a team beloved by all Phoenicians, were involved in a play-off game with the San Antonio Spurs in San Antonio, and the game was being televised at exactly the same time as my autographing. I'm glad I didn't know ahead of time.

The day ended as a great success. I got to hold my handsome new grandson while I tried to figure out what color his hair and eyes would be. He has the greatest smile.

Oh, the Phoenix Suns won their game.

May 17

I am sitting in my room at the Alexis, in Seattle, a little after nine in the evening, enjoying a fat hamburger. This morning, from my room at the Biltmore before flying to

Seattle, I did a thirty-minute live program on the phone with George Chamberlain at KCEO Radio in San Diego before visiting KHEP Radio, in Phoenix, to do *Studio Bea* with Bea Hoeksema.

After registering at the Alexis, my Seattle escort, Tamara Rinaldi, drove me to Waldenbooks in the South Center Shopping Center, where I signed for almost two hours.

While searching through my oversize attaché case this afternoon I discovered a scribbled saying on a legal pad that I remembered writing down, before commencing this grueling trip, in anticipation that its words might help someday. It's all about perseverance and was written by one of England's greatest contributors to the world of letters, Samuel Johnson:

> All the performances of human art, at which we look with praise or wonder, are instances of the resistless force of perseverance: it is by this that the quarry becomes a pyramid, and that distant countries are united with canals.
>
> If a man was to compare the effect of a single stroke of the pick-ax, or of one impression of the spade with the general design and last result, he would be overwhelmed by the sense of their disproportion; yet those petty operations incessantly continued, in time surmount the greatest difficulties, and mountains are leveled, and oceans bounded, by the slender force of human beings.

And thus are best-sellers made—one interview and one autograph session at a time.

I can now see the finish line, thank God.

May 18

My multipage tour itinerary informed me that I would receive a telephone call in my Seattle hotel room this morning at eight-thirty from a reporter for the *Everett Herald*, so I hastily showered, shaved, and dressed after my early wake-up call. Then I packed, raced through my room-service breakfast, and sat waiting for the phone to ring. However, the phone didn't ring until eight fifty-five, and the so-called "interview" lasted no longer than ten minutes. I'm very proud of myself. Not once did I ask why the hell I was being called twenty-five minutes late, and I even thanked the woman for calling. I must be getting old.

As soon as I hung up, I checked out of the hotel and was waiting in the lobby with my luggage when Tamara arrived just before ten. We loaded up her trunk and then went to KIRO Radio, one of Seattle's best, where Jim French, host of their *Midday* show, and I were on the air together again after many years. Waiting in the lobby, before going on, I happened to look up as Mary Higgins Clark, famous mystery writer, was walking out of the broadcasting studios behind the lobby. Mary and I had both been so-called "honored guests" at a southern writers' dinner several years ago, and it was good to see her again. I congratulated her on the special multimillion-dollar contract she had just signed, and she just grinned sheepishly and replied, "Not too shabby, Og."

Jim French, as always, asked some very perceptive questions, and the time flew much too swiftly. On our way out of the studio we were stopped by Bill Yenne, who said he did morning news for the station. He asked me if I'd be willing to do ten minutes or so with him, which I did gladly.

We autographed at noon at Brentano's Bookstore,

Westlake Center, where there was a fine crowd. Then, on the way to the airport, we stopped at Pacific Pipelines, a book distribution center and warehouse, where they were waiting for me, and I signed every copy of *The Twelfth Angel* they had in stock.

At three-thirty this afternoon I was on an American Airlines flight for Chicago. I am writing this on a huge desk in my room at the elegant Mayfair Regent on East Lake Shore Drive before I prepare some bags of laundry and dry cleaning to be picked up in the morning while I am making appearances in the Chicago area.

May 19

Memories. They almost overwhelmed me today. After breakfast in my room I did a one-hour phone interview with Dan Diorio and his *Morning Drive* show on WMBD Radio in Peoria. Then drove for forty minutes or so until we arrived at Borders Bookstore on South Waukegan Road in Deerfield.

Memories. Thirty years earlier Bette and I and our first child, Dana, had arrived in Chicago, where I was going to work in the sales promotion department of W. Clement Stone's Combined Insurance Company of America. We arrived with most of our belongings strapped to the top of our old Ford and we fortunately found a small apartment we could afford—in Deerfield, on North Waukegan Road. If anyone back then had ever told me that three decades later I would be back on Waukegan Road autographing copies of my sixteenth book and that the first fifteen would have already surpassed thirty million copies sold in twenty languages, I would have laughed in their face.

Attendance for my autographing on Waukegan Road was very small. The manager apologized, saying that the store was so new that they had not had much opportunity to advertise. It didn't matter a bit to me. Waukegan Road never looked nicer.

We drove to Naperville, a long ride, where I autographed between six-thirty and eight o'clock, signing perhaps 150 books at the Crown Superstore.

May 20

Still in the "Windy City." Our first program of the day was a taped thirty-minute interview with Cheryl Dobnikar at CRIS Radio, *Access Chicago*. Then to the Board of Trade Building, where we taped thirty minutes on WCIU-TV. Audry Shimp asked excellent questions, and although the program is called *Stock Market Obs*, they had made an exception in my case, and I guess they were pleased.

Autographed at Krochs & Brentanos on South Wabash between noon and one and was surprised at the large size of the crowd. Signed perhaps a hundred books before I was driven out to the Hilton Suites in Oak Terrace. For the next twenty hours or so I am not on tour. Tomorrow, at the ungodly hour of seven A.M., I'll be next door at the famous Drury Lane Theater picking at my breakfast before standing to address the Executive Breakfast Club—a paid performance after these seemingly perpetual days of performing for a book. I've been told that the maximum length of my speech has to be forty-five minutes, so I've done lots of cutting. Hope it doesn't hurt things too much.

May 21

Today was a day I'll always cherish. All hits and runs—no errors! Almost a thousand were at the Drury Lane Executive Breakfast Club breakfast, the largest crowd of the year, I was told. After such a long layoff, so far as my speeches are concerned, I was worried about my delivery and timing, but it turned out very well. A lovely standing ovation when I was finished from a crowd that I imagine could be very tough. My agent and longtime friend, Cheryl Miller, drove over from Long Grove to check me out and said she was very pleased.

Departed O'Hare Airport shortly after noon—to Washington, D.C. Arrived around four, picked up by chauffeur, and driven to the U.S. Chamber of Commerce Building, where I was to tape the nationally syndicated *America with Dennis Wholey* popular television show. Dennis and I are old friends. He even visited me, when we were living in Scottsdale, to interview me for one of his books, and I've appeared on his television show twice in the past ten years. Interview went great, with Dennis's usual laid-back and casual style, although he did ask me some very perceptive questions, one of them being, "Og, you are always talking about your mother and the great influence she had on your life. You never mention your father. What about him?"

I told Dennis that my dad arrived on Ellis Island from Italy when he was only six, with his mother and father. He had always been a hardworking man and was very strict with us kids, but I had loved him very much and miss him, now, just as much as I miss my mother.

What a great day it was! A packed house at Drury Lane followed by what I'm pretty sure was a very powerful thirty minutes on national television.

May 23

Spent most of this day in my studio trying to catch up on all the mail that had accumulated during the past couple of weeks, and although I may have been growing weary, a single phone call from Pierre O'Rourke in Phoenix, struggling so hard to put together our Save ASU Gymnastics program, was all I needed to make my day. Willie Nelson, vacationing in Hawaii, contacted Pierre and offered his services for the fund-raiser, saying, "If a man like Mandino thinks it's so important to help the coach and his team, that's enough for me. Og is one of my favorite writers and I'm just so glad to come there and be with him." Willie Nelson opening for me? And that's not all. A great group of young kids called Four Boys and a Babe, who stole the show on *Star Search* last year, week after week, have also offered their services, and they will go on before Willie. Wow!

May 24

With no time off for good behavior, this morning I boarded a United flight in Manchester, and now, slightly after six in the afternoon, I am sitting in my room at Caesar's Palace in Las Vegas. However, this time there is a big difference. I have my Bette with me. Several months ago when I told her that Cheryl had booked two speeches for me on consecutive days in Vegas, she quickly said, "Count me in."

The speeches are scheduled for tomorrow and Wednesday. We'll then stay here, relax, and play a little until Saturday, when we'll fly down to Phoenix to attend our new grandson's christening on Sunday. Then we'll stay in Phoenix to do the benefit for Arizona State gymnastics on Thursday, fly home on Saturday, and collapse.

Caesar's Palace continues to grow and grow. Now that it has added the Forum Shops, with almost two hundred very classy stores, such as Gucci and Cartier, one need never leave this magnificent complex for any reason except possibly a breath of fresh air, since smoking is still allowed throughout most of the huge building. Our room has a mirrored ceiling as well as a circular shower and bathtub setup only six feet from the bed!

After doing all my packing and unpacking during the recent promotional safari, it's great just to sit back and let Bette do it for a change.

We're going downstairs to tour the place and have a bite to eat. Then, knowing Bette, I'm sure we'll give the slots a little exercise.

May 25

This turned out to be a very special day. I am back in my room at Caesar's Palace suffering the usual letdown that follows a speech but also feeling very good about the "performance." No one ever has to tell me when I did a good job, nor does anyone ever have to tell me when I've bombed.

My first speech this evening was part of the Impact Lecture Series, sponsored by the First Church of Religious Science Life Center. Recent speakers have been author Wayne Dyer and astronaut Edgar Mitchell. I was picked up late this afternoon, at the front entrance of Caesar's, by a dynamic little blonde named Veneta "Skipper" Flippin and her husband and driven to the Cashman Field Theater, where I was scheduled to speak at seven-thirty, so that I could familiarize myself with the lectern, microphone, and lighting. On the way to the theater, Skipper pointed out a huge signboard along the road that announced in bright lights that Og Mandino was speaking at the Cashman Theater this evening! My name in lights in Las Vegas! Move over, Sinatra!

After checking out the theater, we proceeded to the

church, where an outdoor reception was being held for me, and I was warmly greeted by Dr. Fred McCoun, the church's minister, and many of the congregation. As I was shaking hands and visiting with the crowd, one of the members, who looked vaguely familiar, extended his hand and said, "Og, I'm Buddy Greco. Your books saved my life a few years ago, and it's an honor to meet you." Later, as we were munching sandwiches and enjoying a soft drink, a lovely blond woman, Nancy Mead, stood and said that her friend, Buddy Greco, had written a song called "Miracles" after reading Og's book *The Greatest Miracle in the World*. She sang it to us while Buddy accompanied her on the piano. The song was beautiful and truly touched me. I walked over to them after she had finished and embraced both Nancy and Buddy.

Slightly more than a thousand were at the speech. Great audience. Skipper and her husband then drove me back here to Caesar's, where I now think I'll go in search of Bette—and since there are several thousand slot machines in this gaudy empire of Caesar's, it might take me a little while.

For tomorrow's speech I don't have to leave this building. I'm speaking in the Colosseum Complex, to Floyd Wickman's Third Annual Master Sales Academy, a gathering of the nation's top realtors all seeking ideas on how to be better at what they do so that they can become "the greatest salesmen (or saleswomen) in the world."

May 30

The speech to the realtors on Wednesday went very well. Floyd smilingly told me that it was a record-breaking crowd for his company, and I autographed books for a long time after the speech.

The rest of the week was perfect. Bette and I never left Caesar's Palace. We ate when we felt like it, joined Caesar's Emperors Club so that we could amass credits toward merchandise every time we played a slot machine, stood with hundreds of other guests and watched in awe as the artificial sky, high above our heads in the Forum area, exploded with thunder and lightning while costumed gladiators and pretty maidens paraded about. This place is a complete and magnificent world of make-believe for adults. Providing one can control one's gambling, and we both do, Caesar's can be a lot of fun and a marvelous change from the daily routine of living.

We departed the land of make-believe on Saturday morning, and this morning, in Phoenix's lovely Shadow Rock Church, where his mom and dad were married, we watched proudly as William Augustine Mandino was christened. The handsome little guy, in his special heirloom christening gown that Bette had labored over for months, remained fairly calm during the brief ceremony before regular Sunday services began.

Holding Bette's hand tightly, I prayed that Will would live healthy and happy days and be as bright as his mom and dad. I think it was James Russell Lowell who wrote that children are God's apostles, sent forth, day by day, to preach of love and hope and peace. You've got a lot of work ahead of you, Will. . . .

June 2

This morning I appeared for an hour on Phoenix's leading radio station, KTAR, with my old friend and talk-show host, Pat McMahan. What made this hour so unusual is that another old friend, Guy Atchley, from Channel 9 in Tucson, drove the hundred miles or so from Tucson with his crew and television equipment and set up his camera at KTAR to tape part of the "on-air" discussion between Pat and myself. It was a fun hour, and the phone-in calls couldn't have been better.

Pat, who has agreed to act as the master of ceremonies for our function at Arizona State, arranged for Coach Don Robinson to drop by during the live hour to plug our efforts to rescue the gymnastics program. Of course, I did manage to get in a few plugs for *The Twelfth Angel*, which I had learned in an earlier phone call with my editor has now gone back for its fifth printing!

Afterward Coach Robinson acted as my chauffeur and drove me down to Arizona State University, in Tempe, to take me through Gammage Auditorium so that I could familiarize myself with the place. A lovely hall. Hope it's filled tomorrow night!

June 4

Last night, at Arizona State's Gammage Auditorium, was an evening that will live in my memory as long as I have one. By the time our publicist for the event, Pierre O'Rourke, and KTAR Radio's Pat McMahan had greeted the crowd, the estimate was that around fourteen hundred were in the audience. Not a full house, but still a great crowd. As part of the fund-raising, on the gymnastic team's behalf a silent auction had been held before the evening festivities began, featuring such items as a script of the television show *Evening Shade*, sent by Burt Reynolds, and a black fedora autographed by my old friend, Michael Jackson.

The evening opened with several varsity gymnasts doing their thing for the friendly and appreciative crowd, and they were followed by Four Guys and a Babe, who were both adorable and sensational. Then I stood in the wings as Willie Nelson walked out on stage with his guitar and told the audience how honored he was to be a part of such a special evening. I just stood and listened, finding it very difficult to comprehend that Willie Nelson was opening the show for me! The man did a great job, and then I went out and did my thing. This was not the night to bomb. I truly gave it my all, and the standing ovation touched me deeply.

A very talented Arizona entertainer, Jimmy Cicero, followed me with a lovely song he had written titled "The Greatest Miracle in the World Is You," and then we closed the evening with Pierre, Pat, former governor Rose Mofford, and myself holding hands on stage while Willie Nelson sang "Amazing Grace."

Afterward Bette and I were taken to Willie's bus, where we sat and gabbed with the great man and his dynamo of a wife, Annie. Annie said that while they were supposed to be vacationing in Maui, she considered this unexpected trip to Arizona her real vacation since she didn't have to tend to their two young kids, who were still back in Hawaii. She said she had already spent most of the afternoon in the quiet bus, reading *The Twelfth Angel*.

We probably won't know for several days whether we succeeded in saving Arizona State gymnastics or not.

June 6

United Parcel Service delivered two very special gifts today from a retired dentist, Dr. Lewis R. Jensen, of Orem, Utah, who invented the world's first straight high-speed dental drill a few years ago and now heads one of the fastest-growing privately held companies in the nation.

One of the gifts from Dr. Jensen was a walking stick on which he had used his specialized carving equipment to carve sentences from my books as well as his name and mine. What a treasure!

The other gift was a Little League–size baseball bat, cut down the middle, on which Dr. Jensen had carved the figure of my Little League hero from the cover of *The Twelfth Angel* and also my name and the words *The Twelfth Angel*.

Both gifts are now leaning against a wall in my studio and will be here as long as I am. Dr. Jensen's gifts, as his letter stated, were just his way of saying thank you for the lasting effect that *The Greatest Salesman in the World* had on his life.

June 8

During the past twenty years or so I guess I've been asked to read and then write testimonials for at least a thousand manuscripts by both friends and strangers struggling to get their work published. I've done so willingly, even when pressed for time, feeling it was my small way to give back a little of the good fortune that God has bestowed on me.

Two manuscripts I received today have finally convinced me to change my policy. The first, weighing a pound or more, included a cover letter that, after going through the usual sales pitch, told me how much my work was admired and asked for my testimonial by the end of the month. It then went on to state, "If you cannot do so, I would greatly appreciate your returning the enclosed." One problem: no return envelope and of course no enclosed postage for the return trip.

The cover letter of the other manuscript, after describing the book in detail, stated, "As I prepare a highly select list of whom I consider to be the most influential leaders of our time to endorse this book, I placed your name on this list."

Now, for that little bit of stroking I am supposed to spend at least two hours reading a very long manuscript and then writing words of praise to hype the book in public.

I spent a short amount of time yesterday preparing the following letter. I'll make plenty of copies of it and mail one out, from now on, to just about everyone who sends me a manuscript to read:

Dear Friend,

I am highly complimented by your request that I read your work and write a testimonial endorsing it. In the past twenty years or so I have read and endorsed hundreds of manuscripts.

However, I can no longer do it. I am still trying to write a new book every fifteen months or so plus give my usual twenty or thirty speeches per year, somewhere in the world, and as I approach my seventh decade, my goal is to work less and play golf more.

Therefore I have regretfully decided that I shall not spend any more of my precious hours reading manuscripts, whether written by friend or stranger.

I sincerely hope that you will understand.

If you have enclosed a return envelope and postage with your manuscript, your work is being returned in it along with this note. If you have not, and wish your work to be returned, I will hold it for *twenty days* before disposing of it. Let me know.

Needless to say, I wish you every success with your writing. Just remember, if I can do it, you can do it.

God Bless.

June 9

The head is beginning to clear. I've been home now for three days and awoke this morning feeling it was time to get on with my life—and what better way than to work in our garden. In the past week, on my instructions, Bobby Compton and his Homestead Landscaping people rototilled our small vegetable garden directly across the street from the house, and this morning, armed with rakes and hoes, I set about making the soil ready for planting.

For a few years now agriculturalists have been experimenting with a new strain of corn called supersweet hybrid. These varieties can be twice as sweet as the older varieties, convert their sugar to starch more slowly, and can be kept for a longer period after picking without losing their flavor. However, these sophisticated seeds are not to be planted near the usual varieties of corn, or everything gets fouled up in the cross-pollination.

I had ordered, and received, three varieties of supersweet hybrid from my Burpee seed catalog and planted four twelve-foot rows of "Sweet and Tender," which promises two nine-inch-long ears on each eight-foot stalk, and "Honey and Pearl," an All-American Winner with yellow and white kernels.

While I had been on tour, Bette shopped the area, and although it was getting a little late in the planting season, she did manage to find "Better Boy" and "Jet Star" tomatoes as well as some bell, chili, and jalapeño peppers, which I carefully planted in very straight rows as my dad taught me to do a long time ago. Tomorrow I'll plant three varieties of beans, and then in a week or ten days I'll put in four or so rows of "Illinois Xtra-Sweet" corn for a late harvest. This one's ad promised that it would be four times as sweet as standard hybrids even forty-eight hours after picking.

Thoreau wondered why he should bother to raise his beans. He was never quite sure of the meaning of his devotion to making certain that the things he grew received the proper care, but I cannot even begin to describe the incredible feeling of peace that captures me when I am outside grubbing in my little plot of land while robins line up on the stone fence and watch. From Caesar's Palace to a row of corn in just a few days, and I enjoy one as much as I enjoy the other. Maybe the key word is *planting*. When I am writing or speaking, I am trying to plant hope, and when I am gardening, I am planting food, and both are absolutely necessary for survival.

June 16

The special metal plaque that I ordered two months ago arrived yesterday, and Edd Houghton, who does all things around here requiring the use of a hammer, saw, or screwdriver, hung the beautiful thing for me. It looks like an old knight's shield, has the letter *M* on its top in a rather flowery design, and below are the words *Enchanted Haven*, which Bette and I had decided, soon after we moved in, is what this place should be called. The company who sells the plaques, Home Decorators Collection of Saint Louis, will cast any words one wants in aluminum, and the finished product looks just great with its lettering in gold on a black background.

Out near the road, perhaps seventy feet from our house, stands a huge boulder, perhaps seven feet tall and twelve to fifteen feet wide and deep. A monster. The front section facing our road is almost flat. Edd drilled three holes in the stone and screwed our plaque into it so that coming down the road, just before arriving at our precious abode, one will read ENCHANTED HAVEN.

The old-fashioned roses that we ordered from Wayside Gardens arrived while Bette and I were in Arizona. Jim, our UPS deliverer and good friend, placed them in the darkness of our garage, and this morning Bobby Compton and his guys planted them where I had placed stakes after Bette and I walked the property last Sunday.

Our ducks have apparently moved on. We have not seen them on the pond since our return. Our loss.

June 21

Since our present president has made his prime target the reduction of our $4 trillion national debt, a figure none of us can even begin to comprehend, I was interested in what Arizona State's great gymnastics coach, Don Robinson, has printed on the back of his business card: "Putting A Billion In Perspective."

First of all I wasn't quite sure how many billion went into making a single trillion until I consulted my Webster's New Collegiate Dictionary and learned that a thousand billion is equal to a trillion, so we are now more than $4,000 billion in debt.

Can we get any kind of a handle on what a single billion represents?

The figures on the back of Don's card help greatly:

One billion seconds ago—Harry Truman was president of the United States.
One billion minutes ago—Jesus walked the earth.
One billion hours ago—there were relatively few people on the earth.

One billion dollars ago—was yesterday afternoon in the U.S. Treasury.

To count to a billion, at the rate of eight hours a day, five days a week, it would take fifty-seven years!

To repeat, our national debt exceeds $4,000 billion!

June 23

On my wall of memorabilia is a framed letter on embossed White House stationery from Pat Nixon, dated October 10, 1973, thanking me for the "warmly inscribed" copy of *The Greatest Salesman in the World,* which I had sent the Nixons at the request of W. Clement Stone.

Richard Nixon may have been guilty of poor judgment in many matters, some of which caused his downfall, but when he proposed to Pat way back in 1940, he was right on target. Pat provided her man with love, loyalty, and understanding through all their travail, and during the years of Nixon's presidency she was a "first lady" in every sense and meaning of the word.

Pat Nixon died yesterday at the age of eighty-one. I pray she has found the peace she certainly deserves.

July 11

Back in 1955 when my country-girl spouse graduated from her tiny high school, there were eleven in her class.

Last night her old school, now nonexistent, had a reunion of all graduates of every year in a hall not too far from our home. One old gal, from the class of 1916, received much-deserved attention and admiration from the three hundred or so who attended the dinner. Four, counting Bette, checked in from her class.

Commencing with the earlier years, the names of every former graduate who had purchased tickets to attend was called after dinner, and each stood smiling at the applause and shouts. After the master of ceremonies read Bette's name, he pulled his little surprise and introduced "Bette's famous, best-selling-author husband, Og Mandino," and I had to stand, feeling rather foolish, and bow to the applause.

In a way, as Bette pointed out on our drive home, it was a great honor. I was the only non–high school attendant who had his or her named called out.

My hat size is not one iota larger today.

July 14

Our youngest son, Matt, along with his wife, Lori, and first baby, Will, is visiting us from Arizona for a few days, so Matt and I had the opportunity to play a rare round of golf together. I can still remember when Matt was only four and I placed a tiny plastic golf club in his hands for the first time. Through the years he worked at his game and now has as lovely a swing as I have ever seen. He also whipped me handily. Somewhere during the round I remember leaning toward him in our golf cart, touching his arm lightly, and saying, "I sure hope God lets me hang around long enough for us to have a threesome that includes Will."

Hopefully my new grandson will like the game and be swinging clubs in seven or eight years. I should be able to make that okay. I'll be seventy in December, but I just read an article on longevity that said if one makes it to seventy, the mortality tables indicate that he or she still has twelve years to live. I'll take it.

July 17

What a great sight! Two young moose bathing themselves in our pond as the temperature hovered slightly above ninety. As quietly as we could, we opened our kitchen door, and Bette took several shots with her new camera while I managed to capture the two visitors for about four minutes of videotape before they both glanced casually in our direction and then slowly waded out of the water, stepped up on the beach, and trudged off into the woods beyond without even looking back.

Coincidentally earlier in the day I had received a copy of the *Inland Empire Business Journal*, for whom I am speaking in San Bernardino late in September. Their quote of the month, from James Anthony Froude, in 1894, was, "Wild animals never kill for sport. Man is the only one to whom the torture and death of his fellow-creatures is amusing in itself."

The hunting season will soon be upon us. I wish those two poolside visitors all the luck in the world. They will probably need it to avoid providing amusement for some of my fellow men.

July 27

Our flower garden has been an absolute thing of beauty this summer. Bobby took Bette's advice and added many more perennials and annuals to each of the beddings that make up that large, precious, square wonderland to the east of our home. I'm ashamed to admit that I do not know the names of all the lovely plants we now have, so Bobby patiently walks both of us through the flowers at least twice a summer.

After we enter through a white trellis covered with pink

clematis, we find tall lavender liatrus, small yellow coreopsis, moonbeam, gold and orange marigolds, white and pink phlox, astilbes in many hues, daisies, irises, white cosmos, pink coral bells, yellow Japanese primrose, tall and multicolored columbine, purple coneflowers, and daylilies in several shapes and sizes.

The many chrysanthemum plants are also all looking healthy as they prepare to give us a fall season of colors that will pretty much last until the first frost.

The old-fashioned roses that I ordered and planted are all doing fine, blooming constantly and sprouting many new branches. By next summer they should be a show unto themselves.

Henry Ward Beecher, a long time ago, wrote that "flowers were the sweetest things that God ever made and forgot to put a soul into." I'm not sure he was correct. I think the flowers on our Enchanted Haven do have souls.

August 3

I see that this week's issue of *Time* is offering its subscribers a hardbound collector's edition celebrating its seventieth birthday. The edition is promising a nostalgic journey back in time to witness the events and meet the people who have shaped the past seven decades from 1923 to 1993.

Since *Time* and I share the same birthday year, I just cannot resist this offer covering all the accomplishments as well as insanities that have occurred on our tiny, perplexed planet since we both first saw the light of day.

August 4

What a thrilling experience! Last night Bette and I drove to the Hadley Barn in Peterborough to watch the

Peterborough Players perform brilliantly in Thornton Wilder's *Our Town*.

Wilder wrote his magnificent version of life in a small town while he was a resident at the MacDowell Colony in Peterborough before World War II. Almost daily the talented author and playwright would take long strolls through the tiny town of Peterborough and often sit for hours in Moulton's Drug Store observing and listening to the local townspeople and their problems while he was working on his powerful play.

For more than half a century now, conjecture has continued on whether or not Grovers Corner, the setting for *Our Town*, was Peterborough. Wilder, whenever he was asked, would only reply that Grovers Corner was created through observations of humanity he had made in several small New England towns.

This presentation of *Our Town* was the sixth by the Peterborough Players since 1940. Bette and I had never seen the play but reasoned that there would never be a better place to enjoy it more than the century-old Hadley Barn Theatre in the actual town where the play was born.

My lady and I sat with an overflow crowd on flat boards, built like football stadium bleachers, rising on both sides of a small stage below, watching enthralled as small-town events, with little or no seeming importance, enlarge until they were all powerfully proclaiming our most basic human values, such as family, love, neighbors, and God.

Wilder has written a masterpiece that will live as long as there is theater. With good reason it has been acclaimed as "the great American play."

I'm glad we finally spent an evening in Grovers Corner, and we'll never forget it.

August 15

I guess I will always be amazed at the amount of mail I receive from Mandino readers in other countries. A month or so ago I received a lovely letter from a gentleman in Norwich, England, praising my book *The Return of the Ragpicker*. In my reply to his letter, since I try to respond to all who write, I mentioned that I had been a bombardier in a B-24 Liberator and had flown thirty combat missions over Germany from an airfield near a tiny village called Tibenham, not very far from Norwich.

Today the British gentleman's reply arrived. When he received my letter he and his wife had driven to Tibenham and discovered that my old air base was now the location of a glider club. Club officials gave him permission to shoot some photographs and I sat at this desk, with tears running down my cheeks, as I looked at the old runways, a signpost indicating the road to Tibenham which I remembered, an old stone church in the village, and several photos of a black granite memorial, flanked by American and British flags, that had been dedicated by the townspeople to the 445th Bombardment Group.

Also in the mail was a loving note from the wife of John, the man I had stopped in at the hospital to visit in Toledo back in January. Her note was to inform me that John died of leukemia only a month after my visit. She wrote that she had just purchased twenty-two copies of my latest book, *The Twelfth Angel,* and wanted to know if I would autograph them for her nine children, John's nine brothers and sisters, and three special friends. Of course, I replied that I would.

For any of us to complain that life has no joy while there is a single person whose life we can reach out and lift up is so sad. I think we need to revise what is meant by "counting one's blessings."

August 22

Finished *The Spellbinder* early today after a couple of months of the most intense and concentrated writing I've ever experienced. I let my garden pretty much go to hell this year and played golf only four times, but I'm truly proud of the book.

I've noticed that with each new book I seem to be trying harder and getting fussier. Sentences and paragraphs that would have immediately won my approval a few years ago now end up in the wastebasket as I rewrite more and more instead of just coasting on whatever I have for laurels. I'm beginning to believe it all has a lot to do with pride, and because of the amount of mail I receive and answer, I feel very close to my readers—readers I dare not disappoint. The final chapter, for example, is just a little more than a page, double-spaced, in length, yet I rewrote it at least a dozen times in the past three days. Even now there is no guarantee that it will not be rewritten again and again before I finally send it off to Fawcett.

I spent the rest of this day reading the entire manuscript—all twenty chapters of my blood and sweat. I read slowly, after asking Bette not to interrupt me for any reason, closing my studio door (one of the rare occasions when I do so), and concentrating with all my ability on each sentence with a red felt-tip pen in my hand to make any necessary corrections or changes. On several pages I made so many changes that some sentences were illegible to anyone but me, so I retyped those lines on another sheet of paper, cut it to fit, and taped it onto the original page.

When I finished, I was completely spent emotionally, but I knew in my heart I had written a good book. I set it aside and decided to read it again tomorrow before bringing the manuscript to Walt, my printer friend nearby, to produce the final and good-looking copies on his computer and printer that I send to my editor and to Alice, my agent. However, after lunch I changed my mind, deciding not to read it again tomorrow, which would probably produce another series of corrections and alterations. This would go on, I knew, even if I read the thing each day for two weeks. Author's insecurity. A reluctance to let go. I remember reading that when Truman Capote completed a new book, his publisher would have to go to his apartment and almost physically tear the manuscript away from the man, and even after he received the page proofs from the publisher for his final review before the book went to press, he would still correct and change and rewrite giant sections while the publisher despaired. Even charging Capote for all those last-minute changes in the final typesetting did not deter him.

So, late this afternoon, I brought *The Spellbinder* to Walt to retype on one of the good-looking fonts in his computer. He assured me that it would be done in about ten days, as he would try to squeeze it in between all his other printing.

I feel as if I have just parted with a beloved child this evening. *The Spellbinder* is now out of my hands after more than a year's work, and I am already suffering the familiar withdrawal of feeling at completely loose ends with myself. In a day or two I'll be fine and will hopefully enjoy the rest of our summer and the gorgeous fall to follow while making an entry or two in this journal, which will be my only writing, along with answering mail, at least for a while. I know I'm going to enjoy not having a deadline until I must deliver all the pages of this journal approximately a year from now.

There are 165 pages of my messy typing that I delivered to Walt. Since I started *The Spellbinder* more than a year ago, that means that I didn't quite write half a page of good copy per day! Also, I probably should have kept count of how many wastebaskets I filled with pages I did not like upon a second reading on the day after they were written. I've never been certain whether the prime attribute of anyone hoping to write a book should be talent or persistence, and as I get older, I'm beginning to lean toward persistence. I cannot recall who wrote, "There is no royal road to anything. One thing at a time and all things in succession. That which grows slowly will endure."

That person knew one of the great secrets of success.

August 23

Today's mail included a brief note from an old friend who lives in Wooster, Ohio, informing me that I was in the September issue of *Reader's Digest.*

Well, I had to do some driving before I found a store with two copies of September's issue, which I purchased, and yes, there I was, in their monthly "Points to Ponder" feature. Ten lines of mine from *The Choice* explaining that the greatest legacy we can leave our children are a few happy memories. Right above me, Sir Arthur Conan Doyle on the hope that flowers deliver to our soul. Not bad company.

August 24

I see that a young junior high school teacher in Fond du Lac, Wisconsin, and his fiancée recently won more than

$100 million in one of their state's lotteries but he has announced that not only is he keeping his $35,000-per-year job but he's going to donate his salary to the school. When asked why he was still playing golf with his old set of clubs and driving his five-year-old Plymouth, his response, which should be memorized by everyone who believes that acquiring a fortune assures happiness, was that if the moment ever arrives when one is able to afford everything he or she desires, only then will they realize, as he already has, that none of those things are really very important.

Solomon told us the same thing a long time ago when, one day, after surveying all his treasures and mountains of gold, he cried out that it was all vanity and a striving after the wind and that there truly is no profit under the sun. Most of us have been raised to believe that material success is the most important goal of life, when one of the real keys to conquering life and being contented is just being true to the highest and best *we know* and *can do*.

August 26

During my Scottsdale years, before we returned to the New England land of our birth, I often played golf at the Fountain Hills Country Club, which was approximately a thirty-minute drive into the lovely hills and mountains to our east. The town of Fountain Hills derived its name from a giant man-made fountain that sent a geyserlike stream of towering water at least fifty feet into the air from a small pond situated in the center of this colorful western town. I have parked my car and watched the jetting water perform its own unique aerobics on more than one occasion.

Now Bette and I have our own giant fountain. Bobby, our landscaper, came to me several weeks ago and said that our pond, Little Walden, was accumulating algae much too swiftly and from his experience the best way to rid the water of the fast-multiplying vile stuff was to aerate with some sort of fountain.

And so Bobby, with the help of two other good friends, Curt Cisco, builder and plumber, and Jerry Gilbert, master electrician, ran electrical cables under our lawn from the house all the way down to the road, across the dirt road, and into our old shack, which sits close to the pond's northwestern edge. In the shack Bobby set up an electrical motor, Curt added a pressure tank, and Jerry finished with all the necessary wiring. This morning, Alan, one of Bobby's helpers, rowed out to the fountain pipe that Bobby installed in the middle of the pond and adjusted the nozzle to get the most effective and tall stream of water. We then turned the thing on, and a thick spray rose twenty or more feet into the air. Magnificent! Henry David would have probably turned his nose up at this metallic intrusion by man into the natural habitat, but I'm pretty certain that his old Walden didn't have the algae problem that my pond does.

Several weeks ago, after we knew the boys would be digging a shallow trench down both sides of our driveway to install electric wire to power the fountain, Bette went to our favorite electrical store in Concord and selected two brass carriage lamps to match those on both sides of our front doors and the garage, and while the boys were laying down their electric lines, they mounted the lamps atop two black metal poles and raised them on both sides of the foot of our driveway. Through an electric eye that Jerry installed at the side of our house, the driveway lamps now go on at dusk each evening, casting Enchanted Haven in a lovely golden glow until midnight. We can't wait to see the place at night this winter after each snowfall.

September 1

Last night, despite a light overcast, we could see the blue moon shining high in the heaven—that rare phenomenon that occurs every two or three years when we have the second of two full moons within the same month. I'm ashamed to admit that not until this morning, as I was shaving and listening to the radio, did I know the derivation of the phrase *blue moon*, which, according to an old dictionary of mine, means "infrequently recurring." The moon, by the way, was not blue.

For Nana's seventy-seventh birthday today we put her wheelchair in the trunk of our car and drove her and Gramps across New Hampshire to York Beach, on Maine's lovely seacoast, where we treated the old folks to a dinner at Fox's Lobster House. Only a short distance away, on a tiny windswept island rising high above the Atlantic, was the famous Nubble Lighthouse and a small home, once the lighthouse keeper's domain but now unoccupied. It seems that back in their courting days Nana and Gramps would drive to this spot, park their automobile, and watch the waves roll in. Memories again—one of love's best preservatives.

I think the old folks had a good day. They both dozed off in the backseat on our way home.

September 3

These last two days pretty much exemplify the "double-life" that I have been leading for many years.

Yesterday Bette and I went to the Hopkinton State Fair, which is becoming an annual event in our lives. Holding hands and eating popcorn, we didn't miss many of the arts-and-crafts exhibitions, the steer-pulling contests, the elephants performing, and the livestock showing as the Four H kids competed for blue ribbons. It was a wonderful day under a blue sky, and we were children again, even riding the merry-go-round without holding on.

Today I was the "other Mandino." Sitting at my desk, here in the studio, I did two thirty-minute radio interviews on the telephone with stations in the San Bernardino area promoting my forthcoming appearance for the *Inland Business Journal* at the National Orange Show Fairgrounds in San Bernardino on September 23rd. The interviewers were kind and complimentary and very helpful in letting me plug a very powerful two-day program titled "Master Your Future," which will feature four or five of the very best speakers in the business and myself. My speech will close the two-day event, and they tell me that two thousand are expected in the Future 2000 auditorium. Following that very powerful lineup I had better be damn good!

September 8

I see that the Glenn Miller Orchestra is coming to New Hampshire to give two concerts in a week or so. A long article on the band and its legendary leader, in a local paper, was accompanied by a photo of the current nineteen-member band, and even though the memory of Glenn's disappearance over the English Channel in 1944 is still painful to me, I couldn't help chuckling at the photo of the orchestra that would be playing locally. Studying the faces of the band members closely, it was clear that not a single one of them was even born when Glenn vanished in a single-engine plane on his way to France.

During my high school days and later in the service, I was, like most, an avid Glenn Miller fan. Like all the other kids I bought just about every new record he made, from *In the Mood* to *Moonlight Serenade*, and played those ten-inch vinyl disks on my windup Victrola until they wore out.

I shall never forget the excitement on our base, while flying bombing missions in 1944, when the announcement was made that Glenn Miller, a major in the Army Air Force, was bringing his famous band to our airfield as part of a long tour they were making to most air force bases in England. Then, on the evening before their scheduled concert at our base, my heart nearly broke. Our crew was one of thirty-six bomber crews scheduled to participate in a mission to Homburg, Germany, on the following day. We flew the mission, and it was a success, but even so there was no celebration in our hut that evening. We had missed the Glenn Miller concert.

Then our hearts were truly broken two weeks later when we received the terrible news that Glenn was missing on a flight to France to rejoin his orchestra, who had gone ahead of him in a large transport plane. Although half our air force searched the English Channel waters for days, no trace of Glenn or parts of his plane were ever found.

Authorized by the Miller estate, a new Glenn Miller orchestra has been touring the nation since 1956, playing many of the band's old arrangements as well as melodies of today arranged in that same familiar Glenn Miller style. On several occasions I've been tempted to go listen, but I finally decided that listening to the real Glenn Miller band's recordings on my cassette player is as good as it is ever going to get.

September 15

During the past Christmas holidays, when both sons were here at the Haven with their precious families, they expressed concern on more than one occasion at my shortness of breath whenever I exerted myself very much. They wanted me to see a doctor, which they knew I hadn't done since Dr. Lou retired. I promised them I would go after I had finished *The Spellbinder*. Well, this was the day, my first appointment with a new doctor, Frank Fuselier, whom I liked on sight. He put me through most of the usually embarrassing examinations that one endures when having a thorough medical and then told me that I had two problems he wanted to explore further.

Dr. Fuselier told me that I had a small nodule on my prostate that he wanted looked at, plus I had a heart murmur that he suspected was one of the valves acting up. Before I left the office, I was scheduled for several examinations in the weeks to come, including a biopsy of my prostate, an electrocardiogram, an echocardiogram, and several blood tests.

I arrived home feeling truly sorry for myself, with my vivid imagination working overtime on all sorts of thoughts, from cancer of the prostate to open-heart surgery of some sort to replace the old valve. Bette, who had come with me to the doctor's office, kept reassuring me that everything would be all right, but the man who tries to teach others how to deal with life, no matter how tough, was now having a difficult time dealing with his own personal problems. Then our mail lady arrived, and after Bette had sorted it all, she gave me the usual pile of fan letters, which I took into my studio.

After spending a couple of hours reading and replying to

the mail my own possible medical problems suddenly no longer seemed all that difficult.

September 19

Earlier today the weather reports on our radio indicated that there was a strong possibility of frost tonight, so I went out and picked our tomatoes, dividing them into two baskets—those that were ripe right now and those that still needed a week or so. Since Nana is back in the hospital and has been there for two weeks with terrible headaches, Bette is once again, like last year, making her daily trip to visit the old girl, also driving her dad, who seems to be getting weaker each day. So I just put the tomatoes out in the garage until we can figure out what to do with them or find someone who can use them.

The vegetable garden as a whole this year was a disaster. I spent so much time in the spring touring the country and promoting *The Twelfth Angel* that everything was planted much too late. Most of the corn never matured enough to even produce the head of a single ear and the weeds gradually took command. Only the tomatoes survived and produced despite all adversities.

Next year it will all be different. I realize that one has to be an eternal optimist to be a gardener, especially in New England, but when I'm close to nature, whether in my tiny garden or just strolling under the whispering pines, I always feel very near to the real truth. Pascal once wrote that "Nature imitates itself. A grain thrown into good ground brings forth fruit; a principle thrown into a good mind also brings forth fruit. Everything is created and conducted by the same Master, the root, the branch, the fruits, the principles, the consequences."

All of us, each day, are closer to the secret of living a good life, of conquering life, if you will, than any of us realize.

September 23

During our dozen or so years in Arizona it seemed as if I was constantly making transcontinental flights to deliver my speeches somewhere on the East Coast. Now that we are living in New Hampshire, Cheryl is booking more speeches in the far West than ever, or at least it seems that way.

Flew into California's Ontario airport last night and was driven to the Radisson Hotel in San Bernardino, where I am the closing "act" on an all-day program that includes such heavy hitters as Mark Victor Hansen, Brian Tracy, Dr. Laura Schlessinger, and Harvey McKay at the National Orange Show Fairgrounds. The ambitious program is titled "Master Your Future" and is being presented by the *Inland Empire Business Journal.*

Met with a gentleman this morning in my hotel room whose firm is in the process of acquiring the necessary dramatic rights to my all-time best-seller *The Greatest Salesman in the World* and its sequel, *The Greatest Salesman in the World, Part II, The End of the Story.* His plan is to combine the two books into a single dramatic stage presentation with actors and slides and special effects to dramatize the principles of success that were featured in both books. This "road show" of sorts would hopefully be featured at corporate conventions from coast to coast.

Although different publishers own all rights to those two books and can consummate a deal of any sort without consulting me, they still must share the financial reward from any such enterprise with me, and the gentleman came to call this morning seeking my reaction to his plans, even offering to take me on as a consultant when the production begins to take shape so that the finished product would be true to the two books.

Sounds interesting. I may decide to act as consultant, as requested. It would be the surest way I could amply protect the integrity of the fictitious little camel boy who changed my life forever.

September 24

As the final speaker on the program yesterday I was scheduled to go on at four-fifteen and talk for an hour. We had a great crowd of more than twenty-five hundred who truly seemed to be enjoying the all-day program that had commenced at 8:30 A.M.

However, one of our speakers got carried away with the sound of his own voice and he went so much over his allotted time that by the time I was introduced to the crowd, it was after five-thirty.

I walked out on the stage mentally prepared to see a gradual migration of humanity toward the exits. After all, they had been sitting and listening and applauding and taking notes, with only a few small breaks, for almost nine hours. Certainly their fannies were getting sore, and by now their stomachs were probably rumbling as we approached the dinner hour.

To my surprise I received a standing ovation as I walked out onto the stage and I saw only a small handful of individuals leave during my presentation!

Following another noisy standing ovation when I had finished, I was led to a table at the side of the huge auditorium where a long line was assembling for me to autograph books as well as pose for a picture with each of them. When I signed the last book for the final person in line, it was eleven P.M.! After such a long day those who were at the end of the line had waited more than an additional three hours for my autograph! I cannot think of a greater compliment.

September 25

Many times, while autographing books after a speech, I hear the same question again and again. "How old are you, Og?" And when I tell them that my next birthday will be my seventieth, they usually shake their head and say, "Wow!" or their eyes open wider in amazement.

Actually I never think about my age until I'm asked, because I don't consider myself "old." Not when I'm stacked against other senior citizens of history who were working miracles far beyond my years. Albert Schweitzer was still lovingly treating his patients when he was ninety; Grandma Moses was still painting at a hundred; Edison was still inventing things when he was eighty; Shaw was still writing plays after his ninetieth birthday; Frank Lloyd Wright worked until ninety; so did Picasso; Rubinstein received a standing ovation at Carnegie Hall when he was eighty-eight; and Monet was painting his famous water lilies well into his eighties.

Another question I hear often is "When are you going to retire?" I'm always so tempted to use Dr. Peale's great response: "I can't. There are still too many out there who need my help."

I'd like ten more years at least. Michelangelo was still building Saint Peter's in Rome when he died at eighty-nine. A lucky man!

September 27

I believe it was Longfellow who wrote that perseverance is a great element of success and that if one knocks long enough and loud enough at the gate, one is certain to wake up somebody.

Well, it has been a long time and I have done a lot of knocking since I was inducted into the International Speakers Hall of Fame, but now, at long last, another "hour" has befallen me. I have been invited to become part of a "wall of fame," which is actually a wall displaying photographs of great trainers and motivators that is located at Ed Morse University in Delray, Florida, the permanent training facility for all seventeen Ed Morse automotive dealerships.

As requested, I mailed them an eight-by-ten autographed photo this morning. Forgot to ask who the others were that adorned that special wall.

October 1

It is near noon, and I am still in my pajamas in my room at the San Francisco Marriott waiting for lunch to be delivered.

I arrived yesterday evening, and after unpacking I was escorted downstairs to the Sea Cliff/Buena Vista Ballroom, where I'll be speaking this evening. I met with the soundman and the woman in charge of lighting, checked out the lectern and its microphones, and returned to my room pleased with all arrangements. My audience will be approximately one thousand distributors of Matol Botanical International from nearly every state.

Awoke this morning feeling a little blue about some of the possible physical problems still ahead for me—until I sat down to breakfast and looked over this morning's *San Francisco Chronicle* and *USA Today.* Then I realized how small and insignificant my potential difficulties really are. A terrible earthquake, their most devastating in fifty years, struck southern India yesterday, burying entire villages and towns under many feet of earth and debris. It is feared that more than thirty thousand are dead in the rubble, and several hundred thousand are homeless.

Also, Erma Bombeck, who has already endured a mastectomy, has suffered complete kidney failure and is now hopefully awaiting a kidney transplant while she remains homebound and gives herself dialysis four times a day. All the while, this special, very brave lady is working on her next book and doing the laundry, grateful that she's still alive and telling the world that she feels "terrific"!

It always seems to come down to our attitude as the deciding factor between our suffering hell or enjoying heaven here on earth. Attitude is the prime motivating force for each of us, whether we conquer life or life conquers us. In a few hours, in the ballroom downstairs, I'll try once again to get that simple message across.

October 2

I am on United Airlines flight 940 on the first leg of my journey home.

The speech last night in San Francisco, judging from the crowd's reaction, was a success. I really do not understand what has been happening lately, but once again I received a standing ovation as I walked out onto the stage after being introduced by a Matol Botanical vice president.

The lighting in the ballroom was unusually dramatic, and I'm certain it contributed much to my words, while the audience seemed to be hanging on everything I said, with many taking copious notes.

I guess I walked off the stage, after my speech, around 8:45 P.M., to another standing ovation, and then I was led to a table where I signed and personalized the Heirloom Edition boxed leather sets of my three earliest best-sellers until well past eleven! Almost everyone whose books I signed also asked for a hug as we posed for pictures, and of course I had to stand for each photo, which is probably a great new method of exercising. I know that as soon as my head hit the pillow, I was sound asleep.

Tomorrow, Sunday, I can take it easy. However, on Monday I'll be heading for the airport again. I'm speaking to the Re-Max Real Estate people, in Merrillville, Indiana, on Tuesday morning. Then I fly on to Minneapolis for another speech on Thursday. A good time to be busy. No time to think of my own problems.

October 6

I am writing this as I sip my breakfast coffee in an unbelievable suite of rooms at the Radisson Star Plaza in Merrillville, Indiana. Besides an elegantly furnished sitting room with greenery and television, the huge separate bedroom has a king-size bed, a console television, *plus* a Jacuzzi! Then, just off the bedroom is a wood-paneled sauna and a regular bathroom with tub and shower! Tough to remain humble in such an environment!

All this luxury through the kindness of Re-Max of Northern Illinois. I was the closing speaker yesterday morning at the Midwest Conference of this fine group of realtors, and they were enthusiastic, attentive, and respectful. Great gathering!

I am flying on to Minneapolis this evening to speak to-morrow night in the Minneapolis Convention Center, on a program being presented by Peak Performers Network.

Following my speech yesterday, several realtors approached me as I was autographing books, with tears in their eyes, and thanked me. One gray-haired well-dressed gentleman said it was the most powerful speech he had ever heard. There is no greater reward than a kind word or two. Unless it is a much-needed helping hand. There is no better way to deal with our own life than to touch the life of another, with love and a smile.

October 8

It happened again last night at the Minneapolis Convention Center. Another miracle! A crowd exceeding two thousand actually stood to applaud as I walked out to the podium. Dan Brattland, whose company presented the motivational program, said that he had never witnessed such a welcome in all the programs he had ever produced. I didn't know how to respond to him.

Another thrill. I'm in the November issue of *Vanity Fair.* Three celebrities were asked what book they were currently reading, and singer Janet Jackson said *The Greatest Salesman in the World* by Og Mandino. She went on to give her highly complimentary opinion of the book. Very nice. *Reader's Digest* in September and now *Vanity Fair.* I wonder how Henry David Thoreau would handle this. Probably ignore it.

October 11

Last night the towering ninety-foot-plus ash tree with huge branches that lovingly embrace our old home cast off

almost its entire cloak of brown leaves. With the temperature dropping to its coldest night since last February, eighteen degrees above zero, Bette and I expected the old
tree's annual autumnal shower and we were not disappointed.

The deck behind our house was already blanketed by
several inches of tiny leaves when we awoke. We both
stood at our second-floor bedroom windows completely
enthralled by the steady downpour, each leaf spinning its
way downward as if it were the blades of a tiny helicopter.

The woods beyond were putting on another kind of
show, not visual but auditory. Acorns were crashing down
from oak trees in a crescendo of drumbeats as they
bounced off limbs of tree branches and then lower limbs
and lower until they finally landed on the pine-needle-
covered ground with a soft thud.

More than ninety percent of the ash's leaves have now
fallen in only a few hours, and I have just swept most of
them off the deck, creating a huge mound of leaves that
the landscape crew will have to deal with when they come
mowing our lawn later this week.

In just a little more than two months it will be Christmas. Bette and I are already making plans to spend a week
or so shopping in Phoenix in November.

Still have not heard from my publisher. They have not,
as yet, notified me that they have accepted *The Spellbinder*.
Hope they are satisfied, because this is certainly not the
season when I want to get involved in any more rewriting.

October 13

Had a biopsy of the prostate this afternoon, not one of
life's most pleasant experiences. The urologist who took
the biopsy also informed me that the reading from my

PSA blood test had just come back and was high enough to cause concern. The PSA measures something in the blood called prostate-specific antigen, which increases when there is a tumor present, a red flag that cancer may be lurking. Of course, the PSA count increases in any enlarged prostate, whether it is cancerous or not, and although it is a marvelously effective warning alert, a test that every male over forty should take at least yearly, it still does not provide the final answer as to whether one has cancer of the prostate or not. Only a biopsy will do that.

We will learn the results of the biopsy next week. In the meantime I am trying very hard to keep my mind off all the possible dire consequences that might affect my future and my life. If it is determined that I do have cancer, I've been told there are two ways of treating it—through radiation or a complete removal of the prostate, which can be risky. Either would put me on the sidelines for about eight weeks, since the radiation treatments are daily for that length of time and the operation would require six to eight weeks of recovery. The radiation treatments would probably also leave me bald, which I guess wouldn't be that much of a loss, but I now know that the only certain method of getting rid of all the cancer is to get rid of the prostate—assuming the problem has not spread to other areas.

Bette and I, when we returned home, checked our calendars. After Christmas I don't have my next speech booked until February 24th, in San Juan, Puerto Rico, so if I need an operation and have it right after Christmas, I should still be ready to walk out on the stage by late February. And that way, waiting until after Christmas, we would not have fouled up Christmas for our kids and grandchildren.

I truly believe I am married to the gutsiest girl in the world. Worried about her mom and dad as she tries to prepare them for their forthcoming move into the Odd Fellows Nursing Home in Concord, she now has the additional load of my problems to weigh her down. And yet she keeps smiling, keeps doing her thing, and has even begun teaching sewing classes locally. Also, she is making plans for Christmas. What a great lady!

October 20

Dr. Fuselier just phoned with the results of the prostate biopsy. Not good. Apparently I do have a higher-grade tumor of the prostate, and the concern now is whether or not the cancer has spread to the pelvis.

I have been scheduled for a bone scan on Friday to learn if the cancer has traveled beyond the prostate. If it hasn't, we can tackle it with an operation or radiation. If it has spread outside the prostate, we have a major problem and will not be able to do much except try to treat it with chemo or hormonal therapy. And . . . pray a lot.

I will know on late Friday afternoon, two days from now, what the results are. In the meantime I am catching up on my mail and doing some Christmas shopping with Bette.

For many years I have bragged that I've never missed a speaking engagement for any reason. What we learn Friday may cause me to cancel the remainder of the year's schedule, and if I am hospitalized, it will play havoc with our Christmas, the most important day of the year in our home. When I told Dr. Fuselier that I couldn't possibly cancel my speech scheduled in Houston on October 28th and the one in Salt Lake City on October 30th, he asked, as if he were talking to a child, if I considered those two speeches worth my life. If I have hopes of continuing my career, and I certainly do, then I must deal with the enemy soon, he reminded me.

Strange that when I decided to keep a journal for publication, nearly four years ago, I suggested to my publisher that we title it "How to Conquer Life."

October 21

Spoke to both my editor and her boss at Fawcett several days ago and learned that although they both liked *The Spellbinder*, they thought I had spent too much time and effort in the early chapters dealing with the many facets of the speaking profession, its challenges, and the various types of individuals who make a living behind a lectern.

And so, with red pen in hand, I have been conducting painful surgery on my latest offspring and have managed to remove a total of 524 lines, or twenty-one pages, from the first seven chapters. I'll have my friend Walt retype the shortened version and send it off as soon as possible. We are also making a slight change in the book's title. Our pride and joy will henceforth be called *The Spellbinder's Gift*.

October 22

Drank some vile stuff last evening that I was told would commence the process of causing my insides to glow. Drank more of the same this morning before Bette drove me to the hospital. Had a CAT scan and received an injection and then was told to return in three hours for the bone scan, which I did shortly after noon. Then Bette and I went to Friendly's for lunch, and by the time we returned home, there was a message from Dr. Fuselier on the answering machine that both scans indicated no spread of cancer beyond the prostate. What an insane feeling! I have cancer, but now I know that I've got at least a fighting chance to lick it. What's that old saying about feeling sorry for myself because I had no shoes until I met a man who had no feet?

Dr. Fuselier, when I phoned him, told me that he had set up another meeting with the urologist, Dr. Murata, on Monday, October 25th, but that he now saw no reason why I couldn't fulfill my speaking engagements in Houston on October 28th and Salt Lake City on October 30th, and that is exactly what I am going to do. I told him that both Bette and I had decided on surgery rather than radiation since that was the avenue that presented the best opportunity of removing all the cancer. The prostate was going to be completely removed from my body, dangerous as that might be. He agreed with our decision and said he doubted that arrangements could be made for my hospitalization and operation for at least a week but he would get right on it.

After I hung up, Bette and I decided that we would pack a small suitcase in the morning, Saturday, and get out of the house. The last thing the two of us were about to do was to sit and suck our thumbs and bow our heads in self-pity. There is a new casino called the Foxwoods that was recently opened on an Indian reservation in the southern part of Connecticut, probably a four-hour drive for us. I think we'll just leave the real world behind for a day.

October 24

A dear friend, Jim Adams, came to our rescue yesterday morning. Bette had packed us for a two-day journey, but I failed miserably in trying to get us a room reservation anywhere within fifty miles of the Foxwoods Casino. We had just about decided to head north into Maine for some factory-outlet shopping when Jim, who had called us earlier to learn of my health condition, phoned us back to tell us that he had made a reservation for us at the Saybrook Point Inn, an hour or so drive beyond the casino.

This was a typical and enchanting New England autumn day, and the drive through oak and maple country, in all its colors, was like drifting through many acres of heaven. The town of Old Saybrook had been settled by Indians near a large river that flowed into what is now Long Island Sound, and the Inn was a lovely and cozy spot. Since it was Saturday, the casino was jam-packed with humanity by the time we arrived. We actually had to stand in line and wait in order to get to play any of their hundreds of slot machines in what is now being called the largest casino in the Western Hemisphere.

Early this morning we drove home, relaxed and ready to deal with my problems. The first one may be tomorrow, when we meet with the urologist to plan our next step.

October 25

The die has been cast. In our meeting with Dr. Murata, after listening to him carefully review our various options, we informed him that I had definitely selected surgery. I wanted the prostate removed, before the cancer spread, so that I could get on with my life.

And so, on November 1st, I shall go to the Cheshire Medical Center in Keene for a chest X ray, blood tests, and Lord knows what else, and at that time I'll be told when they want me to check in on the following day, November 2nd, for my operation.

Recovery time for such an operation, I've been told, is

approximately two months, so I'm going to notify the Church of Today, in Warren, Michigan, that regretfully this will be the first year in fifteen that I will not be able to visit with the congregation on the first Sunday in December. I'll also phone my old friend John Hammond, president of the American Motivational Association, and tell him that I will not be able to appear on the program with him in Anaheim on December 7th. That will be the first booked speech I have missed, for any reason, in more than twenty-five years of appearances! Strange that it should be on John's program, since the very first speech I ever made, back in 1968, was for John's company. Round and round we go . . .

I am working very hard at searching for the good in what is ahead for me. I realize that if the cancer had not been discovered and if we didn't remove the prostate, my life would be considerably shortened. A wise old American clergyman, John Moore, once wrote, "The real test in golf and in life is not in keeping out of the rough but in getting out after we are in."

We have talked with both our sons about the forthcoming operation. Dana received the news very quietly, and Matt replied that he thought I had made the right choice.

October 29

I am relaxing in a penthouse suite of the Westchase Hilton in Houston, sipping my second cup of coffee after a great breakfast. It is raining and a light fog hovers over one of my favorite cities.

Last night I addressed a capacity crowd at the Unity Church of Christianity for my friend of many years, Reverend Howard Caesar. Also on the program was another dear friend, Jan Frichot, from Shawnee, Oklahoma, who opened the program with a lovely song, "Dream On," which she announced that she was dedicating to me.

It was another warm and loving audience, thank God, with standing ovations before and after my speech. Although I hadn't planned to do it, at the close of my talk I told the group, as my voice broke several times, that I would be going into the hospital for some heavy-duty surgery next Tuesday and I asked them if they would please say a little prayer for the old man. Following my speech Jan closed the program with what she said was everyone's prayer for me as she sang—what else?—"Amazing Grace."

This afternoon I'll be flying into Salt Lake City for my speech in the morning to representatives of the NU SKIN Corporation. I understand that my name does not appear on any of their national-convention promotional materials and that my spot on the program is being billed as a "surprise attraction." George Bush and Paul Harvey are also on the program. Good competition.

Just spoke to Bette on the phone. She has made all arrangements with the hospital for my examinations next Monday and then we'll be told when they want me on the following day. I am working very hard at restraining my vivid imagination with all its corroding anxieties and trying to picture instead how much healthier I will be after Dr. Murata lays down his instruments and removes his rubber gloves.

October 31

Yesterday morning there were more than seven thousand NU SKIN representatives from around the world filling the massive Accord Arena in the Salt Palace Convention Center, Salt Lake City, when I walked out on stage.

What a wonderful audience! I'm sure that speakers can

sense the love and respect that is occasionally reflected in people's faces and react accordingly. I believe I did a good job, and toward the end of my talk, as I had done in Houston at the Unity Church, I told the crowd that I was going in for some serious surgery in a couple of days and asked for their prayers. When I did, something very magical seemed to happen in the huge auditorium. Suddenly there was a stillness that was almost frightening—as if everyone were sitting motionless and holding his or her breath. It was a very special moment for me.

When Bette picked me up at the airport, it was snowing—snowing in October! There were at least a couple of inches on the ground by the time we arrived home. Can Christmas be far behind?

Today I managed to catch up on my mail and most of my phone calls. Tomorrow, early, Bette will drive me to the Cheshire Medical Center in Keene for a chest X ray, EKG, and blood work. On the following morning I will check in and, hopefully, have all of my prostate, with its high-grade malignancy, removed. My life, at least for a while, will be controlled by others, and it's a helpless feeling I have never enjoyed. I should know what to do by now when these rare occasions arise in my life. Pray.

November 1

All the various tests seemed to go well at the hospital this morning. I am scheduled to be back there for the real thing tomorrow at seven-thirty in the morning.

Bette has been very quiet all day. I hug her at every opportunity and she forces a smile, but I know she's worried about me. The next few days will probably be a lot tougher on her than on me.

December 14

Forty-two days—forty-two days that were filled with fear and doubt and prayers and tears have passed since my previous journal entry!

Montaigne, the great sixteenth-century French essayist, once wrote, "He who would teach men how to die, should, at the same time, teach them how to live."

When one reverses that great truth, it is equally powerful. In order to teach others how to live, one must learn how to die, and I've had a few lessons on that during the past six weeks!

My memory, especially of those early hospital days in November when death was my unexpected companion, is extremely foggy, primarily induced, I am sure, by drugs prescribed to help me forget all that I had endured while nurses and physicians struggled bravely to save the old boy's life. Fortunately Bette made daily entries in a notebook, covering those dark days, and I am now relying on them heavily to bring my life up-to-date.

Even if I could, I would not enter here a day-by-day or hour-by-hour "overdramatized" report of my close encounters with eternity. I have only been home four days as I write these words and I still tire easily. When I was admitted to the hospital, I weighed 207 pounds. This morning my weight is 166 pounds! Even striking these keys on my old IBM Selectric requires all my effort, but it is time that I get on with my life, and the best way to do that is to deal with the past and put it all to rest.

On November 2nd, Bette and I arose at 5:30 A.M. and drove to the Cheshire Medical Center in Keene. I remember going into "pre-op," giving Bette my clothes plus a kiss after changing into that strange hospital gown, before walking down the hall toward the operating room, trying very hard to keep a smile on my face. Bette returned to the lobby after being told that the prostate operation would take three or four hours. One of the nurses said that in this instance "longer is better." Shortly after noon Dr. Murata reported to Bette that it had been a clean operation, the lymph nodes had come back negative, reconstruction had gone well, and she should be able to see me in about two hours. I do not recall her visit. Bette later said that when she eventually returned home, the phone was ringing constantly and continued to ring well into the night. She said she couldn't believe the number of people who called and said they were praying for Og. She hoped someone was listening.

On the following day we received frightening news. A postoperative EKG disclosed that I had suffered a heart attack while my prostate was being removed! More tests were run and they indicated that I was continuing to have small heart attacks. Dr. Wiese, a cardiologist, called for more tests, concerned, as he told Bette, that what I was experiencing was just the tip of the iceberg, and yet time was needed for the prostate operation to heal before they could deal with my heart problems, whatever they were.

More tests disclosed that we could not wait very long. The doctors discovered that I had a blocked artery and a dysfunctional heart valve and that if we didn't act quickly, my problem would be fatal. I talked with both my sons in Arizona before I was wheeled out to an ambulance, with wires and tubes protruding from several places in my body, and rushed to the Dartmouth-Hitchcock Hospital in Lebanon, New Hampshire—for heart surgery. In a long meeting with Dr. Wiese, both Bette and I had told him that if I couldn't have the same quality of life I had enjoyed in the past, we would prefer that he just give me something to ease my pain and allow me to die quietly. I did not want to live for years as a vegetable, squatting helplessly all day in some wheelchair while others tended to my needs.

At this point all my charts indicated that I was in grave danger. I was having trouble with the prostate catheter, my kidneys had all but shut down, my body was slowly filling with fluid, and I continued to have heart attacks. Now it was estimated that I had approximately thirty-six hours of life remaining unless a miracle occurred or action was taken swiftly.

The greatest fear was that I might have a major heart attack before anything could be done, and the damage to the heart might be fatal. We made another decision. Despite the fact that my prostate operation site was still bleeding, my heart had to be repaired immediately, or it would be too late. I signed two permission slips—one for a heart bypass and one for the replacement of my right aortic valve.

Meanwhile the urology team was moving at a frantic pace. They were working swiftly to reposition the catheter implanted during my prostate operation as well as trying desperately to stop the internal bleeding.

For the valve replacement I was given a choice of one made from pig tissue or a mechanical valve. Since I had been told that the pig-tissue valve would probably have to be replaced in five years or so, I opted for the mechanical one. I didn't think I wanted my chest sawed open more than once during the rest of my life.

Dr. Charles Marrin, one of the finest cardiac surgeons in New England, who was literally going to have my heart in his hands, dropped in to explain all the risks we faced. His major concern was about the possibility of severe bleeding and that I might continue to lose blood faster than it could be replaced. However, we had to risk it. The clock was ticking.

I don't recall any of this, but Bette tells me that at this point I asked everyone to kindly leave the room. I wanted a few precious moments alone with my son, Matt, and Bette, and she tells me that we were all trying very hard to be courageous for the others. I guess I began rambling on about this unfinished journal, my royalty statements, and where other files of importance had been left, but they told me not to worry and that I could deal with everything when I got home. Positive mental attitudes in action! Another kiss and hug from Bette and Matt and then the staff returned and resumed their preparations. The anesthesiologist came in with his list of risks, and I signed the permit slip. Dr. Marrin looked in once again to tell us that the operation would take about six hours, if all went well. Commencement of the heart surgery was delayed, however, until 7:30 P.M. since the urology people had found it necessary to insert a second catheter through my prostate incision to facilitate the draining. There was also another major attempt made to stop the internal bleeding that still concerned everyone.

At around 11:00 P.M. Dr. Marrin entered the room where Bette and Matt were waiting and told them that I was being "closed up." The bypass and valve replacement, he said, had gone very well. I had received an amazingly large amount of blood, four units, during surgery and continued to receive more since the prostate operation site was also still bleeding. All in all, Dr. Marrin sounded very optimistic and told Bette and Matt that they could look in on me in ninety minutes. Bette's notes state that my color was good and I was sleeping soundly, although on a respirator with 100 percent oxygen output, plus I was receiving a transfusion and lying under a warming blanket. Matt, Bette told me later, sighed and said he would believe Dad was truly okay when he got him on the golf course next spring. To perform the heart operation, with its bypass plus valve replacement, my heart had actually been stopped and then "kick-started" again. It is almost impossible to grasp the fact that I was really "dead" for several hours while the heart was being repaired. Sorry, I heard no angels nor did I see· any white lights.

The following ten days or so were a living hell. With respirator tubes down my throat I was unable to converse with anyone, plus my kidneys were not functioning well, which concerned the doctors a great deal. Dialysis was now a possibility, but the danger of attaching that machine to remove the uric acid and other foreign matter from the circulating blood was that the machine might become a permanent part of my life, which I certainly didn't want. Bette told me that when my oldest son, Dana, arrived from Arizona I held his hand tightly, squeezing hard to let him know I knew he was with me.

Twenty-four hours later my oxygen requirements were down to sixty percent and all other signs were positive. Although I still had at least six tubes protruding from my body, my color remained good and everyone was now very positive. The respirator tube was finally removed from my throat, to be replaced by an oxygen mask, which I hated. Kept pulling it off and the nurses patiently but angrily kept replacing it. Oxygen requirements then dropped to forty percent, and there was no more talk of dialysis. Thank God!

My voice sounded terrible. Bette's notes indicate that I was very worried about my speaking career until we were assured by a nurse that my condition was perfectly normal and that I would sound a little better each day. Yes, I hope to be back on the platform again. The sooner the better. Retirement or a rocking chair will never be on my schedule.

Lori brought my new grandson, Will, to see me. Bette said there was a big smile on my face when I saw the little guy. However, I was still having great difficulty with the thought process. I could identify everyone but I kept talking about my briefcase and my airline tickets. I was also concerned about my wristwatch and my wallet, positive that I had lost them somewhere, although Bette kept assuring me that they were safely at home.

Two days later I was actually out of bed and sitting in a chair. Tiring but necessary in the slow process of regaining my strength. Still had several tubes protruding from my body, but every day or so another one disappeared. Finally I was transferred to a room in the Intermediate Cardiac Care Unit, a lovely room with a magnificent view of the nearby mountains. Still, for days after my move I gave the hospital staff a difficult time, even requiring a "sitter" for a while to prevent me from pulling on my tubes and getting out of bed, once "to catch a plane." At that point my speech was still slurred, all four bed rails were pulled up to slow down my "escapes," and I still had two tubes in me.

Three days later my heart monitor was removed and I had a milk shake. Another step closer to the good life. That same afternoon, while I was having dinner in bed, Bette removed a notepad from her purse to read some of the names of friends who had sent their love in words or flowers, such as Taylor Dayne, Cindy Landon, W. Clement Stone, Willie Nelson, Michael Jackson, Harvey Mackay, Pierre O'Rourke, Jim Tunney, Sheila and Bill Bethel, Larry Gatlin, Paul Harvey, my two wonderful agents, Cheryl Miller and Alice Martell, John Hammond, and my editor, Susan Randol. Finally I was also taken off morphine and so was able to talk with my lady intelligently for the first time in weeks.

A few days later I was transferred to the Cheshire Medical Center in Keene for rehabilitation. For two weeks I then took exercise instructions from their people as if I were a mindless zombie. I skipped rope, I rode the stationary bicycle, I walked and walked and walked. Finally, on December 10th, Bette took me home. Borrowing from one of my all-time favorite movies, *Field of Dreams*, as we turned on our dirt road and approached our old farmhouse, I turned to Bette and asked, "Is this heaven?"

She nodded, again and again, as the tears ran down her cheeks.

December 16

Piled high in my studio is six weeks of mail. The two sofas are filled to capacity, and there are several mounds of envelopes on the floor, each at least three feet high and just as wide!

I have always prided myself on answering every letter written to me, but I have decided that there is absolutely no way that I can respond to all the get-well cards I have received.

Bette and I opened several hundred envelopes this morning containing cards from strangers with handwritten messages of love and encouragement. So many touching gestures from people who really care! We spent most of this day packing the envelopes into cartons to store. There is no way we would ever throw away such a wonderful gift from so many. As near as I can tell, I actually received more than 2,700 loving cards from NU SKIN people who heard me ask for their prayers in Salt Lake City in early November! I'm going to write an open letter of "thank you" to all of them and send it to their president, Blake Roney, with a request that it please be printed in their monthly magazine.

I also received a very special gift from the wonderful congregation of the Church of Today in Warren, Michigan. On the face of a large, folded get-well card that measured approximately 2 by 3 feet, were the words "We believe that the thoughts of those who love you can make a difference"—hand painted. When I opened this huge card, I saw that it contained hundreds upon hundreds of signatures, each with a message wishing me a speedy recovery! The back side contained hundreds more. Never have seen anything quite like it, and I have lovingly placed it on the floor near my studio fireplace, where it will remain, to cheer me up, as long as I live.

December 19

A week ago today I passed a big milestone in my life—my seventieth birthday! Despite all the difficult and traumatic moments of recent months I truly never lost faith that I would make it. Many times in the past few years I have said that the ten years between seventy and eighty would be good years, and now that I have a rebuilt heart and that deadly prostate is gone, I have no doubt that I'll enjoy those years.

Bette held off my birthday celebration until today so that our youngest son, Matt, his pretty wife, Lori, and new young son, Will, who arrived today to spend Christmas with us, could also join in the celebration. Yes, there were a few tears when I blew out the candles on my cake.

The nineteenth-century American theologian Tyran Edwards once wrote, "Some men are born old and some never seem so. If we keep well and cheerful we are always young, and at last die in youth, even when years would count us old."

December 21

Each day, as I get stronger, my appetite also improves and I am having a difficult time trying to adjust to my new diet that will lower my cholesterol so that no more arteries clog up, endangering my life again. With all the knowledge that we now have, with all the discoveries we have made in the past decade or so, it is amazing that so many continue to commit suicide daily through the food we eat.

More than 1.5 million of us have heart attacks each year and almost half a million will die—most before they ever reach a hospital. Each year more than 350,000 of us have coronary-bypass graft surgery which, in almost all cases, we have brought on ourselves because of our terrible eating habits.

I love cheese, eggs, and ice cream. I no longer eat any of them. In place of cheese I now eat Formagg, a cholesterol-, butterfat-, and lactose-free cheese alternative that tastes great; in place of the eggs I always enjoyed I now eat Egg Beaters, which are cholesterol- and fat-free and extremely low in sodium, and instead of my most favorite food in the entire world, ice cream of any flavor, I now eat a frozen yogurt, which tastes almost as great, is free of all fat and cholesterol, and is also low on sodium. (Fortunately I stopped smoking several years ago, so that's a deadly habit I don't have to work on.)

There is so much great literature out there on how to diet safely and sanely that there really is little excuse for any of us to have to suffer through the nightmare of open-heart surgery when we can prevent it with a little common sense at the table. In place of regular milk, drink skim (you'll get used to it); in place of a T-bone or Porter-house steak, have a lean piece of top round or top sirloin; in place of tuna or salmon in oil, buy the cans packed in water; in place of a fat, juicy hamburger, loaded with cholesterol and sodium, eat a grilled chicken sandwich.

A sane diet plus thirty minutes of daily exercise, even if it's just walking, will add many years to our life. As usual, it is up to us. We decide our own destiny. We always do.

December 26

Yesterday was Christmas. Although it was the first in all our married years when I hadn't put up the tree with all its trimmings, I still savored every moment of that special day. Bette, with all her concerns and time spent caring for me, had still managed to Christmas shop and wrap scores of presents for everyone, as always, and our old friend, Edd Houghton, came over and helped her put up and decorate the tree so that it was already glowing in our living room on the day that I came home from the hospital.

Fortunately I had done some Christmas shopping also, long before my health problems had surfaced, and so as usual everyone made out quite well, and our newest grandson, Will, now a year and a month old, truly enjoyed all his new toys.

Every precious hour of yesterday was very special to me. Bette apologized to everyone, again and again, for not baking any Christmas cookies as she has always done, but there just had not been enough hours in the days for her to accomplish any more than she had.

For almost thirty years I have saved thousands of quotations that have touched my heart, on many subjects, and I am constantly amazed at all the words of love and reflection that Charles Dickens wrote, through the years, regarding the Christmas holiday. Since I knew full well that I was enjoying this Christmas through what had seemed to me to be several miracles, another of Dickens's Christmas gems expresses so well how I felt all day yesterday.

From the pen of the brilliant genius and creator of Scrooge, Marley's Ghost, and Tiny Tim came these words:

> We write now, many miles distant from the spot at which, year after year, we met on that day, a merry and joyous circle. Many of the hearts that throbbed so gaily then, have ceased to beat; many of the looks that shone so brightly then, have ceased to glow; the hands we grasped, have grown cold; the eyes we sought, have hid their luster in the grave; and yet the old house, the room, the merry voices and smiling faces, the jest, the laugh, the most minute and trivial circumstance connected with those happy meetings, crowd upon our mind at each recurrence of the season, as if the last assemblage had been but yesterday.

And I, of course, had received the greatest present of all—the gift of my life. Thank you, God.

1994

*For those who will fight bravely and not yield, there is trium-
phant victory over all the
dark things of life.*

James L. Allen

January 2

A sad day. I have just learned that my dear friend Norman Vincent Peale passed away in his sleep on Christmas Eve. I'm sure he already has the angels thinking positively as they flit about their daily activities.

January 10

This morning I attended my first cardiac rehabilitation session at the Concord Hospital. To my great surprise I enjoyed it. For the next eight weeks, on Monday, Wednesday, and Friday, I'll be attending lectures covering a wide range of subjects, from nutrition to exercise. These will be followed by an hour of five- to ten-minute sessions walking a treadmill, riding a stationary bicycle, working a rowing machine and an arm exerciser, as well as doing a series of exercises, all watched over constantly by a registered therapist, Jean Kane, and also Beverly Aubert, the hospital's cardiac rehabilitation director. While all this activity is taking place in a bright and colorful gymnasium, to the accompaniment of swing and jazz recordings from the 1940s, I'll be wearing a portable heart monitor so that my heart rate can be watched carefully throughout the various physical activities.

It is almost an hour's drive, both ways, to and from the Concord Hospital, and Bette, bless her, is still functioning as my chauffeur. I have not yet received permission from my doctor to get behind the wheel, and I feel quite helpless and dependent, but this morning, as I was exerting myself on the various exercise machines, I began to feel as if I were finally on that yellow-brick road toward full recovery, especially when comparing what I was doing to some of the fifteen or so other participants in the session, each of whom, like myself, had survived heart surgery of one kind or another.

An amazing fact I learned today was that heart disease is also the number-one killer of women in our nation. I had thought it was almost exclusively a man's disease, but, according to the American Heart Association, almost a quarter of a million women die of heart disease every year, making it truly "an equal-opportunity killer."

I never concerned myself very much about my diet before, but now the words *sodium, cholesterol,* and *fat* are bright red danger flags, and both Bette and I spend a good deal of time in grocery stores studying the nutrition information on food packages. I've always been pretty heavy-handed with the saltshaker, and it is no longer even on the table while we eat, not to mention a long list of my favorite foods that are now forbidden, such as potato chips, cheese, salted crackers, cold cuts, hot dogs, bacon, and canned soups. However, doing without any and all of them is not that difficult now that I finally realize how easy it is for any of us to shorten our lives through ignorance or carelessness.

January 14

Yesterday afternoon, after the snow had stopped, we tossed our packed suitcase into the trunk of Bette's Town Car and drove northeast across the state of New Hampshire to Lebanon and the Dartmouth-Hitchcock Medical Center, scene of my open-heart surgery in November. We checked into the Radisson Hotel and after breakfast this morning drove to the hospital for my scheduled examination by Dr. Marrin, who had performed the major surgery on my heart.

Following an electrocardiogram and an X ray I waited in a small room, shivering in that silly nightie hospitals make one wear, until Dr. Marrin arrived carrying my fat file folder. His eyes opened wide as he came through the door and exclaimed, "You look great!"

While he was examining me, he inquired as to whether I had any pains and if so where, and I replied that the only time I felt anything was when I coughed or sneezed and the chest he had cut open reacted a little, but outside of that I felt great. He shook his head, looking very pleased, and suggested that I should have a general heart checkup yearly. I asked if he would do it and he said he would.

As we were parting, I grasped his hand and I'm sure my voice broke a little when I said, "Doc, I thank you for everything. You saved my life."

He smiled and replied, "My pleasure, Og."

January 16

Usually the best decisions that Bette and I have made have been spur-of-the-moment things, including even the buying of houses, and this morning while having breakfast we both decided that we felt like going on a cruise. We phoned Nancy McLaren, our travel agent, and are now booked on the *Royal Princess* in mid-April for an eighteen-day junket to Europe including Ponta Delgada, Portugal; Cork, Ireland; Amsterdam; Brussels; Paris; and London. When the cruise terminates in London, we will spend a couple of days seeing a play or two, sight-seeing, and shopping before we fly home.

January 18

The thought and the words are certainly older than Solomon's utterances, but it is absolutely amazing how many of the good things in our life we take for granted until we no longer have them.

This morning I drove an automobile for the first time in almost three months when I climbed up on the seat of our Jeep Grand Wagoneer and drove downtown to get a much-needed haircut. What a thrill! I was more than a little nervous as I backed down the driveway.

My return to the world of automotive transportation stirred up many memories, taking me back even to that day more than fifty years ago when I received my driver's license after I was certain I had fouled up the driving test. I remembered the days when my son, Matt, not much more than five, would sit on the front steps of our first home in Arlington Heights, Illinois, waiting for his daddy to come home from work. When I would pull into the driveway, he'd come dashing across the front lawn and wait, impatiently, until I stopped the car, opened the door, and lifted him onto my lap. Then I would hold my hands high off the steering wheel as I gently applied pressure on the accelerator while Matt, gripping the steering wheel tightly and proudly, guided the car into the garage. Memories.

It felt good to be behind the wheel again. Another step toward full recovery.

January 19

The sight that greeted our eyes when we awoke this morning was the perfect setting for a children's fairy story. Because of a combination of snow and rain, last night the snow froze as it landed on the branches of pine and oak and birch trees so that everything is now glistening brightly in the morning sun. Since the temperature is below freezing, it appears that we will have this scene, which seems to be taken directly from the movie *Dr. Zhivago*, for many hours.

We have a three-tree clump of birches on our front lawn that were planted soon after we moved in. They reach perhaps twenty feet into the heavens, and this ice storm weighted down the treetops so much that all three of the pliable trees leaned over and buried their heads in the snow. Bette, fearing they might snap in the cold, put on her deep boots and walked out to rescue them, the snow halfway up her thighs with each step. One by one she tugged at the tree limbs until they escaped from the snow and slowly reached toward heaven again.

This must be a terribly difficult winter for the birds and squirrels. Every time it snows, I go out and clear the feeding area again so that the little guys can return. Word must be getting around, because we are beginning to get quite a crowd during most of the daylight hours.

January 24

There is a large sign hanging on one of the walls of the Concord Hospital Rehab gymnasium that reads:

Relative Perceived Exertion

7–8	*Very, very easy*
9–10	*Very easy*
11–12	*Fairly easy*
13–14	*Moderately hard*
15–16	*Hard*
17–18	*Very hard*
19	*Extremely hard*

After we have labored on the treadmill, which is speeded up a little more each day while the incline is made a little steeper, Jean, our therapist, will always come over and ask how much effort was expended. After glancing at the board, we will reply with a number indicating whether our effort was "fairly easy" or "very hard" or whatever, which she enters on our record.

Since I have spent so much of my life speaking and writing about the subject of success, the Relative Perceived Exertion chart fascinates me. I've been wondering how we would respond if a Saint Peter–like figure approached us with a golden clipboard and asked us each to give a rating on how much effort we believe we had exerted in our daily lives. How many could honestly say that they had tried "very hard" to achieve a better life compared with those who had chosen to travel at a much slower pace with little challenge or "steepness of incline" and yet wondered why their lives were filled with failure and tears. So many of us forget that the shaping of our destiny is our own work. It is a thing of pride and accomplishment or of shame and defeat, as we ourselves make it.

January 28

We decided not to risk driving to Concord for my rehab session after we looked out our bedroom windows this morning. The seventh major snowstorm in January commenced last night, and then, although the temperature was still below freezing, the snow turned to rain. Every street this morning is a skating rink, and last night, according to this morning's paper, the temperature in Concord was a record-breaking twenty-seven degrees below zero.

I plan to spend this day in my studio catching up on an "in"-box full of mail.

February 27

Since my first scheduled speech is on March 7th, we couldn't put off any longer the painful task of trying on some of my dress clothes to see if anything would fit after the weight loss from my operations. I weighed only 165 pounds or so when I came home from the hospital, but now that my appetite is back, I'm weighing in these mornings at 182 pounds, and I have decided that will be my limit. No more evening snacks.

Still, most of the dress suits, sports jackets, and slacks purchased in the past year or so were for when I weighed around 205 pounds, so the trying on of my favorite suits and sports jackets was an awful experience. The most recently purchased Hart Schaffner & Marx suits and other clothing were just too large. There were several inches to spare at the waistline, and the jackets were so huge on my new body that they looked comical.

Fortunately Bette had saved some of my clothes from several years ago, including a couple of old suits, four sports jackets, and probably half a dozen pairs of slacks, but by the time I had finished trying on my entire wardrobe, we both decided that I needed some new clothes, and soon.

I've not given a speech since early November of last year, so I've been going over my notes, time and time again, as if I were some rookie preparing for his first ordeal on the platform.

March 5

For years I had been proudly boasting that I have never missed a speaking engagement for any reason—and then my open-heart surgery took care of that quarter-century record. I had been originally scheduled to speak for my old friend John Hammond and his American Motivational Association in Buena Park, California, on December 7th. Bette and I are flying west, early tomorrow morning, so that on March 7th I can finally fulfill the engagement. Bette is coming with me, not to attend to my needs, she reminds me, but to check out my performance on the platform. If she decides that the past four months of operations and therapy have taken too much out of the old man, so that his delivery doesn't, as she put it, "raise the dead," then she is going to suggest that I "retire" while I'm ahead. Ha!

For several days now I have been nervously thinking about the speech, with feelings I haven't had for a lot of years. I'm not sure that it is stage fright, but I've been reviewing my speech notes often, even speaking some sections aloud in order to revive that old feeling of confidence. It has been a long road from early November, and Dr. Fuselier, yesterday in a checkup exam, reminded me once again what a very sick man I was only a few months ago.

Went to our bank this morning and put the file folders containing all these journal entries of the past four years into our safe-deposit box, since we'll be gone for a week. Just in case, perish the thought, our old farm burns down, I'll still have this journal. Unlike a fictional piece, which could probably be rewritten, there is no way I could ever reconstruct all these entries.

On the morning following the speech Bette and I will be flying to Las Vegas, where we will spend four days at Caesar's Palace, just relaxing, shopping, and seeing a show or two—activities all designed to replace work and worry with something called "sacred idleness." We're ready.

March 8

Worrying about impending events in our lives can become a terrible habit that will cast a pall over every day. My old friend Reverend Bob Schuler says that if we played the piano as frequently as we worried, we would all be first-class piano players.

In early January of this year I wrote an open letter to all those who had purchased tickets to hear me speak in December, apologizing for not being able to appear and informing them that, God willing, I would see them all in March. The speech was scheduled for the large ballroom in the Sequoia Conference Center in Buena Park, California, and when John Hammond introduced me last night, the huge audience stood and applauded as I walked to the microphone. As I began to speak, someone shouted, "Welcome back!" and I just turned away from the lectern, trying to collect my thoughts.

Afterward Bette gave me a huge hug and said, "You passed the test. You can keep on working." Maxine McIntyre, who had preceded me on the platform, approached me when it was all over and said softly, "In all my years of speaking I have never before seen a speaker get a standing ovation before he or she said a single word. Does this happen to you often?"

I just grinned and said, "For the last couple of years."

Later that evening, back in our hotel room, Bette turned toward me and asked, "What are you thinking about? I haven't seen you this quiet for a long time."

I kissed her forehead and replied, "I've been thinking of all those days and nights in my hospital beds, with tubes and wires stuck into my body, when the events of tonight were an absolutely impossible dream."

"Good material for a book." She smiled as she patted my shoulders.

March 18

It is early evening and I am waiting for room service to deliver dinner to my room here in Nashville's Opryland Hotel. Actually the word *hotel* does not begin to describe this huge complex with its more than a dozen restaurants, shops, and boutiques everywhere plus two thousand rooms and new construction under way to add another thousand in 1996.

A petite blond chauffeur picked me up at the airport and delivered me to Opryland in her stretch Lincoln Town Car. Soon after I had checked into my room, I was brought to the Jefferson Ballroom, at my request, so that I could check the lectern and sound equipment. Tomorrow at nine in the morning I am keynoting the annual international convention of the TCBY Corporation.

Early in January, when my future was still in doubt, Cheryl had phoned to tell me that TCBY's president,

Charles Cocotas, had been in the NU SKIN audience at the Salt Palace in Salt Lake City when I had told that huge crowd that three days later I was going into the hospital for some heavy-duty surgery (at that time I had no idea how "heavy-duty") and asked them to say a little prayer for me.

Cheryl said that Mr. Cocotas was very impressed with my speech for NU SKIN and wanted me to keynote the TCBY convention in March. I told her I'd be willing to try but that we both owed it to Mr. Cocotas to inform him that I had undergone open-heart surgery and was slowly recovering, so we weren't sure how strong I'd be in March or whether I could still perform on the platform. He responded that he would gladly take that risk, so we booked the date. What a great feeling it was to open my calendar book and mark in a speech for March 19th, the first newly scheduled speech since my operations!

TCBY ("The Country's Best Yogurt") is a fabulous American success story. Fifteen years ago Frank Hickingbotham opened his first yogurt shop in Little Rock, and now the organization has more than twenty-five hundred locations throughout the nation plus more than twenty foreign countries, and they are still growing and growing.

When I walked into the ballroom this afternoon, to check the sound and lectern, I was wearing slacks, an open shirt, and leather jacket. On the stage, behind the lectern, a man was talking into the microphone . . . about Og Mandino . . . and I quickly realized it was the company president, Charles Cocotas, going over the introduction of me he would deliver tomorrow morning.

I walked slowly down the ballroom's center aisle until I was close to the stage and stood there, hands folded, saying nothing. Suddenly Charles stopped saying all those nice things about me, leaned forward on the lectern, squinted, and then broke into a great smile, saying, "Og, is that you? My God! Wow!"

Charles rushed to the edge of the stage, bounded down onto the main floor, and embraced me. Soon we had a crowd of TCBY people surrounding us, including the company's founder, Frank Hickingbotham, and his son, all warmly welcoming me and telling me they were looking forward to my speech.

I pray to God I'm sharp tomorrow. Would hate to let this great group down.

March 19

My speech was scheduled for nine this morning, so I set my alarm for six-thirty and phoned room service with a breakfast order. When the young man finally arrived at my room, pushing my breakfast on a cart, he greeted me warmly as he entered my room.

"Are you enjoying your stay here at Opryland, sir?"

I told him that I was and that I was preparing to address a group of people here for their national convention.

"Oh," he said, "are you a motivational speaker?"

"Yes," I replied, "I guess you could call me that."

"Well, sir," he said, "there is one man whose books I've been reading for ten years now and I just think he's fabulous. His name is Og Mandino. Do you happen to know him?"

Well, I had just signed the dining-room tab he presented to me and I handed it back to him so that he would be sure to see my name. He did the greatest double take I believe I have ever seen.

"No . . . no . . . is it really you? I can't believe it. Sir, may

I have your autograph on a piece of hotel stationery or something?"

He was still shaking his head as he departed.

The TCBY people were a wonderful audience, and they honored me with a standing ovation when I finished. What a lucky man I am!

March 22

Lewis Grizzard's down-home and clever redneck humor has kept me chuckling for years. I've probably read at least six of his books, always enjoying and admiring his rare ability to combine wisdom and laughter in easy-to-read sentences.

While I was still in the hospital recovering from all my problems, I read that Grizzard had a new book out, published by Villard Books, called *I Took a Lickin and Kept On Tickin*, relating his most recent hospital experiences involving his third heart surgery in the past ten years. Since his latest trip involved open-heart surgery, a bypass, and an aortic valve replacement like me, I asked Bette if she would buy me a copy, and it had been one of my Christmas presents.

Loved the book. Like me, Grizzard couldn't recall very many of his day-to-day hospital experiences because of the medicines he was given, but his graphic narration did provide me with a much clearer view of all I had been through.

Most touching was this tough guy's comments that he's pretty certain the prayers of so many of his readers contributed to his survival. It seems that in his last column before entering the hospital, Grizzard had asked his readers to pray for him, reminding me, once again, of my experience in Houston and Salt Lake City when I had asked the audiences to say a prayer for my recovery.

What I found difficult to understand was that Grizzard refused to follow some commonsense rules of good health after his latest surgery. He continued to eat fatty foods, drink alcohol, and do very little exercise as if his heart were completely healthy.

Two days ago Lewis Grizzard died. He never regained consciousness from a fourth heart operation.

I recall that when comedian Richard Pryor was asked to talk about his multiple sclerosis a year or so ago, he replied that since there was nothing he could do about it, he just said a prayer each morning thanking God for the gift of another day. Recovering heart patients, on the other hand, have much they can do in the way of diet and exercise to prolong their lives.

Rest in peace, Lewis Grizzard, and thank you for so many funny and touching moments. Wish you had taken better care of yourself. We'll all miss you!

March 24

Writing these words in my room at the San Francisco Marriott. Spoke to more than 1,700 this evening in one of the hotel's larger ballrooms. This was a ticket sale event produced by Dan and Kerima Brattland and their Peak Performers organization. Since I have spoken for them before, I was more than a little interested in their evaluation of my "performance," the first for them since my surgeries. They were not only both pleased, they said they liked me a lot more in my new "twenty-pound-lighter" mode.

March 30

Ever since Frank Sinatra collapsed on stage while performing several weeks ago, there has been a ton of discussion on talk shows and in the press about people who should have retired because of their advanced age and settled quietly into a rocking chair. Very often I am confronted with similar questions in my interviews—why am I still flying around the world giving speeches, why am I still writing books—at age seventy? I certainly, my questioner assumes, don't need the money, so why am I doing it?

A look of courteous doubt appears on faces when I reply that I still love what I am doing. Money is no longer a motivating force, but appearing before a huge crowd or holding the very first copy of my latest book is a thrill that I am not yet ready to curtail. Why should I?

Sinatra is exactly eight years older than I am (we were both born on December 12th) and I'm certain that neither he nor Katharine Hepburn nor many of the other "old-timers" who are still performing and working are doing it strictly for the money. Instead they are probably living each day to the brim, savoring the adventure of life to the fullest.

A long time ago Canadian humorist Stephen Leacock wrote,

> The child says, "When I am a big boy." But what is that? The big boy says, "When I grow up." And then, grown up, he says, "When I get married." But to be married, what is that after all? The thought changes to "When I'm able to retire." And when retirement comes, he looks back over the landscape traversed; a cold wind seems to sweep over it; somehow he has missed it all, and it is gone. Life, we learn when it is

much too late, is living and enjoying every moment of every day, whether we are ten or eighty.

I believe I'll slow down when I hit eighty—slow down to just golfing and gardening and reading.

April 3

Having completed twenty-four sessions, ninety minutes each, three times a week, I am now graduated from the Concord Hospital Cardiac Rehab Program. It has been one of the best investments of my time that I have ever made, alerting me especially to the amount of danger I bring into my life when I am careless with my diet or don't exercise enough.

Yes, there are problems with my diet, but I control the solution. I love eggs, for example. Always have. However, they are no longer a part of my food intake. A single egg yolk contains 275 milligrams of cholesterol, almost the maximum allowed limit for the entire day!

Sodium is another hazard. Consuming the daily limit of 3,000 grams doesn't take much food when most cans of soup (I love soup) contain a thousand or more grams.

The treadmill I ordered arrived today. In my garage's empty third stall I now have a stationary bike, a rowing machine, and the new treadmill. Earlier today I put myself through the paces on all three. Thirty minutes. Hard minutes. Heart rate hovered around 100 while I was exercising. Perfect!

Bette is already starting to lay out clothes for our cruise to Europe, sailing from New York on April 18th. Neither of us can wait.

April 8

The messengers of spring have finally arrived. On the front lawn, right outside my studio window, at least fifty robins are searching among the thatched grass for food.

The ice on Little Walden has started to melt, and the tiny green tops of tulip and lily plants are just beginning to show themselves. As Goethe once wrote, "It always makes a pleasant impression on us when we open again at these pages of the book of life."

April 11

Victor Hugo has always been, to me, the great talent who wrote *Les Misérables*. Period. I knew little more about the man and his ability to write an epic poem or even a powerful journal in a life also filled with living.

I stumbled across a short work of Hugo's this morning in an old book and read it with awe, thinking he could have been the "self-help" author of all time had he put his mind forcefully on the subject. His short piece was titled "Providence—An Apologue." He wrote,

> The other evening I was a little late in going down to dinner and this was the reason: I noticed a number of dead bees lying on the floor of the lookout where I am accustomed to work—a sight that I encounter every spring. The poor things had come in through the open window. When the windows were closed they found themselves prisoners. Unable to see the transparent obstacle, they had hurled themselves against the glass panes on all sides, east, north, south and west, until at last they fell to the floor exhausted and died. But, yesterday, I noticed among the bees a great drone, much stronger than the others, who was far from being dead,

who, in fact, was very much alive and was dashing himself against the panes with all his might, like the great beast he was. "Ah! my fine friend," said I, "it would have been an evil day for you had I not come to the rescue. You would have been done for, my fine fellow; before nightfall you would be lying dead and on coming upstairs, in the evening with my lamp, I would have found your poor little corpse among those of the other bees." Come now, like the Emperor Titus I shall mark the day by a good deed; let us save the insect's life. Perhaps in the eyes of God a drone is as valuable as a man and without any doubt it is more valuable than a prince.

I threw open the window and by means of a napkin began chasing the insect toward it but the drone persisted in flying in the opposite direction. I then tried to capture it by throwing a napkin over it. When the drone saw that I wished to capture it, it lost its head completely. It bounded furiously against the glass panes as though it would smash them, took a fresh start and dashed itself again and again against the glass. Finally it flew the whole length of the apartment, maddened and desperate. "Ah, you tyrant!" it buzzed. "Despot! You would deprive me of liberty! Cruel executioner, why do you not leave me alone? I am happy, and why do you persecute me?"

After trying very hard, I brought it down and in seizing it with the napkin, I involuntarily hurt it. Oh how it tried to avenge itself! It darted out its sting; its little nervous body, contracted by my fingers, strained itself with all its strength in an attempt to sting me. But I ignored its protestations and, stretching my hand out the window, opened the napkin. For a moment the drone seemed stunned, astonished; then it calmly took flight out into the infinite.

Well, you see how I saved the drone. I was *its Provi-*

dence. But (and here is the moral of my story) do we not, stupid drones that we are, conduct ourselves in the same manner toward the providence of God? We have our petty and absurd projects, our small and narrow views, our rash designs, whose accomplishment is either impossible or injurious to ourselves. Seeing no farther than our noses and with our eyes fixed on our immediate aim, we plunge ahead in our blind infatuation, like madmen. We would succeed, we would triumph; that is to say, we would break our heads against an invisible obstacle.

And when God, who sees all and who wishes to save us, upsets our designs, we stupidly complain against Him, we accuse His Providence. We do not comprehend that in punishing us, in overturning our plans and causing us suffering, He is doing all this to deliver us, to open the Infinite to us.

I guess that what has touched me so deeply, upon discovering this great essay by Hugo, is that I had gone through a startlingly similar personal experience with some bees and butterflies, in the old shack across the road, nearly two years ago, and I even made it a journal entry, dated June 9, 1992!

April 16

The temperature soared to eighty degrees yesterday afternoon, and the banks of snow around our place have all but disappeared except in the deep woods. A heavy fog hangs over the ground today, but I still had to drive downtown to put some material back into our safe-deposit box.

We depart on the first leg of our trans-Atlantic journey in two days, and the cruise line strongly recommends that we take along sales receipts, an insurance policy, or jeweler's appraisal for any valuable trinkets we are bringing with us so that U.S. Customs, upon our return, can see proof that they are not dutiable articles purchased in foreign ports.

Yesterday I had removed from our bank safe-deposit box our insurance policy, which contains a listing of Bette's jewelry and furs. She made a photocopy of the policy this morning before I returned it to the bank, and she is now upstairs ironing and making notes and lists of items she wants to remember to take with her.

We are both beginning to get very excited about the trip. I deliberated for several days before deciding to take my video camcorder instead of my old and trusty 35 mm Olympus. Rather than have another piece of luggage to carry, the camcorder is going right in my oversize attaché case along with several books, cruise material, and legal pads so that I can document our trip for this journal.

April 18

Our cruise ship, the *Royal Princess*, departed New York Harbor at seven-fifteen this evening.

As we passed close to Ellis Island, I said a silent prayer to my dad, who, with his mother and father and so many thousands of others seeking a new life, passed through Ellis a long time ago.

Neither Bette nor I have ever been so close to the Statue of Liberty. We held hands tightly and said nothing as we sailed past the lady.

We have now left the lights of New York City far behind, and it is very dark and blustery as we sail out into the North Atlantic.

April 19

I don't know how Bette worked such a miracle, but she has unpacked our five suitcases, put all our clothes away in the tiny closets and drawers, and slid all our luggage under our beds.

This first full day onboard was one of orientation and getting organized. We went through the Panama Canal on this same lovely ship, eight years ago, so finding our way around was fairly easy.

The *Royal Princess* has a gross weight of forty-five thousand tons, is almost eight hundred feet in length, and holds twelve hundred passengers, but numbers just don't describe the vastness of this huge liner with its nine decks and two acres of deck space with jogging track.

Our minisuite is on the Aloha deck, so we have our own veranda with sliding door. It's a little chilly out there today but still quite a thrill to push open that sliding door and step outside for our own private view of the Atlantic. There are two chaises out there, so we can settle down with a good book and listen to the swirling ocean far below.

During our last cruise on this lovely ship, Gavin Macleod, the original *Love Boat* captain, came onboard to do some commercials, and he kindly offered to pose for a picture with anyone who asked. Bette and I got in line, and we now possess, on my bulletin board at home, a photo of "Captain Stubing" with his arms around each of us.

Of the twelve hundred passengers aboard, I would guess that at least a thousand haven't cracked a single smile since they came onboard. It must be tough to be old and rich and cranky.

We played bingo in the International Lounge this afternoon and visited the casino for a short while this evening. We are now watching CNN on our room television set. News of Richard Nixon suffering a stroke reminded me, as if I need to be reminded, of my own recent problems. This morning after breakfast I went up to the gym on the sun deck and did some work on the stationary bike and rowing machine. My only companions were younger people with spandex tops and shorts covering their svelte figures. The older overweights on the trip, who really need to exercise, are all sprawled out on deck chairs with a glass of booze in their hands.

April 20

It is absolutely mind-boggling to glance through the ship's daily publication, *Princess Patter*, and see the wide variety of activities available to the passengers.

Today, for example, some of the planned events include a lecture and slide presentation on two of our forthcoming port destinations, Cork and Amsterdam; men's shuffleboard and trapshooting; a ladies' table tennis tournament; a bridge lecture; a dance class; bingo; golf putting; a fine jewelry seminar (on Bette's list); a gathering of bridge players; a lecture on handwriting analysis; another on the history of trans-Atlantic crossings; deck quoits; afternoon tea; a trivia contest; a country-and-western barn party; a gathering of Alcoholics Anonymous; a musical variety show; plus a first-run movie in the cozy theater.

At around midnight tonight we'll be passing approximately two hundred miles south of the Grand Banks of Newfoundland, an area of the Atlantic that is prolific breeding grounds for codfish and was immortalized by Rudyard Kipling in his *Captains Courageous*.

Tonight, for the third consecutive night, we will advance our clocks and watches an hour—and already our body clocks are starting to raise hell in protest. It's not easy to enjoy the fabulous meals available, especially for supper, when they are serving at seven P.M. ship's time but four P.M. body time.

April 22

The past two days have been restful and relaxing as our ship, on fairly calm seas, continues its easterly course toward our first destination.

We expect to dock at around two P.M. tomorrow afternoon at the port city of Ponta Delgada, on the island of São Miguel, one of the nine fertile tops of undersea volcanoes that make up the Azores.

One frightening sign of the times yesterday morning—a bomb drill. At ten A.M. a stern voice on the public address system asked all passengers to return to their rooms and to search for any suspicious objects. We were to inform a member of the ship's company if anything strange was discovered, and upon completion of our search we were to remain in our staterooms, with the door open, until we received further instructions.

Approximately an hour later another announcement over the speakers informed us that the drill was over. Imitation bombs had been discovered in two staterooms, and both couples would receive a bottle of champagne for their good work. Life . . . as we approach the twenty-first century. It just seems to get cheaper and cheaper.

April 24

An extremely turbulent sea greeted us when we awoke today. Yesterday morning our captain, Ian Tomkins, announced over the public address system that because they had been unable to locate the proper helpful currents, our ship would not arrive in Ponta Delgada until after five P.M. instead of two P.M., so the on-land tours we had signed up for were canceled because we would still be departing the port at eight P.M.

It was Saturday afternoon and we had been warned that almost all stores were closed, but we still went into town on the shuttle buses provided and walked from the old Ford de San Braz, on the Avenida Infante D. Henrique, along the colorful waterfront.

We did find one or two small gift shops that were open, but the huge crowds from the ship made it impossible to do any shopping. After strolling for a mile or so along the harbor road we returned to our waiting buses and climbed the gangplank shortly after seven P.M.

Because our huge ship was rolling so severely today, Bette and I decided to remain in our room and had our great steward, Luis, bring us our meals.

We'll now be at sea another full day before docking on the following morning in Cork, Ireland. The tour we have purchased there is scheduled to take almost eight hours, and hopefully it will be filled with castles, countryside legends, and plenty of leprechauns.

I continue to be amazed at the general attitude of most passengers. Here they are on one of the most luxurious cruise ships in the world, being pampered and overfed and entertained as if they were royalty, yet most of them walk around all day looking unhappy and uncaring. Sourpusses unlimited! Of course, most of the ship's passengers are much older than the general population. Our younger generations, still struggling to get a firm hold on our crazy world, have far more important things to spend their time and money on than a cruise, although I am convinced that they would appreciate this wonderful trip far more than the generation onboard.

I think the explanation for our dour passengers is a simple one. They have forgotten, as they grew older and their assets increased, how to count their blessings. I wonder how many of these so-called senior citizens remember to thank God for the gift of a new day when they awake each morning.

Amazing what a little open-heart surgery does for one's perspective of life.

April 26

After docking at Cork this morning, on the south coast of Ireland, we boarded shuttle buses and listened attentively as our bright guide, Valerie, pointed out some of the city's attractions, including the square tower of Red Abbey, all that remains of Cork's oldest building, an Augustinian friary founded around the year 1300.

The River Lee meanders through the quaint setting of the old city, and when Valerie told us its name, a chill went up my spine since my mother's folks had come from Galway and her maiden name was Lee.

After a brief stop in the quaint village of Bandon, we returned to a great lunch at the Metropole Hotel in Cork before riding out to Blarney Castle, home of the Blarney Stone. It has been said that when one kisses the stone, one is immediately blessed with eloquent speech and persuasive ability. I should have kissed it a long time ago.

We did a lot of browsing in the nearby Blarney Woolen

Mill but somehow couldn't get into the buying mode and ended up with just a couple of Blarney Castle T-shirts.

The most touching and precious moment of the day came after we were back on the ship. Apparently we are the first of a dozen or so cruise ships that will visit Cork this year, so at least a thousand townspeople came down to the pier to bid us farewell. There was even a brass band playing somewhat strange-sounding arrangements of American favorites such as "Anchors Aweigh" and "America the Beautiful" as everyone on shore waved and blew kisses when the *Royal Princess* gradually pulled away from the dock.

Memories of the lush green countryside and smiling faces will remain long after we are back home. The two hundred days of rain that fall each year have done nothing to dampen the Irish appreciation of life. Gutsy people. We could learn plenty from them.

April 28

After a seemingly long night of moaning foghorns we docked in Amsterdam this morning just as the sun appeared.

There is an old saying in the Netherlands that although God created the world, the Dutch made Holland. Evidence of this is most striking along the waterfront with its countless dikes, dams, and levees designed to protect the small nation from tidal flooding since half the land area is below sea level. When the sea has been permanently excluded from an area, these industrious people work very hard at washing all the salt from the soil until they have more rich sand, called polder, which they then use for agriculture. Amazingly this tiny nation, about half the size of New

England, has doubled its size through the years by this process.

We had a great day, and I did try to preserve some of it with my video camera. Our tour bus first took us to the old city of Delft with its cobbled alleys and quaint homes where we visited the world-famous Delftware Porcelain Factory. Bette spent her year's allowance there, and the hand-fashioned pieces she purchased will all be shipped to our home, I hope.

We then visited the Mesdaq Panorama Museum in The Hague, with its awesome painting of more than a hundred feet of village houses and buildings completely circling the inside of a tower so that an illusion of depth is almost hypnotic, with its forefront of actual white sand and stone.

We then rode to the Kurhaus Hotel in Scheveningen, with its vaulted dome area of antique paintings and incredible inlaid mosaics, where we were served a lavish buffet lunch. On the way back to our ship we received a special bonus. Marge, our guide, had our bus driver take some unscheduled back roads so that we were treated to the awesome sight of vast fields of bright tulips, at the peak of their bloom, being grown by commercial seed companies.

In the evening we took the Amsterdam twilight canal cruise and spent two hours on man-made waterways reeking of character and history. No one spoke a word when we sailed slowly past the Anne Frank house with its black exterior. Bette and I had visited that tiny canal home six years ago, and neither of us will ever forget our climb up the narrow winding stairway to the garret where the Frank family hid from the Nazis for more than two years.

April 30

After docking at the small Belgian port of Zeebrugge yesterday morning, we spent most of the day on an almost hypnotic trip back in time as we walked and rode on the cobblestone streets of Ghent and Bruges. Both towns were bustling areas of trade and commerce way back in the sixteenth century, but now the swans travel languidly along the dark waters of hundreds of canals and life moves at a much slower pace.

There are more than two hundred bridges in Ghent because of the old city's many waterways. With its ancient castles and bridges and rows of mansions and guildhouses, all with striking towers, we felt as if we were walking through a children's fairy tale. Bruges remains a wonderful source of handcrafted lace, and of course Bette had to own some of it.

Today we turned back our "time machine" again. After arriving at France's huge port of Le Havre, our tour buses took us to the awesome cliffs and lazy beaches of Entretat, which Monet and Isabey had captured on so many canvases. In Fecamp we visited Le Palais Benedictine, an awesome building worthy of any royalty but which is actually the factory where Benedictine liqueur is distilled.

Our bus was very quiet when we rode through the green of upper Normandy. It wasn't necessary for our guide to remind us that here was where Allied troops fought and died on D day, a long time ago.

May 1

Sometime during the early-morning hours, the *Royal Princess* arrived at Southampton, England, having traveled a total of more than 5,200 statute miles since leaving New

York Harbor. Those of us planning to spend a few days in London, as part of an additional package offered by the cruise line, were escorted to buses, with our luggage, for the two-and-a-half-hour trip into London and our ultimate destination, the Gloucester Hotel in Kensington. However, our trip to the big city took considerably longer because along the way our bus broke down and we all had to sit or stand by the side of the busy highway until relief finally arrived and we boarded another bus, all the while of course worrying about our luggage, which was left behind.

The Gloucester Hotel is not listed in *Fodor's London Companion* as either a "dream deluxe" or even a "deluxe" hotel, but we found our room clean and comfortable and were too weary to be very fussy. Since we had to wait quite a while before our luggage finally arrived, we decided to have dinner in the hotel and get some rest so that we can truly enjoy tomorrow.

Bette and I did the tourist bit here several years ago, so we decided to forgo another look at Westminster Abbey, London Bridge, the Houses of Parliament, and so on, and to spend tomorrow instead visiting what is probably one of the best shopping areas in the world, Regent Street. Also high on our prayerful agenda was Andrew Lloyd Webber's *Sunset Boulevard* at the Adelphi Theatre, and our hotel concierge had said she would try her very best to get us tickets but could promise nothing.

May 2

There is a permanent magical aura that seems to hover over all of London that I have only felt in one other place—Rome. For more than two thousand years this special metropolis, which once occupied a gravel site of only

350 acres on the north bank of the Thames, has played major roles in the evolution of our planet. Whether one is a history buff or not, however, there is so much to see and do here that one could never possibly get bored.

Received some great news right after breakfast. The concierge phoned our room as we were leaving to inform us that we have two tickets for *Sunset Boulevard* tomorrow night! Wow! After breakfast downstairs we took a cab to Regent Street. Conceived by the Prince Regent, who was later to become King George IV in 1811, the fabulous thoroughfare was designed by Britain's leading architect of the time, John Nash, who spared no expense in creating one of the city's prime jewels. In London, where shopping is almost as important as breathing, Regent Street is second to none. Our cab dropped us at 214 Regent, as we had requested, and we commenced our day at the place recognized as London's most original store, Liberty.

There are five huge floors in Liberty and Company's old building, each with its own distinguishing characteristics, whether it be stained-glass windows, wood carvings, or even creaky floors. The rear of the store, I had read somewhere, was actually built from two old ships! Bette had long ago decided that this very special store needed to be covered thoroughly, so we began in the basement and slowly worked our way upstairs, finally inspecting the last counter on the top floor four hours later! We purchased fabric, silk neckties, Waterford crystal, Royal Doulton china, several books, some English samplers, and a Liberty-print address book. Then we had an omelet in the store's small and cozy restaurant.

Fortunately, early in the day at Liberty a pleasant clerk gave us some great advice. He told us to go to their business office and apply for a shopping card, which meant that all our purchases would be shipped directly to our

home back in the United States and we would avoid paying the value-added tax, which tacks an additional fifteen
percent on all purchases. So, without armfuls of shopping
bags to load us down, we finally emerged from Liberty
looking for new stores to conquer. They truly spread out
before us for as far as the eye could see.

In the next several hours, on a rare and bright sunny
day, we spent time and money in Hamley's, a six-floor toy
store, probably the largest in the entire world, for both
kids and grown-ups, which has been in existence since
1760; Garrard's jewelry store, which was Queen Victoria's
favorite and where one can actually observe master craftsmen as they assemble one-of-a-kind valuable pieces; the
Scotch House, filled with all sorts of sweaters, scarves, and
cloaks in cashmere, camel's hair, and Shetland wool, as
well as Harris tweed; Burberrys of London, with its tempting collection of tailored clothes for both men and women;
Henry's, with its awesome display of luggage and leather
goods; Waterford Wedgewood, with its fine bone china, elegant earthenware and quality crystal, as well as more
than one hundred tableware patterns! We even wandered
into the Disney Store, at 140 Regent, God help us, the first
of its kind in the United Kingdom. Then I bought Bette a
bag of hot chestnuts from an old street vendor and we
were peeling and chewing when we were finally able to
flag down a cab and wearily return to the Gloucester.

We are now both in our pajamas. Bette is doing a little
ironing on some of our more formal clothing so that we
will not look like two country bumpkins at the magnificent old Adelphi Theatre tomorrow evening.

May 3

We spent much of this morning strolling hand in hand along Oxford Street, which had once been a Roman route that circled the city twenty centuries ago. Browsed for the longest time in Selfridge's Department Store. Bette just had to visit and "sample" their perfume department, which is supposed to have the largest collection of fragrances for sale in all of Europe.

When we returned to the hotel to rest up for our big evening on the town, we asked the concierge to recommend a good restaurant that would be within short walking distance of the Adelphi Theatre, and without hesitation she said, "Rules." She also suggested that she make a reservation for us and that we allow at least two hours for dinner, which we did.

Rules is the oldest restaurant in London, having been in business 196 years, and through all that time it has had only three owners. Able to seat two hundred on three floors, its walls, glowing warmly from the light of many chandeliers, are covered with hundreds of framed photos, drawings, paintings, and cartoons depicting both the literary and the theatrical history of London. The restaurant, I learned, was my idol Charles Dickens's frequent hangout as well as a favorite dining spot for H. G. Wells, Graham Greene, Evelyn Waugh, Laurence Olivier, Charles Laughton, Clark Gable, Charlie Chaplin, and John Barrymore. According to their colorful brochure, Rules even owns an estate in the High Pennines, which supplies game for the restaurant, where it is able to exercise its own quality controls and determine how the game is treated.

Bette and I had delicious poached salmon with new potatoes and creamed peas, followed by a huge apple tart with ice cream and rich coffee. We have both eaten in hundreds of restaurants through the years, but the ambience of this special place was so powerful that we often caught ourselves talking in whispers.

The brochure we were given after we had been seated in Rules included a photo of the Charles Dickens Room, which seats up to eighteen. On the way out I asked if we could look in, and the waiters, who were very kind and gracious since the room was being set up for a dinner party, let us. As a young boy, Dickens often wandered through the streets and alleys of Covent Garden, his wages from the blacking factory where he toiled allowing him only a sniff of the mouthwatering aromas that rose from the kitchens of Rules. He never forgot those hard times when he could afford to enjoy the restaurant later in his life. The place was also a favorite spot of the Prince of Wales for wining and dining the lovely actress Lily Langtry, and Rules finally installed a special and private door for the future king so that he could enter and leave without the other diners seeing him. There is now, although we didn't get to see it, another private room that seats twenty, called the King Edward VII Room.

A short walk, just around the busy corner, brought us to the Adelphi Theatre. A theater playhouse, of one sort or another, has stood on the same site for almost two centuries. It was rebuilt, reconstructed, and refurbished many times through the years. When the revival of the long-running musical *Me and My Girl* ended in 1993, Sir Andrew Lloyd Webber became a co-owner, initiating a lavish restoration and rebuilding project in preparation for his musical stage version of *Sunset Boulevard*, which had its world premier last July.

After having thrilled to *The Phantom of the Opera* with its original cast in New York, Bette and I were a little concerned that Webber would find it an almost impossible task to approach the power and glory of that blockbuster, but we needn't have worried. The gripping tale of Norma Desmond, silent-movie idol to millions, trying to adjust to a life and world that has passed her by, was mesmerizing. From the opening scene outside Desmond's mansion on 10086 Sunset Boulevard we relaxed in our comfortable seats and relished every moment as Betty Buckley and John Barrowman handled the two lead roles to perfection. During intermission we strolled through the foyer with its restored black-marble walls, stenciled coving, and many chromium-plated fixtures before stopping for some lemonade at the crowded Billy Wilder Bar.

Sometime during the final act Bette nudged me, leaned toward me, and whispered, "Are you okay? You look strange."

"I'm fine, I'm fine," I said, patting her hand. "Was just thinking what a long trip it has been from that intensive care unit at Dartmouth-Hitchcock Hospital, in Lebanon, New Hampshire, to this old theater on Strand Street in the heart of London."

May 4

For many, many years I have dreamed of this very special day, and it was everything I had hoped it would be.

Back in 1944, when I was flying bombing missions over Germany, each time we completed five flights and were still alive, we were issued a forty-eight-hour pass, and of course we all caught the first available train for London, where we drank too much, chased girls, and raised general hell for two nonstop days and nights. Why not? We couldn't possibly survive another five combat missions anyway, went our rationalization, so let's eat, drink, and be merry now because our days were certainly limited.

Piccadilly Circus, in the heart of London, was the prime destination of nearly all Allied servicemen on leave and, war or not, every day and night looked and sounded like New Year's Eve in what was Britain's own version of Times Square. Not even German bombing raids at night, while the whole city was in their blackout mode, dampened our search for a little fun.

The word *Piccadilly* is believed to trace its origin to an old tailor shop in the area that made lace collars called piccadells, and *Circus* meant no more than that it was a circular street. To all of us, however, the gaudy area was truly a perpetual circus.

In the heart of the giant circle, seemingly always filled with noisy traffic and pedestrians, stood the famous statue of Eros, which had been fashioned of aluminum and raised high above a stone fountain and a series of steps that always seemed to be packed with people. Actually the statue is not of the goddess of love but of the Angel of Christian Charity, and it was erected more than a century ago to honor philanthropist and statesman Anthony Ashley Cooper, a true "angel" to the poor and homeless.

On my very first visit to Piccadilly Circus, in 1944, I sat on the uneven steps beneath the statue of Eros, a confused and frightened kid from the country, all dressed up in his spiffy air corps uniform and silver wings and yet . . . and yet I was certain that I would never survive another five deadly missions in combat. I vividly remember sitting there, that very first time, and saying a prayer as my mother had taught me to do, asking God to please watch over me.

Back then, however, I *never* saw the statue that all Britons referred to as Eros, high above my head. The Germans were still bombing London almost nightly, so the precious and beloved figure had been boarded up to protect it from anything but a direct hit.

That unique spot, in the heart of Piccadilly, became my very special shrine of life. On every trip to London, after completing another five missions, I would make it a special point to go to Eros, sit on its steps, and repeat my short prayer to God. In my mind and heart those brief visits became a special sort of good-luck pilgrimage, and that crowded base of the statue was my personal haven from the world and all its dangers.

So today, with the sun shining brightly, Bette and I took a taxi to Piccadilly—and I finally got to see the lovely and graceful statue in all her shining glory. After walking around the statue several times, holding Bette's hand, I climbed up on the uneven stone steps and waited for Bette to move back far enough to take a few snapshots. So many disjointed thoughts raced through my head: German fighter aircraft almost wiping out our entire squadron one morning. A U-2 rocket landing on London one evening while I was having dinner only two blocks away. Jimmy Stewart, with clipboard in hand, interrogating me at length after what had been a difficult but successful mission. Memories. Memories.

A strange thought struck me as I was sitting in just about the same location, in relation to the statue above, where I had always sat. My overactive writer's mind was at work. What would I have done, way back then, if someone came up to me as I was sitting on the hard stone and said, "Lieutenant, all your prayers will be answered and you will survive all your missions. Son, you will be back here, in fifty years, sitting on the same stones, and during that half century until that moment of your return you will marry your childhood sweetheart, have a daugh-

ter, buy a house under the G.I. Bill of Rights, get a job selling life insurance, begin drinking until alcohol rules your
life, lose your wife and daughter to the booze, then your
job and your house, become a bum, almost commit suicide
in Cleveland, begin reading success books in libraries as
you search for some answers, meet a girl who had more
faith in you than you had in yourself, get another job selling insurance, marry Bette, have two sons, Dana and
Matt, get promoted to the company's home office to write
sales promotion material, become editor of W. Clement
Stone's magazine *Success Unlimited*, write an article about
Ben Hogan that caught the eye of a New York publisher
who surprisingly publishes your first book, *The Greatest
Salesman in the World*, which eventually becomes the best-
selling book of all time for salespeople. In the following
years you will write sixteen other books with total sales of
more than thirty-five million copies in twenty languages,
plus you will also become one of the highest-paid and
most honored motivational and inspirational speakers in
the nation along with being inducted into the International Speakers Hall of Fame."

If anyone had come up to that young kid as he sat below the boarded-up statue in 1944 and spelled out the
chapters of his life still ahead, he probably would have
run off and vanished forever into the distant British countryside.

Today was a day I shall never forget. That angel, I am
positive, is still watching over me.

May 6

It was an exceedingly calm and uneventful eight-hour
flight from London's Heathrow Airport yesterday, and last
night we slept in our own king-size bed.

I made a trip to our small post office first thing this morning and returned with three weeks' accumulation of mail, which our postal friends had packed into several large plastic baskets.

After we had separated the catalogs and junk mail from the first-class variety, we also had a huge pile of fan mail on the kitchen table.

Bette sighed, shook her head, and placed both her hands on the sides of the tall stacks of envelopes. "Hon," she asked, "do you remember the Blue Plaques in London?"

I nodded. Throughout the old city there were many houses that displayed circular Blue Plaques indicating that someone who had had some sort of impact on history occupied that particular residence at one time. Our concierge at the Gloucester had even suggested that we visit some of the homes and buildings on the printed list she gave us and have our own unique "Blue Plaque tour." Lord Byron's plaque is on Holles Street, Mozart's is at 180 Ebury Street, Shelley's is at 15 Poland Street, and George Bernard Shaw's at 29 Fitzroy Square. We took a stroll to see T. S. Eliot's in nearby Kensington Court Place.

"Og, do you remember reading about Wren's plaque?" she asked.

Sir Christopher Wren's architectural creations still dominate the London skyline, and after more than two hundred years at least fifty of the architectural wonders he erected are still standing.

I shook my head. "No."

"Well," Bette continued, "Wren's greatest achievement was the rebuilding of Saint Paul's Cathedral after the Great Fire. The man is buried in the church crypt, and the Blue Plaque on his huge tomb states, 'Reader, if you seek his memorial, look all round you.' "

Bette then pointed to the huge mound of mail, which we both knew, from years of reading them, were mostly letters of gratitude for the help and lift that one or more of my books had given to the writer. She reached toward the pile, removed a handful of envelopes from the top, and one by one read the envelopes' return addresses as she let them drop back to the table.

"Atlanta, Georgia . . . Dayton, Ohio . . . Perth, Australia . . . San Diego, California . . . Lima, Peru . . . Houston, Texas . . . Rome, Italy . . . Denver, Colorado . . ."

When her hands were empty, she raised them slowly out to her sides. Her voice broke as she nodded toward all the mail and said slowly, "If you seek his memorial . . . look all round you."

ABOUT THE AUTHOR

OG MANDINO is the most widely read inspirational and self-help author in the world today. His eighteen previous books include *The Spellbinder's Gift* and *The Twelfth Angel.* He and his wife, Bette, live in New Hampshire.